NEW TRAIL ADVENTURES
for CALIFORNIA HORSEMEN

Doni Hubbard

Foreword by Sharon Saare
Illustrated by Deborah Young

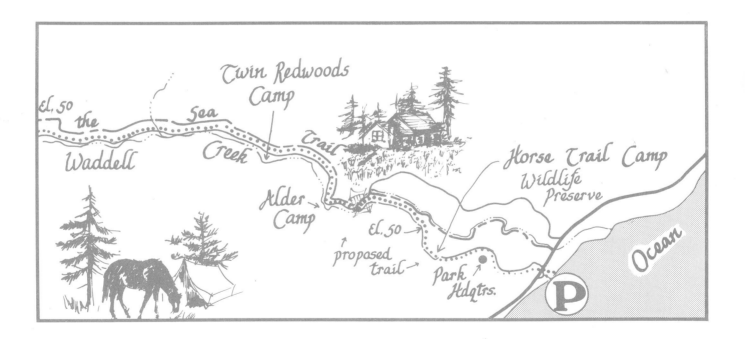

Hoofprints
Redwood City
California

Nancy Stuart

Cover photo: George Cardinet
Copyright © 1985 Doni Hubbard
First Edition — First Printing   Printed in United States of America
Photographs by author unless otherwise credited.

Write to: HOOFPRINTS
         P.O. Box 5765
         Redwood City, CA 94063

ii

Managing Editor
Walt Peterson

Illustrations
Deborah Young

Calligraphy
Ellen Pofcher

Graphic Production
Blankenburg Design Group
Design Vivace

Composition
Kathleen Schrader

Printing
Griffin Printing & Lithograph

Advertising
Pat Corwin
Barbara Tryon
Sonic Reproductions

Photographers
Charles Barieau
Carolyn Caddes
George Cardinet
Sandy Darby
June Fallaw
Chris & Jean Haughsten
Melinda & Paul Hughes
Carol Ivie
Tony Look
Alexander Lowry
Charlotte MacDonald
Lynn Quam
Ron Reisterer
Anna Robertson
Jon Saunders
Nancy Stuart
Robert Toren
Tom Upton
Alice Watt
Sheldon Woodward
Cal Yeats

CONTENTS

You see, I am alive.
You see, I stand in good relation
   to the earth.
You see, I stand in good relation
   to all that is beautiful.

Like the Most High Power ways are beautiful
   so are horses,
As I become one of them...

Before me peaceful,
Behind me peaceful,
Under me peaceful,
All around me peaceful ~ ~
Peaceful voice when he neighs
I am Everlasting and Peaceful.

I stand for my horse.

— from the songs of the Navajo and Kiowa

ACKNOWLEDGEMENTS

IF *NEW TRAIL ADVENTURES* had been my project alone it would have drowned in a relentless wave of personal challenges which just happened to coincide with the production of this book. But no book is only one person's achievement, and this book survived because it is the product of generously shared ideas, work, and joy. Above all, it is a testament to the dedication of people who love horses and trails. Over 100 individual horsemen and representatives of various agencies advocating trails played a part in the development of this book. I cannot list them all, but to each I owe a lasting debt of gratitude.

Ironically, the two people to whom I am most indebted for the completion of *New Trail Adventures* are rarely on a trail and quite indifferent to horses. It is impossible to adequately convey the degree of unswerving support and tangible assistance received from my friend and husband, Sid Hubbard, and my friend and editor, Walt Peterson. Both are survivors of my first book, *Favorite Trails of Northern California Horsemen*, and both have been creatively involved in every phase of this one.

With eagle eyes and good humor Walt applied his 32 years' experience with Stanford University's Publications Department to the task of editing and overseeing production. Words cannot do justice to his uncanny perception as an editor and his unflagging support as a friend.

Patiently, unselfishly Sid applied his 21 years' experience as my husband to the task of seeing me through each crisis that threatened completion of the book. In addition, he developed a few basic skills as a cook and laundress, and even joined me along some rugged trails on days well suited to golfing.

The contribution of the research-riders featured in this book will be obvious to you as you read the text. Their meticulous attention to detail is the heart and soul of the book.

One close perusal of the carefully illustrated maps and you have been introduced to the talent and integrity of Deborah Young. Again, as in *Favorite Trails*, Deborah has gone the extra mile to enrich your experience. From start to finish she was assisted by East Bay horsewoman Ellen Pofcher, whose skill as a calligrapher and warmth as a person made her a valuable addition to our trail book team. Supervisor of the Tahoe Basin Management Unit, U.S. Forest Service, Frank "Mac" Magary's careful review of the maps was invaluable.

In the Santa Cruz Mountains area rich sources of information were Bill Carter; Tony Look, Director of Sempervirens Fund; Park Ranger Les Clark; and Melita Oden, Emerson Shaw, and Willis Peck, members of the Saratoga Historical Foundation.

For a review of Wine Country trails I am indebted to the Army Corps of Engineers staff at Lake Sonoma; Jack London State Park staff members Anna Monroe, Greg Hayes, and Wendy Sharpe; Park Ranger Larry Perkins at China Camp State Park; Genevieve Day and Stephanie Lieber.

In the Gold Country I received invaluable assistance from the State of California Department of Parks and Recreation, the Placerville Ranger Service of the U.S. Forest Service, the Nevada County office of the U.S. Forest Service, the El Dorado National Forest Information Center, and the California State Department of Forestry in Auburn. The following individuals were of particular help: David H. Helton, C. Vic Maris, Joe Kilgore, Eric Holtz, Don Pearson, Bill Haire, Robert Chapin, and Mike McHook.

The San Francisco Peninsula section benefited from the careful scrutiny of San Francisco Water Department Manager Ed Fonseca, Bob Emret of the San Mateo County Parks Department, and Del Woods of the Midpeninsula Regional Open Space District.

The update on East Bay trails was made possible by the Heritage Trails Fund and Bob Doyle for the East Bay Regional Park District.

For the sharing of family albums I am immensely grateful to Vince Garrod, Chris and Jean Haughsten, and Joe and Joan Case.

Very special help came from very special friends who joined forces with me in assembling the beginnings of a directory of services for horsemen on the move: Pat Corwin, Lee Adair, Bill Tisher, Victoria Raucci, Nancy Dupont, and Sandy Brooks.

In addition to all of the above who were vital to this project, I must mention a potpourri of people. Their great and small deeds, and kind words of encouragement on timely occasions "made all the difference:" my in-laws, Barbara Hubbard and Bea Hubbard; old friends Millie Scranton, B.J. Davis, Bev Tibbitts, Michelle Ventura; new friends John Christensen, Carrie Curlee, Ann Duwe, and Kenny Pugh, and numerous readers of the first book who urged me to do a second one. If you're surprised to find your name on this list it's because you are unaware that your pat on the back or helpful act moved me forward on days when the task seemed overwhelming. I am most grateful.

—*D.H.*

Dedicated

To the memory of my father-in-law,
Wesley L. "Bud" Hubbard . . .

He blazed the most important trail of all,
the example of a good life . . .

FOREWORD

THE KEY WORD of *New Trail Adventures for California Horsemen* — and trailriding — is ADVENTURE!!!

As a youngster growing up in Santa Rosa, riding all over Sonoma County and later Marin, I remember the thrill it gave me to see what might be behind the next hill! Sharing that delightful excitement with a friend, my saddle horse, is something I've never gotten over, and still experience today.

Over the years professional commitments have taken me to every state in this nation, also to Canada, Mexico, Australia, England, Hungary, and West Germany. Quite a bit of formal sightseeing has been included in those tours, but the best parts have always been by horseback, experiencing beautiful country in a way that for me, and trail riders like me, just can't happen without a horse.

The more I've traveled, the more I realize what a unique opportunity California trail riders have in the multitude of public lands and trail systems available to them. (This isn't the case in many other parts of the country.)

The special opportunities for riders in the Golden State are a reality for two reasons. First, nature generously endowed California with a variety of spectacular mountains, foothills, grassy slopes and valleys, and miles of accessible seashore. The setting and our climate in which to enjoy it are ideal. Secondly, and most important, our access as horsepeople continues as a result of the dedicated work by those who realize that it isn't automatically guaranteed.

Fortunately there were horsemen who initiated and participated in the planning and political processes as our state's recreational programs were being developed. Their foresight and exhaustive efforts occurred before it was too late, enabling our present use. But the planning process is ongoing, and pressures always exist that would squeeze us out. In most cases exclusion need not happen; however, it will be up to trail riders and drivers like yourself to become involved to assure that it doesn't! Hopefully, your thoughtful attention to the "Trail Patrons" featured in this book will give you some specific ideas on the contribution *you* can make to saving trails. For instance, each state horse council or horsemen's association, each endurance and competitive ride association, and each saddle club should assign a committee or an individual to immediately start working with key land use agencies to make your interest known. Your riding access will be affected for the next ten years by what you do or fail to do in the next few months.

Now for the fun part! Select any or all of the riding tours presented in *New Trail Adventures for California Horsemen*. Load up your horses and gear and discover for yourself the glorious beauty of our state (and Nevada, too, if you're on the Tahoe Rim Trail). Besides offering splendid enjoyment of open country, your excursion will give you the opportunity to achieve a level of companionship with your horse that will occur in no other way, as the two of you develop a strong bond of interdependence and confidence.

The trails carefully described in *New Trail Adventures for California Horsemen* are offered by some of the most experienced trail riders in our state. These riding areas are for the most part relatively close to home. And don't forget the driving trails. Driving is again coming into its own, not only in this country but on a worldwide basis as well.

With stories, maps, and photographs Doni Hubbard and her research-riders have brought excitement and adventure right to your door step.

The opportunities and information you need to hit the trail are right here, right now! Let's take advantage of our good fortune!!!

Sharon Saare

A chance encounter along the Tahoe Rim Trail.

INTRODUCTION

I F YOU DON'T immediately see the connection between the photograph of a baby, a dog, and a deer and a book on horse trail
adventures, don't be concerned. I'm confident the relevance will be
clear to you one day as you return home, tired but invigorated,
chock-full of memories and tales of your first horse camping
experience, or carriage drive on the trails, or trail competition — or
any other form your new adventure may take. As surely as I sit here,
pen in hand, I know that regardless of all the planning that preceded
your excursion, in spite of how much you anticipated the beauty
promised to you by maps and photographs — what you will cherish
for years to come are your encounters with the unplanned,
unpromised, and unexpected.

No, it doesn't offend me to know that in spite of exhaustive efforts
to supply you with facts and details — armor against uncertainty — it
is the very elements of uncertainty and surprise which will reward
you with the tonic of the adventurer, exhilaration. Like the good trail
guide that he is, George Cardinet had armed me with topo maps and
detailed descriptions to aid in my pursuit of the Tahoe Rim Trail. I
had viewed trays of gorgeous colored slides. Nevertheless, I was not
prepared for the intensity of my delight, the sheer joy of being alive,
as I rode through an August landscape of alternating snow and
wildflowers; the well-being that permeated as I breathed clean,
unused air; the almost piercing happiness in the unity I felt with
horse and friends as we watched two hawks dipping in and out of a
sapphire sky. Nor had George foretold the unexpected fun of a
campsite meeting with a baby, an old dog, and a fawn!

Not all unexpected experiences are so delightful. To spend hours
and miles getting to a trailhead only to find a locked gate or a trail
sign, "Closed to horses", or the sudden appearance of a motorbike
on a narrow trail — these are aggravations, not adventures. This
level of uncertainty is what I've tried to remove by a year-long effort
to research trails. In addition to renowned trail blazer George
Cardinet, I have been assisted by the research-riding of San Mateo
County trail boss Lewis Reed, Santa Cruz County endurance rider
Julie Suhr, Midpeninsula Trails Council president Carolyn Lekberg,
Marin County veterinarian and Morgan Horse breeder Dr. Henry
"Hank" Boyd, and numerous Gold Country horsemen, including Ray
Sherman, Maxine Stahl, Bab Verdugo, Carol Jones, Marianne Jordon
and family, Jon and Carol Saunders, and members of the Twin Lakes
Riding Club from Sacramento. Our combined efforts have produced
thirty-eight "new" trail adventures divided into six geographical
sections. Each section is introduced by a story featuring the research
rider. These riders were selected, first, because they are
knowledgeable trail riders who know inside-out the trail areas
presented. Secondly, they represent a wide variety of experience not
only as horsemen, but also as activists in promoting horse access to
trails. Hours run into years when you measure the time they've spent
fighting for trails at public meetings as well as enjoying the trails on
horseback. Their stories embody the old adage, "One isn't lazy about
what one loves." We who love trails but are a little lazy about
meetings are in their debt.

This book directs you, primarily, to trails that have been established for horse use since the publication of my first book in 1980,
Favorite Trails Of Northern California Horsemen. In some instances, the
trails aren't truly "new", except to me. In other instances, trail areas
are featured because of new or improved horse facilities. A third
category of newness is where the trails have recently been built, or
are so new that they are just approved on paper but are not yet on
the ground. Some segments of the Tahoe Rim Trail are in the last
category. In this case, besides your courageous spirit you'll need our
maps and consultation with the U.S. Forest Service, Lake Tahoe Basin
Management Unit. The information presented here is current
(Spring, 1985) but since both weather and politics can have an
adverse effect on trails (trees fall, policies change), **it is strongly
recommended that you phone ahead to confirm both your overnight
stay and current trail conditions.**

My favorite cookbook groups its recipes according to "easy,"
"easier" and "easiest." It's not quite that simple with trails. With even
a little horse experience you are familiar with the variables that make
it difficult to categorize a ride. You may be on a "difficult" trail but it's
an "easy ride" if your usually difficult horse behaves well. Then a
mile or two further down the trail the terrain gets easy, the horse gets
difficult, and you're having a heck of a time 'til a spectacular view, or
a chance encounter with a cordial ranger or a fellow horseman,
leaves you with good memories of the trail and an eagerness to
repeat the experience. Who's to say whether you'll label that
particular ride easy or difficult? Still, risking the boggy soil of
semantics we have attempted to designate some rides as beginner

areas, suitable for novice trail users, good conditioning trails, suitable for carriage driving, etc. These designations are no substitute for your own view of the terrain based on knowledge we don't have — your level of ability as a rider or driver and your horse's condition and level of experience. In other words, this book is no substitute for your own horse savvy and common sense.

At the risk of stating another obvious point, **our reference to beginner and novice trails designates trail experiences suitable to knowledgeable horsemen who are beginners or novices with regard to distance riding or wilderness experiences on horseback. It does not mean suitability for beginning and novice riders or untrained horses or even trained horses with no trail experience.** The assumption in this book is that you and your horse have the fundamentals of horsemanship (especially "whoa"!) down pat. Even the best of horsemen will generally school a horse in the arena before taking him to the uncertainties of the trail. This is said only to clarify wording, not to dishearten the able rider from leaving the well-worn favorite trail and striking out for new adventure. In fact, if you haven't invested in some saddle bags and a decent ground cover shortly after reading this book, somehow we missed the mark!

To be honest, we've aimed to do more than take you out of an easy chair and put you in a saddle. This book is your personal invitation to participate in aspects of horse ownership you may not have realized existed. Considering the high cost of hay and land it makes sense to wring every bit of enjoyment you desire out of your relationship with the noble steed standing in the paddock. Have you caught a glimpse of him winking slyly at the cat as you pass by, up to his eyelashes in the feed bucket, contemplating yet another day of leisure while you, the more intelligent creature, hurry off to work every morning? In a tactful way let him know that you're reading about carriage driving on the trails, contributed by Bab Verdugo and Marsha Jo Hannah. Or you might mention that tiny donkeys and modest mules have been known to work for a living and, according to Robert Miller, DVM, and Joe and Joan Case, to be superior mounts on the trail. If he still strikes you as rather smug and complacent wake him up with Nancy Smith Kasovich's chapter, *Evaluating the Young Trail Horse Prospect.* There's nothing like a younger rival to get you in shape!

The fact is, rather than resist your efforts to add adventure to your riding your horse will welcome them. Quoting NATRC veterinarian judge Bill Throgmorton, "It is the horse's nature to roam, so he too enjoys the feeling of freedom that the open trails provide. Carrying his rider across ever-changing terrain, he is relieved at last of the boredom of stall and paddock confinement . . . the reward of trail riding is an improved partnership with the animal that has served man so well throughout history."

Thousands of Californians are drawn to trail riding for a thousand different reasons: some general such as a love of scenic beauty, an appreciation for the beauty and challenge of the horse, the camaraderie of a trail ride; some personal, such as my own — I can't ride down a mile of trail and stay mad at anyone. Another mile and I have no doubt that this is a good earth and a good time to be alive. Whatever your reasons I hope this book serves you well as you seek a new adventure. The facts we've presented are meant to encourage you, but the desire to meet a challenge, the courage to leave the familiar path, they can only come from you. Like happiness and love, all true adventure comes from within.

x

Hughes

Doni on Misty McQue in trail ride competition.

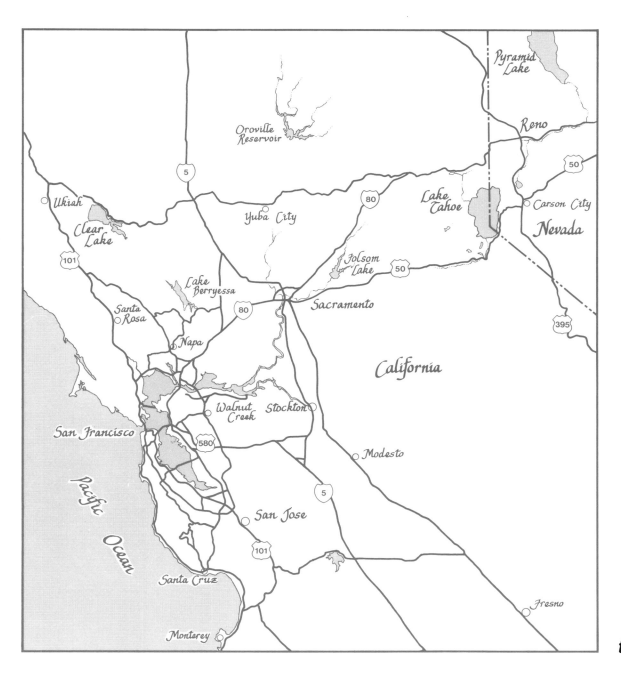

FEATURED AREA

I   Wine Country Trails

II   San Francisco Peninsula Trails

III   Midpeninsula Regional
Open Space District Trails

IV   Santa Cruz Mountain Trails

V   Tahoe Rim Trail

VI   Gold Country Trails

VII   Overnight Camping with Horses
in the East Bay

*Trails range from the seashore
to Alpine rides above the timberline . . .*

Marin~Sonoma Areas

Salt Point
Healdsburg
Calistoga
Armstrong
Redwoods
Guerneville
Austin Creek
Lake
Berryessa
St. Helena
Santa Rosa
116
12
Sugarloaf
Annadel
Napa
Wild Horse
Valley
Bodega
Bay
101
12
121
Petaluma
116
29
80
Pacific Ocean
San Pablo
Bay
Pt. Reyes
1
Sir Francis
Drake Hwy.
Drakes
Bay
Mt. Tamalpais
Marin Headlands

Copyright © 1985 Hoofprints

I. Wine Country Trails

Featuring

☆1 China Camp State Park
☆2 Jack London State Historic Park
☆3 Bothe ~ Napa Valley State Park
☆4 Lake Sonoma
☆5 Samuel P. Taylor State Park

⊛ Neighboring trail areas

The Haughsten family's wagon team provides popular tours of the Wine Country.

DR. HENRY "HANK" BOYD and his wife, Louise, tried with faint success to contain their enthusiasm as they approached an Illinois farmer plowing a potato field. The man, a stranger to them, was clearly intent on his work. He appeared oblivious to the prospect of visitors as he focused his energy on guiding two muscular work horses through the generous crop. It was an impressive picture —sweat-varnished man and stallions digging deeply into Illinois' black earth. Even if the farmer were to view the presence of the California couple as a welcome time-out, it seemed a bit of a shame to interrupt the vivid harmony of human and equine coworkers. But the Marin County veterinarian and his wife had come a great distance to meet the farmer, and with such high hopes. Enthusiasm for their mission drowned out the last tinge of reticence. They just had to ask.

"We walked up to the farmer," Hank Boyd recalls 30 years later, "and said, 'We've been told you have some very fine Morgan show horses. We're getting ready to set up a breeding farm in California, so we've been traveling all over the country looking for the right bloodlines. We'd sure appreciate seeing what you have in your barn.'

'Glad to,' said the farmer without any hesitation. 'Just a minute and I'll get the harness off so you can get a good look at 'em.'

"After traveling all over the U.S. and visiting the finest stables in the country we were expecting the farmer to take us to see some pampered show horses in a nice barn," recalls Hank. "Instead he just matter-of-factly unhitched the horses, brushed them off with a glove, and trotted them down the road. They moved with all the high-stepping action you'd look for in the show ring. Were we ever surprised to find horses of that quality hitched to a plow!"

"We were so impressed," says Louise, "with these gorgeous, magnificent stallions who displayed all the animation of 'park' horses, but whose utility and gentleness we had seen demonstrated moments before as they worked side by side in harness. Right there our search for the kind of Morgan we wanted to breed came to an end."

What the Boyds had discovered in Illinois was the Brunk line of Morgan horses, the oldest line of the present day Morgan families. Brunk-bred horses date back to 1893 when Joseph Brunk of Springfield, Illinois, attended an auction in Nashville, Tennessee, and purchased 10 Morgans for $1,000. At his Cotton Hill Stock Farm in Illinois Brunk used his purchase of two stallions (a son of Ben Franklin 1508 and a son of Ethan Allen 3rd 3987) and eight mares

4

Dr. Henry "Hank" Boyd is an avid fan of the Morgan Horse. As president of the Morgan Horse Association from 1965 to 1968, Hank devoted countless hours and miles to seminars, the Morgan Horse Youth Association, and international travel to promote the Morgan Horse. His wife, Louise, is the author of extensive research on the Brunk line of the Morgan Horse which was published in the third edition of the Morgan Horse Directory. Their dedicated efforts earned them the Morgan Horse Association's perpetual trophy, established by Intrepid Farms, for "most outstanding contribution to the Morgan Horse" in the western states.

The splendor of the Morgan Horse displayed by National Champions "Sam L. Carter," lead horse, and "Dapper Dan," wheel horse. Tandem turn-out being driven by well known Morgan show competitors, Jack and Evelyn Harrod.

"You get great versatility with the Morgan Horse," says Hank. "For many years we used them in NATRC competition. The origin of NATRC can be traced to the Morgan Horse when the first 100-Mile Endurance Ride was held in Vermont in 1936. Traditionally Morgans have been heavily used in that event because it was patterned after the 300-Mile Endurance Ride used by the Cavalry to test their Morgan horses. The Vermont ride is the oldest competitive ride still in existence and is the granddad of the competitive riding we enjoy today. Carriage driving is another great way to enjoy the trails."

"Our horses are well trained in the arena before we take them out in the open. We start to drive them at two years of age and ride them a little at three. That means they're at least four years old before we work them on the trails."

"Louise has the gentle touch," says Hank. "She gets them settled and people-oriented before I begin with the lessons in discipline and obedience. Horse raising and horse showing have always been a family endeavor."

to expand his breeding farm to 150 horses. Brunk-bred horses displayed a combination of brilliant action and kind disposition which made them notable winners in national competition and created a demand for their export to Canada, China, Europe, South America, Cuba, and the Bahamas. After Brunk's death in 1935 the family tradition of breeding quality Morgan horses was continued by his children. Today, Brunk-bred Morgans are a significant influence in the pedigrees of numerous horses bred in the western region of the country, as well as their native Midwest.

Although the Boyds hadn't known which line they'd end up with when they started their search, there was never any doubt that the breed they would devote their energies to would be the Morgan horse. Thirty years later, through the promotion of their chestnut stallion with flaxen mane and tail, Funquest Echo Hawk, their Morgan breeding program is still aimed at perpetuating the qualities of beauty, gentleness, and utility that impressed them in the potato field.

"I married into the Morgans," explains Hank. "My bride convinced me that you can't beat the Morgan Horse for a

5

combination of strength, refinement, and ability to perform with brilliance . . . I had to acknowledge their value as an all-around horse for the family, although through the years I had been very actively showing Thoroughbreds or anything that could jump."

Hank's life had been destined from birth to be filled with horses. He grew up in Mill Valley where the major part of his father's veterinarian practice was treating horses and the dairy animals which used to dominate Marin County hillsides. Showing hunters and jumpers on the weekends was a natural extension of his family's enjoyment of animals.

In the meantime his bride-to-be was growing up in San Francisco, which wasn't such an unlikely place to get a start as a horsewoman as you might think. "Believe it or not," says Louise, "San Francisco used to have many stables and there were horses everywhere, not just in Golden Gate Park. Although my dad prided himself on being a San Franciscan, he was also a real mountaineer. Dad owned

property in the Sierra where we spent our summers, and he always kept a horse for trail riding. I have the happiest memories of those days. Our whole family would pack in for a week of fishing and sharing one horse! It was the beginning of the love for horses and trails that I've had all my life. We still have the cabin that my dad built with real logs, too!"

City trails and wilderness country established Louise's interest in horses, but it was poring over horse books that made her an ardent fan of the Morgan in particular. Like thousands of other little girls she loved the story of Justin Morgan and thought the pictures of the Morgan, with his finely chiseled head and bountiful mane and tail, to be the most beautiful horse of all.

It's not easy to pinpoint exactly the moment when one's childhood dreams take root in reality, but Louise might settle on her decision to attend the University of California at Davis to take animal husbandry courses. She had been a physical education major at UC-Berkeley, but her dream of raising horses kept surfacing as she planned her educational career.

"Believe it or not, I met my husband-to-be in a class on genetics! We had both been students at Berkeley but had never met each other. It took veterinary classes at Davis to get us together. While we were students at Davis we began breeding Morgan horses, and three years after our marriage we were looking for enough property to accommodate four horses, an infant son, and one on the way!"

What they found is a dream come true for anyone who appreciates horses and country living with a little bit of history thrown in for good measure. In 1952 the Boyds settled into a large modern home on 100 acres which included a smaller second home built in the 1800s (a countess's summer home, no less!) with a quaint little fishing village as a next-door neighbor. Thirty-two years later the scenic beauty and hominess of the property are still intact. The Boyd children are grown but return often to the big, "modern" home indelibly stamped with 1940s charm. The little house dating back to the 1800s still stands (square nails and all), and the little fishing village is preserved forever as China Camp State Park. By preserving China Camp as a state park California will spend thousands of dollars to maintain the charm of days gone by for the public to enjoy. Still, when it comes to preserving the ambience of yesteryears they can hardly do better than Hank Boyd, as he returns the waves and smiles of motorists enjoying the sight of a man loving life from the seat of an antique carriage being whisked along the road by a proud-stepping Morgan Horse!

To the water's edge at China Camp State Park with Hank Boyd and his Morgan mare.

7

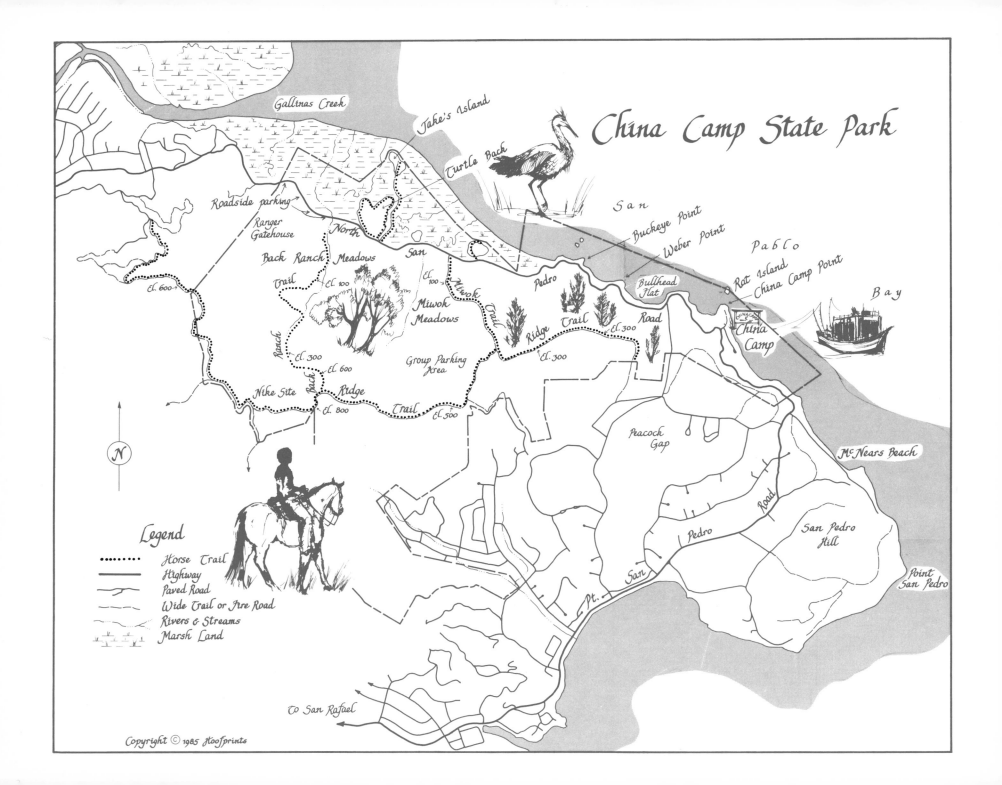

China Camp State Park

Gallinas Creek

Jake's Island

Turtle Back

San

Buckeye Point

Weber Point

Pablo

Roadside parking

Ranger Gatehouse

North

San

Pedro

Rat Island

China Camp Point

Bay

Back Ranch Meadows

El. 100

El. 100

Miwok Trail

Bullhead Flat

China Camp

Trail

El. 600

Miwok Meadows

Ridge Trail

Road

El. 300

Ranch

El. 300

El. 300

Group Parking Area

Back

El. 600

Nike Site

Ridge

El. 800

Trail

El. 500

Peacock Gap

Mc Nears Beach

San Pedro Hill

Pedro

Road

San

Point San Pedro

Pt.

To San Rafael

Legend

.... Horse Trail
———— Highway
———— Paved Road
– – – – Wide Trail or Fire Road
Rivers & Streams
Marsh Land

Copyright © 1985 Hoofprints

N

CHINA CAMP STATE PARK

Superb view of San Francisco Bay ... There just aren't many places in the world where you can relax in the saddle and view a dazzling metropolis, but this is one of them.
— Henry Boyd, DVM

REASONS TO GO: 360-degree views featuring San Francisco skyline, Mt. Tamalpais, Bay bridges and the ocean shoreline . . . put a camera in your saddlebag!

SPECIAL FEATURES: China Camp dates back to the 1860s when it was a thriving fishing village on the San Francisco Bay shoreline . . . still a popular fishing spot if you have a yen for sturgeon, striped bass, and starry flounder . . . daily catches of grass shrimp for sale by Frank Quan, resident China Camp fisherman . . . Dense bouquets of wildflowers in the spring and rich varieties of wildlife . . . snowy egrets, blue herons are two showy residents . . . great variety of vegetation native to marshlands, meadow and oak habitats . . . Horse lovers can hit the trail while unmounted friends or family members play golf at adjacent public course . . . or go for a bay swim . . . there's so much to discover and enjoy here you'll feel like a Renaissance man on horseback!

LOCATION: Park is on the San Pedro Point peninsula about three miles northeast of the city of San Rafael, 13 miles north of San Francisco just off U.S. 101 . . . Park entrance clearly marked from freeway.

WHERE TO PARK: This is a new Park and policies for horsemen are still being defined. As of Spring 1985 the only parking for individual horsemen is along the wide shoulders of North San Pedro Rd. A wide pull-out area on the left side of the road less than 0.1 mile from Park Entrance is your best bet. Reserved area for groups.

TRAIL FEATURES: Four-mile loop trails on unmarked but easy to follow fireroads . . . Park is new (opened in 1980) and new trails are being developed all the time . . . The main Back Ranch trail begins at the Back Ranch parking area leading to the top of the ridge along the south boundary and down to the Bay . . . Bayshore riding is around Turtle Back peninsula for one mile of wooded and grassland trail, narrow but nearly level . . . a second four mile loop is through Miwok Meadows generously sprinkled with oaks . . . more mileage is gained by connecting with the adjacent Marin County fireroads . . . lots of shade on most of the trails and the footing is generally good . . . topography in the Park varies greatly from sea level to 1,000 feet atop the steeply sloped ridges . . . lots to see in this park whether it's animal wildlife (200 species!) or homo sapiens wildly enjoying themselves as sailors, windsurfers, fishermen and swimmers in the Bay . . . of course, you and your horse will be having the best time of all on the trails! **Carriage driving on the trails with permission from the ranger.** Phone: (415) 456-0766. A special treat is carriage driving to the China Camp Historical Area . . . approximately eight miles round-trip on two-lane, paved County road with wide shoulders and minimal traffic except on weekends. If you are interested in Carriage Driving, Henry Boyd will provide you with an update on trail and road conditions. Phone: (415) 472-1341.

ACCOMMODATIONS: Excellent parking for horsemen groups in Miwok Meadows . . . **Reservations required.** (Write to China Camp State Park P.O. Box 244, San Rafael, CA 94901, (415) 456-0766 for reservations). A $25 fee will be charged to reserve group parking area . . . Miwok Meadows staging area is a great place to picnic, complete with barbecue pits, tables, and horseshoe pits (hopefully you don't have any loose shoes to contribute!) . . . Plenty of trees for tying horses but watch carefully for poison oak! . . . Creeks are adequate for watering horses on day rides . . . toilet facilities at Miwok Meadows and Back Ranch Trail staging area.

PARK SERVICES: Ranger on duty . . . map posted at entrance to Park but we're providing you with one for the trail . . . Visitors' Center.

FEES: No charge for day use of trails but $25 fee for reserving group parking area.

PARK RULES: Leave all features of Park undisturbed . . . Leashed dogs may stay in camping area but they aren't allowed on trails.

WEATHER: Temperatures usually cool and pleasant for good summer riding . . . but Park is especially beautiful decked out in the greenness of spring . . .

 CAUTION: Good year-round trails but some feeder trails can be slick after a rain and should be avoided . . . Poison oak in abundance in the meadow area . . . coastal breezes are frequent and pleasant, so a jacket is advised. **Imperative to stay on the trail when riding through marshy area** . . . it may look inviting but it is extremely hazardous footing for horse and rider. North San Pedro Rd. can have heavy traffic on weekends . . . check with Henry Boyd if you're planning a carriage drive.

Deborah Young and Ellen Pofcher take time out from their art work on this book to ride Jack London trails.

10

JACK LONDON STATE HISTORIC PARK

Steep trails and old ranch roads, rich with the history of the Valley of the Moon . . . A wonderful museum here . . . be sure to spend some time out of the saddle!

— Henry Boyd, DVM

REASONS TO GO: This is "Beauty Ranch," the home of Jack London, one of America's best loved writers . . . At the time of his death in 1916 he had completed over 51 books and numerous short stories celebrating his love of adventure . . . His love of the land is preserved for your enjoyment in this historic Park with faithfully maintained trails and ranch facilities . . . The beauty of the wine country crystallized in the 800 remaining acres of the original 1400-acre ranch . . . a welcoming attitude toward horsemen by Park staff, perhaps an acknowledgement of Jack London's love of riding . . . You've missed a choice segment of California history if you haven't experienced this Park!

SPECIAL FEATURES: Almost too many to mention! In addition to all the historic features of the Ranch, this is a great place to introduce your "horseless" friends to trail riding . . . rental horses and guided rides on Park trails are available from the Sonoma Cattle Company . . . Phone ahead and they'll provide you with lunch too! (707-996-8566) . . . Bring your fishing rod . . . there's bass fishing in the lake.

LOCATION: 2400 London Ranch Rd., Glen Ellen, CA 95442, (707) 938-5216. In Sonoma County, 1.5 miles west of Glen Ellen . . . An hour from San Francisco and a half-hour from Santa Rosa.

WHERE TO PARK: At the Park entrance a ranger will direct you to the Overflow parking area which is large enough for group trailer parking (10-15 trailers) and offers easy access to the trail system . . .

Tie rails and a spotlessly clean chemical toilet add to the convenience of this staging area . . . No water.

TRAIL FEATURES: Approximately 15-20 miles of trails which are mostly old ranch roads, but very steep in some areas . . . Additional trail mileage is possible on new trails which connect with the orchard lands of Sonoma State Hospital . . . Maintenance on the trails is excellent and they are well marked . . . Impressive vistas of the Valley of the Moon invite you to ride past the vineyard and pick up a steep forest trail leading to the 5-acre lake used by the Londons as a farm irrigation reservoir . . . Veils of lacy Spanish moss hanging from the trees and a leafy shelter of redwoods, oaks, and maples inspire you to tackle the steep trail leading to the 2300-foot summit of Sonoma Mountain . . . "Fallen Bridge Trail" takes off of main "Mountain Trail" 1.5 miles from parking lot leading to a grassy meadow with a view of Mt. Diablo and San Pablo Bay . . . along the creek the trail is narrow and shaded . . . it makes a one mile loop back to the main trail.

ACCOMMODATIONS: Day use only . . . Picnic tables and immaculate restrooms at the Park Headquarters. For more information: Jack London State Historic Park, P.O. Box 358, Glen Ellen, CA 95442, (707) 938-5216.

FEES: $2 fee per vehicle to enter the Park, plus a charge of $1 per horse.

PARK SERVICES: The Museum is staffed with very knowledgeable and friendly personnel . . . The loving care of the Valley of the Moon Natural History Association is much in evidence through their guided nature walks and historical tours featuring Jack London as writer and rancher . . .

Be sure to ask for the trail map and Park brochures which will increase your appreciation of the area . . . Fishing is OK (license required) . . . A special service on the trails is mounted patrol of the Park by volunteers, members of the Valley of the Moon Mounted Assistance Unit . . . it's nice to know that Certified First Aid help will come galloping to your rescue if needed!

PARK RULES: Leave all features of the Park undisturbed . . . No fires are allowed and smoking is restricted to designated areas . . . Dogs are not allowed on the trails . . . The fenced vineyards are private property and trespassing is prohibited . . . All visitors are requested to observe the opening and closing hours: 10 a.m. to 5 p.m. (6 p.m. daylight time weekends).

WEATHER: Park is open year-round but favorite riding times here are spring and fall . . . Trails can be slick after a rain, particularly Treadmill Rd. and Cowan Meadow Trail should be avoided in wet weather . . . 100-degree summer temperatures aren't unusual here, but hardy horsemen head for Jack London's shady trails and the mountainsides protected by dense stands of timber.

 CAUTION: If your love of wildlife doesn't include snakes and poison oak you'll want to be especially cautious in this Park . . . Hot days make the lake eminently attractive but swimming with your horse is dangerous here because of uncertain footing . . . You're most welcome to go to the water's edge to give your steed a cool drink but lake water is not for human consumption . . . Trails are shared with bicycles, so be especially cautious where the path is narrow and steep . . . Give wide berth to wild pigs.

11

Limited mileage for horsemen in this Park, but the quiet beauty of the redwood and mixed evergreen forest make the trip worthwhile.

Bothe-Napa trails are well marked and there's easy access to the trail system from the parking area.

BOTHE-NAPA VALLEY STATE PARK

In the heart of the vineyard country . . . beautiful wooded trails with the refreshing sight of rushing water and redwood forests . . .

— Henry Boyd, DVM

Cool, shaded trail along Ritchey Creek, but still very hot in the summer . . . spring and fall are favorite times to ride.

REASONS TO GO: Spectacular wine country scenery ushers you into the Park . . . vineyards ablaze with color in the spring and fall . . . dairy farms, orchards, cattle ranches, fruit and vegetable stands provide a visual feast en route to the Park, the ultimate in Sunday drives . . . By the time you get your rig parked and your horse saddled you're so steeped in beauty you can't believe there's more . . . but there is! Park-like trails in wooded areas . . . views of the Park's back canyons and glimpses of Mt. St. Helena . . . Live streams along the trails, redwood orchids and trilliums blooming in the spring!

SPECIAL FEATURES: The Park is home to an abundance of wildlife and numerous plant communities . . . fox, bobcat, coyote, and gray squirrels thrive in the deep cover of the forest . . . six kinds of woodpeckers hammer away in the coolness of the redwood and mixed evergreen forest . . . You'll enjoy your ride even more once you're acquainted with the wildlife . . . so return on foot sometime and enjoy some of the guided programs provided by the Park . . . Numerous picnic areas and the nearby communities of Calistoga, St. Helena, and Yountville are good reasons for "making a day of it".

LOCATION: Easily accessible on good roads well marked with signs, four miles north of St. Helena, on Hwy. 29, Napa County.

WHERE TO PARK: Park ranger at entrance will direct you to the equestrian parking area about a quarter-mile from the main entrance. Parking is in a narrow paved area with room for about 10 trailers. The area can be a little difficult to maneuver in if the lot is full, but the rangers are very friendly and helpful in assisting you to find more space if necessary.

TRAIL FEATURES: Very limited mileage for horses (approximately six miles round trip), but the beauty of the trails and the surrounding area make the trip worthwhile . . . The trail is easy and climbs gradually, following an old roadbed used in the 1860s . . . paralleling the trail is a year-round stream with dense shade and cool undergrowth giving relief on hot days.

ACCOMMODATIONS: Day use only for horses . . . Fifty family campsites otherwise. For more Park information phone California State Parks (415) 456-1286.

PARK SERVICES: An excellent map is available from the ranger which not only features the Park but also highlights other recreational areas and wineries in the upper Napa Valley . . . The Park has a Visitors' Center and an evening campfire program during the summer . . . From mid-June through Labor Day a swimming pool is open to campers and day visitors who have purchased pool tickets.

FEES: $2 per rig and $1 per horse for day use.

PARK RULES: All Park features including wildlife are protected . . . Dogs are not allowed on the trails.

WEATHER: Very hot in the summer . . . spring and fall are the best times to ride, with fall especially beautiful because of the vigorous displays of fall color . . . If summer is your only time to ride, plan a morning trail ride, then go for a swim!

CAUTION: Trails are well maintained but poison oak is in abundance on both sides . . . stay in the saddle and on the trail and remember that poison oak changes from a shiny green in spring to a vibrant orange or red in autumn.

13

LAKE SONOMA

A brand new area . . . tremendous potential for an outstanding trail system . . . barely developed now, but plans are being implemented to make this a favorite recreation area . . .

— Henry Boyd, DVM

REASONS TO GO: Bountiful planning for public recreational use of this exciting new trail area is being spearheaded by the Army Corps of Engineers . . . Don't miss the boat, literally, because this will be a favorite area for horsemen who like tacking and tackle, as well as tacking up! . . . Lakeshore riding, campsites that can be reached only by horse or boat! . . . Trails through cool, mysterious redwood groves and forests of oak . . . Driving through the vineyard country to reach the lake is a joy in itself — the charm of Sonoma County on the threshold of your wilderness ride!

SPECIAL FEATURES: 5,000 acres devoted to wildlife including lion, bear, deer, pig, bobcat, fox, and coyote . . . Nesting habitat for the rare and endangered Peregrine Falcon . . . Views of Pritchett Peaks from the Dry Creek arm of Lake Sonoma . . . 17,600 acres of recreational area with 2,700 acres of water surface for cooling off after a hot summer's day ride . . . At the Visitors' Center you will find the most modern fish hatchery in the State of California starring salmon and steelhead trout . . . boating, fishing (catfish, trout, bass, red-ear perch), swimming, waterskiing . . . something for everyone here.

TRAIL FEATURES: Handmade trails designed for less than 10% grade . . . steep areas for good conditioning rides and stretches of old farm road for taking it easy . . . Varied terrain of chaparral, grassland, oak and bay trees . . . refreshing lakeshore riding. When area is fully developed it will feature 125 miles of riding trails . . . By spring of 1985 plans call for four miles of newly constructed trail plus the existing old farm roads to give you a pleasant day's ride . . . new signs are being made to designate trails, mileages, and campsites . . . **With further development trail competition and carriage drives may be possible** . . . Enough trail area is currently established to give you the varied experience of riding through a thick grove of redwoods, along a ridge trail leading to Bummer Peak, on switchbacks across open grassland, ridge riding with lake views, and a few stretches of trail close to the lake. So stay tuned to the planning process here . . . there's more to come.

LOCATION: In Sonoma County, 10 miles from Healdsburg, at the confluence of Dry Creek and Warm Springs Creek. From Hwy. 101 take Dry Creek or Canyon Rd. exits and travel west 10 miles to entrance of Sonoma Lake recreational area . . . Paved, two-lane road once you leave Hwy. 101.

WHERE TO PARK: It's two miles from Park entrance to equestrian parking area. Stop at the Visitors' Center for most up-to-date information on parking and camping areas . . . Basic directions are to proceed past administrative complex uphill to Stewart's Point Rd., turn left and go one half mile to Lake Sonoma Overlook parking area. This is a large, graveled parking area with room for 40 cars and trailers. There's drinking water for people at the parking area and water for the horses in the lake and in springs . . . The Army Corps of Engineers will be installing some rather ingenious water troughs — jet engine containers cut in half.

"They do the job and they're free," explains the Park ranger!

ACCOMMODATIONS: Great overnight camping areas for riders and hikers . . . campsites have interesting names like Quicksilver, Island View, Lone Pine, etc . . . White Oak Ranch camp area commemorates the fact that you're on the original site of Tom Baxter's ranch. The 14 individual campsites have outhouses, tables, and fire rings . . . Possibly 10 of the sites will be on the lakeshore . . . For individuals the only arrangements are first-come, first-served, so plan to arrive early on a weekend. **Reservations for a group** can be made by arrangement with the Senior Park Ranger, 3333 Skaggs Springs Rd., Geyserville, CA 95441-9644, or phone the Army Corps of Engineers (707) 433-9483.

FEES: None proposed for individual campsites, but reserved area will be $5 per family per night or $25 per night for groups. No charge for day use.

PARK SERVICES: Rangers on foot and boat patrol . . . very cordial Park rangers and a fascinating Visitors' Center add to your enjoyment and safety . . . As trails are more developed a map will be available.

PARK RULES: Dogs are allowed on leash in the campground . . . Protection of wildlife is strictly enforced . . . there's a $10,000 fine and five years imprisonment for disturbing the habitat of the Peregrine Falcon, an endangered species.

WEATHER: Ideal riding times are spring and fall, with redwood-shaded trails giving you a rest stop in the summer . . . Just remember that the same sun that sweetens wine country grapes can make you feel like a raisin . . . be prepared for heat! Still, it's not every trail ride that can offer a refreshing swim as your reward for hard work . . .

 CAUTION: Rattlesnakes, poison oak, and yellow jackets will be sharing the land as much as you . . . stay on the trails for maximum enjoyment of this beautiful area.

SAMUEL P. TAYLOR STATE PARK

You can't help but appreciate the reassurance of well maintained and well marked trails . . .

— Henry Boyd, DVM

REASONS TO GO: 2,600 acres with connecting trails to Pt. Reyes National Seashore and Mt. Tamalpais State Park . . . scenic riding through beautiful, dramatic redwood forests threaded with bright streams and lined with thick, fern-filled ground covers . . . or take a trail through open grassland and watch for deer camouflaged by oak and madrone.

SPECIAL FEATURES: An area rich in history as well as scenic beauty . . . The site of the little town of Taylorville where Paper Mill Creek is named for the paper mill business operated by Samuel Taylor in the 1860s and '70s . . . After the opening in 1874 of a narrow-gauge railroad to connect the area with Pt. Reyes and Tomales Bay, Taylorville became a famous recreation area and was one of the first areas in the United States to promote outdoor camping as public recreation . . . Today there are 68 campsites in the redwood groves and a special camp for horsemen . . . Fishing is allowed along the creeks and in nearby lakes with permission from the Marin Municipal Water District.

LOCATION: North of San Francisco in the hills of western Marin County west of the town of Lagunitas. You have two choices: Exit off Hwy. 101 on Sir Francis Drake Hwy. and travel through the communities of San Anselmo, Fairfax, Forest Knolls, and Lagunitas. The road is well paved but curving and congested for about 15 miles, so take it easy, OR take the Lucas Valley Road exit off of 101 to Nicasio Rd., turn left to Sir Francis Drake, turn right (Forest Knolls) and travel on twisting, narrow road to Park entrance. . . . Very scenic and less traffic this way.

WHERE TO PARK: There are many, very wide areas along Sir Francis Drake Hwy. which make suitable pull-outs for parking for one or two trailers. For a larger group or overnight stay, drive in the main Park entrance and a ranger will direct you to Devil's Gulch Camp for horsemen. To use the equestrian area **reservations must be made in advance with Park headquarters.** Phone (415) 488-9897 or write Samuel P. Taylor State Park, P.O. Box 251, Lagunitas, CA 94938.

TRAIL FEATURES: Trails well marked with California Riding and Hiking signs (including mileages) . . . Eight miles of trail within the Park with many more miles possible by connecting with adjacent Pt. Reyes, Mt. Tamalpais, and Golden Gate National Recreation Areas . . . Some trails are quite steep, giving you an opportunity for good conditioning rides (from Shafter Bridge to Mt. Tamalpais) . . . others are fireroads with gentle grades for easy side-by-side riding . . . A suggested route for novice horsemen and unconditioned horses is to park in the equestrian area, ride from Devil's Gulch Camp to Shafter Bridge, and return . . . what you experience on this route is a beautiful two-hour ride on a trail paralleling Paper Mill Creek and bordered by redwood trees, an invigorating ride as the sound of rushing water accompanies you! **Competitive rides are possible here** . . . these

trails are used for a portion of the Drake's Bay 50-Mile Endurance Ride.

ACCOMMODATIONS: Devil's Gulch Campground has corrals, hitchracks, water troughs, picnic tables, and toilets . . . a great overnight area for horse groups! Don't forget to phone ahead for reservations.

FEES: No charge for day use, but $4 per rig for overnight (2 horses).

PARK SERVICES: Maps are available at the ranger's gate for 25 cents . . . Maintenance of a great overnight camp for horsemen is the best service of all!

PARK RULES: All wildlife and natural resources are protected here . . . Remember, no dogs and no smoking on the trail.

WEATHER: A great place to cool off in the summer . . . usually cool with coastal breezes . . . Anytime is a wonderful time to ride here . . . There's good drainage on the trails, so even after a heavy rain most of the trails will be usable.

 CAUTION: Use your good judgment about crossing the creek under Shafter Bridge . . . especially in the spring, water can be too deep for safe crossing.

15

TRAIL PATRONS

Sonoma County Trails Committee

A FULL-FLEDGED ribbon-cutting celebration on February 26, 1984, marked the opening of public access to trails linking Jack London State Historic park with the trails on Sonoma State Hospital lands. The honored guests were 35 hardworking hikers and riders who played a permanent part in two years of negotiations culminating in the happy ceremony. Prominent in that group are members of the Sonoma County Trails Committee, which is playing a significant role in the development of Wine Country trails.

The Committee began in 1980 with the request by the Sonoma County Planning Commission for citizen involvement in the development of the County's General Plan. United by the goal of establishing a multiple-use trail system, hikers, horsemen, bicyclists, and joggers worked to include this concept in the General Plan. The goal was met in 1981, and the following year the SCTC was incorporated as a nonprofit, public-benefit organization dedicated to the development and support of multiuse trails.

Why spend all this energy in support of trails? The SCTC has no problem answering that question! "Sonoma County is unique in its great beauty and ideal climate. It is the site of numerous historic trails and scenic routes already in existence. It is an area of greatly contrasting environments, from salt marshes and rugged coast to lakes, redwoods, scenic valleys, and vineyards. Recreational trails provide healthful pleasure for thousands of individuals and families at minimum expense . . . A strong trail system enhances the total assets of Sonoma County for business and commerce as well."

New goals are set each year, and your help is welcome and needed. Join the fun! For more information: P.O. Box 483, El Verano, CA 95433.

Sonoma County Trails Council

As you ride along the trails of Warm Springs Dam-Lake Sonoma, Annadel State Park, Austin Grove and Armstrong Redwood State Park, and Sugarloaf State Park (just to name a few!) think a few grateful thoughts for the Sonoma County Trails Council. This group which dates back to 1967 is largely responsible for the development of trails in these areas.

Originally it was horsemen groups and a few hikers who were active on the Council, and so the emphasis was put on equestrian trails. But with the involvement of more hikers and the advent of mountain bicycles the Council has been working toward a multiuse trail system. Besides working closely with the Sonoma County Regional Parks Department and State Recreation agencies as "advisers," Council members are known for their well attended trail work parties and barbecue trail rides! By all accounts it's a friendly, hardworking, effective group with a solid record of achievement for trails. In 1982 federal government budget cuts nearly eliminated the money designated for trail construction in Sonoma County's only federally owned installation, Warm Springs Dam-Lake Sonoma. In response the Council spearheaded a petition drive requesting the Corps of Engineers and the federal government to honor their commitment to the people of Sonoma County. According to Genevieve Day, Council president, the hundreds of petitions sent to Washington, D.C., were definitely helpful in reinstating recreational use at Lake Sonoma. Trails, staging areas, and a boat ramp are presently under construction, and a good working relationship has developed between the Corps rangers and the Council.

Your involvement is welcome on the Council, which currently represents 12 riding clubs, individual horsemen, hikers, and a group of mountain bicyclists. Monthly meetings are held the third Wednesday of each month at the Sonoma County Driving and Riding Clubhouse in Santa Rosa. For more information: P.O. Box 832, Windsor, CA 95492-0832, (707) 838-6088.

Northern California Trails Council

You can't fail to be impressed with the Hiking and Equestrian Trail Guide distributed by the Northern California Trails Council. The featured area is the Little Lake-Sherwood trail, described by the Council as "an extensive chain of roads and paths, offering both hiker and rider approximately 45 miles of enjoyment. Through serene redwood groves and heavily forested canyons to open fields and meadows, the trail user will follow roads that have been abandoned as well as those busily used for logging — the Sherwood Trail runs north and south on its western end, and through its feeder trails serves the most populated section of Mendocino County. By its extension eastward the trail serves to connect the inland parts of the County with those of the coast . . . Long-range plans call for the trail to continue to Willits, then to Ukiah, and back over the mountains to Mendocino, completing a loop of more than 150 miles . . . Special thanks to those private corporations who have granted special use permits to Mendocino County: Louisiana Pacific, Georgia Pacific, Masonite, and World Visions."

Credit goes to the Mendocino County Parks Department and the Mendocino County Trails Advisory Committee for the high quality and detail of this Guide. Don't delay in contacting the Northern California Trails Council for your copy. Better yet, join this group which already has a long list of accomplishments to its credit:

- Board of Supervisors adoption of a Master County Trail Plan.
- Establishment of the Chamberlain Creek Horse Camp in 52,000-acre Jackson State Forest between Coast Hwy. 1 and State Hwy. 101.
- Dedication of Pudding Creek-Ten Mile Beach Trail on the north boundary of Fort Bragg.

Future goals include the completion of a "loop" trail around Mendocino County, as well as assisting in the ultimate accomplishment of a coastal trail.

New members are always welcome! Write to: NCTC, Inc. 10511 Wheeler Street, Mendocino, CA 94560, (707) 937-5974.

Marin Horse Council

Nearly 800 members and still growing! That's the prognosis for one of the fastest growing horse clubs in the country. The Marin Horse Council was conceived in December 1980 in response to a call for equestrian information from Pierre Joske, Director of the Marin County Parks and Recreation Department. The discussion centered on whether there was a need for an equestrian facility in Marin County. Out of this discussion "the need was recognized for an independent, central coordinating council representing Marin County's many horse clubs, individual owners, breeders, trainers, veterinarians, farriers, etc." As a result the Marin Horse Council was incorporated on April 22, 1981. An enthusiastic membership has grown by leaps and bounds.

Council officer Deni McNamara gives much of the credit for the club's early success to founding director Rod Peck. The Council's establishment as a nonprofit public benefit corporation was the first step in the development of this highly effective organization serving the interests and needs of persons involved with horses — whether or not they own one. In addition to its work with the Marin Humane Society, the Council has established success through the following activities:

- a NEWSLETTER and a HOT LINE alerting members to issues of concern to horsemen (includes assistance in trailer emergencies!).
- a CALENDAR of horse-related activities.
- a DIRECTORY of information about all equestrian facilities and services.

Mendocino County

NCTC Trailboss Dave Sverko of Mendocino leads riders on Five Day Ride.

- EDUCATIONAL PROGRAMS covering numerous subjects of interest to horse lovers.
- a LIBRARY of books, maps, magazines, and other resource material (at the Humane Society building).
- an INFORMATION REFERRAL SERVICE for any individual, organization, business, agency, or governmental body.
- a proposal for the development of a major EQUESTRIAN AND LIVESTOCK FACILITY/SHOWGROUND.

If you own one of the approximately 10,000 horses in Marin County or just love horses in general, don't miss the chance to join the Marin Horse Council, 171 Bel Marin Keys, Novato, CA 94947.

With the heavy duty equipment of the Army Corps of Engineers behind you, plan on improvements happening fast at Lake Sonoma. Sonoma County horsewoman Genevieve Day consults with Park personnel on plans for new equestrian staging area.

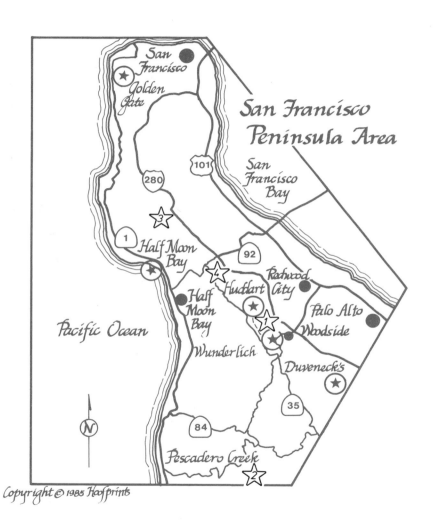

San Francisco
Peninsula Area

San
Francisco
Bay

Pacific Ocean

San Francisco
Golden Gate
Half Moon Bay
Half Moon Bay
Wunderlich
Redwood City
Huddart
Palo Alto
Woodside
Duveneck's
Pescadero Creek

II. San Francisco Peninsula Area

Featuring

☆1 Skyline Trail
(Wunderlich to Huddart County Parks)

☆2 Pescadero Creek County Park
(Jack Brook Horse Camp)

San Francisco Water Department:

☆3 Ridge Trail

☆4 Filoli Trail

⊛ Neighboring trail areas

San Mateo County Horsemen on a spring trail ride.

LEW REED couldn't possibly have guessed that the simple decision to have a second cup of coffee would change the course of his life. With the first cup of coffee he had skimmed the local newspaper, reading in full only the articles of national interest. But with the decision to stretch out the coffee break, (a rare luxury for the harried insurance claims supervisor), Lew's attitude became leisurely as he scanned the Peninsula newspaper with the thoroughness native to his character. Then he saw the advertisement. A Western store not too far from his San Mateo office was having a sale. For just $12 he could own a pair of genuine leather boots! The bargain price caught his eye, but it was the memories aroused by the leather boots that made the ad irresistible.

Lew had grown up on an Illinois farm in the good company of cows, horses, pigs, and chickens. He was only eight years old when his parents presented him with his own horse, buggy, and harness in which they had invested $20. Lew kept the whole rig intact for seventeen years until the day he sold the horse for $30. His enjoyment of horses and farm life had been interrupted first by college at the University of Illinois, then law school, followed by law practice in Chicago, marriage, then with wife and daughter a move to California for health reasons. The "good old days" of rural living seemed gone forever until 1949 when he discovered the Circle H guest ranch in Bridgeport, California. Since then the ranch had been the favorite vacation place for all three members of the Reed family. But in the midst of all the pressures of suburban life, happy memories of farms and ranches had lain dormant until now when they were roused by the prospect of owning a new pair of boots.

"Walking in that Western store was the most expensive decision of my life," recalls Lew 24 years later. "I plunked down the $12 for the boots, then on the way out I saw a belt and a hat and so on. Before I got out the door I'd spent $60 on Western wear hardly needed by a Bay Area insurance man! But that was only the beginning. Pretty soon I found myself at an auction where I bid on a saddle and got it! It seemed kind of silly to own a saddle without a horse so the next thing I knew I was buying a horse. Then we felt like we needed a home in Woodside to keep the horse around so we could try different trails. When we put it all together I'd say those $12 boots ended up costing me about $300,000!"

Even more impressive than the dollars involved is the wide range of community involvement which opened up as Lew's life began to focus on horse activities. Lew retired in 1976. but his life as a retiree makes a mockery of the word as defined by Webster. He is the

20

Lew Reed, trail boss for San Mateo County horsemen.

oppposite of "someone who has withdrawn, has retreated or secluded oneself, kept aloof or apart." For over 25 years he's been esteemed as a dedicated member of the San Mateo County Trails Advisory Committee; member of the Board of Directors and trail boss for one of the oldest organized horse groups in the state, The San Mateo County Horsemen, incorporated in 1943; treasurer of the Midpeninsula Trails Council; planning commissioner for the Town of Woodside; city councilman and newly elected Mayor of Woodside. There's plenty of action on the home front as well including Little League and 4H. Lew and his wife, Veva, have been parents to their grandson Christopher since the untimely death of their daughter in 1971.

While it's difficult to imagine integrating these commitments of energy and time with the additional commitments required of the horse owner, it's easy to see what makes it all possible—Lew Reed and his family express an uncommon dedication to their community and to each other. What are the rewards?

"I see *results* and that's encouraging," answers Lew. "I've seen a lot of active people concerned about trails, or some other issue, come and go, but the ones who are most effective are the dedicated ones . . . the ones who will stick with an issue as long as they're needed. The danger for these people is that they can easily become so overloaded they practically have to give up riding to attend all the meetings. But don't let that happen! You have to keep a balance between your enjoyment of your animal, quiet woods and open country, the peacefulness that you find on a trail, and your willingness to attend meetings and fight for your access to trails. I want to add that the most effective people I've seen fighting for trails have been reasonable people, not the ones haranguing the government officials they need to work with."

The good results Lew sees from dedicated political involvement are only one aspect of the reward he's received from his activity with horses. "I give the horse credit for the fact that I feel hale, hearty, and healthy," he says with enthusiasm. "There's a lot of work, a lot of physical effort required to care for a horse and to work on trails. As I get older I find it very gratifying, very satisfying to accomplish the sometimes arduous physical tasks connected with horses."

The most satisfying and the most physically demanding activity that Lew shares with his purebred Morgan trail horse is the annual Circle H cattle drive which he has been participating in for the past 17 years. This is no dude activity. In the bitter November cold of the High Sierra the Hunewill family moves their cattle herd ranging from

Lew, (far left) is flag bearer for San Mateo County Horsemen's display at the Cow Palace.

500 to 750 head from Bridgeport Valley to winter pasture in Smith Valley, Nevada. The fifth generation ranchers are assisted in this enterprise by a few neighbors, regular ranch hands, and about 12 guests of the ranch such as Lew. All together about 20 people on horseback brave five days of snow, rain, and dust storms to push the cattle out of the mountains and along the road to the milder winter temperatures of Nevada.

"A rough day on the ride is getting up at 4 a.m. and it's pouring rain, saddling your horse at 7 a.m. and it's pouring rain, and still pouring rain when you get out of the saddle at 5:30 in the evening," recalls Lew. "Worst of all was eating lunch in the rain. We ate our lunch standing in a great big stock trailer. I'll tell you one thing for sure, you don't dare drop your sandwich!"

"It sounds pretty miserable, and often it is, but the fact that I haven't missed a trail drive in 17 years tells you how I really feel about it!" explains Lew. "It's a lot rougher riding than you get riding Bay Area trails, but still it's a pretty easy life compared to the old time cowboys. We're up before dawn and in the saddle all day, but when

At San Francisco Water Department entrance to the Filoli Trail, trail boss Lew demonstrates what not to do with your horse when opening a gate!

Robert Toren

A silhouette of Lew Reed and friends on a crisp November morning during a Circle H cattle drive.

the day's over our horses are corralled at neighboring ranches along the way and we're driven back for a delicious dinner at the ranch. It's freezing cold outside but we're cozy in winterproofed cabins. The elements of snow, sand, and rain can make you pretty miserable, but the camaraderie of the group, the excitement of moving down the trail makes it all worth it. Stanley Hunewill, head honcho at the ranch, says that as long as his son and grandson are around to run the ranch they'll continue to operate the cattle drive. Well, his grandson is only a year old so I think there are quite a lot of drives ahead!"

Lew credits his experience at Circle H for giving him a preference for ranch-raised Morgan horses. "Circle H raises good strong Morgans that do well on pasture grass and don't get a lot of pampering and doctoring. They're savvy horses, exposed to all kinds

of trail hazards except for cars and trucks which they rarely see. They cross streams, work cattle, maneuver well on all kinds of terrain, and can lope all day, they're in such good condition. Ranch horses are worked hard all summer, all day every day, but then they're out to pasture the rest of the year so it's a good life. Time spent on a ranch is good for us city slickers too. Bay area riders are used to single file trails, so there's a lot of excitement when you get the freedom to ride cross country with no specific trail. It's very unconfining, it gives you a tremendous feeling for open space."

What advice does this veteran horseman and community leader have for the beginning rider? "Get involved in NATRC, learn about trails on their well planned rides. With NATRC you'll get a good education in horse care, general horsemanship, and an appreciation for a good trail system. If we're going to have riding for individuals and groups we have to have a trail system to support the activity, just like you have to have a bowling alley to bowl. People have to care enough about trails to fight for them, to be dedicated."

Life might have been a lot simpler for Lew Reed if he'd never read the ad featuring $12 boots. But what those boots ultimately cost him in terms of time and money has been recompensed in years filled with achievement and adventures. As we leaf through a family album filled with picturesque photos of trail rides and cattle drives Lew is obviously a man whose dedication has been rewarded along the way.

22

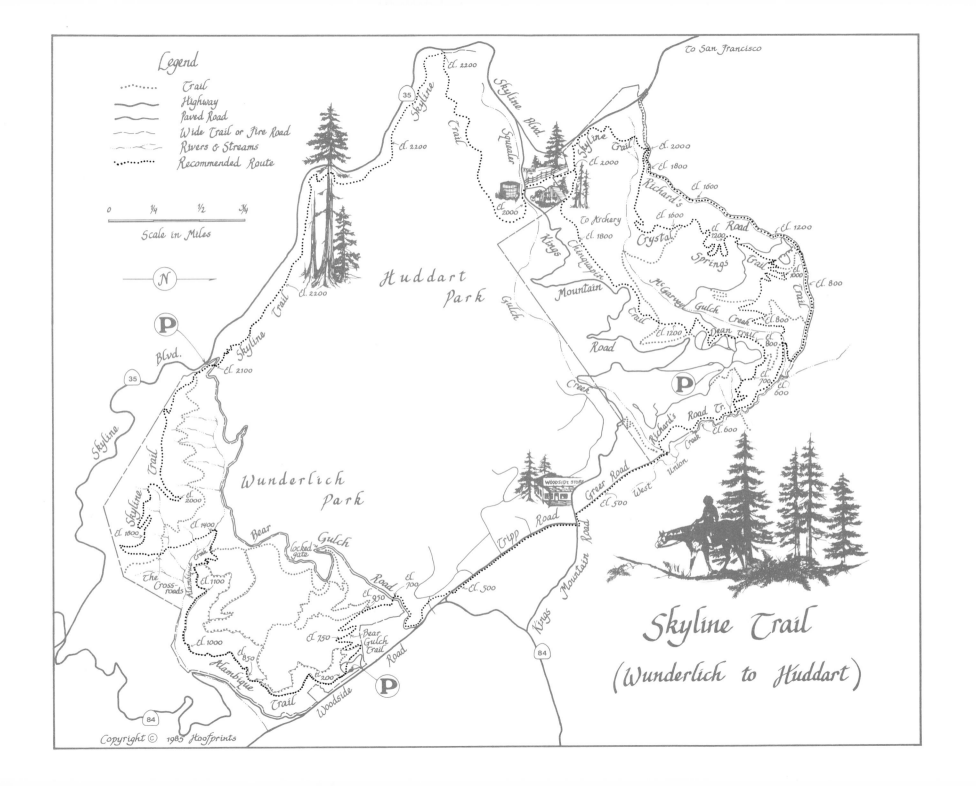

Legend

⋯⋯⋯ Trail
〰〰〰 Highway
〰〰〰 Paved Road
〰〰〰 Wide Trail or Fire Road
〰〰〰 Rivers & Streams
•••• Recommended Route

0   ¼   ½   ¾
Scale in Miles

N

Huddart Park

Wunderlich Park

Skyline Trail
(Wunderlich to Huddart)

Copyright © 1985 Hoofprints

SKYLINE TRAIL
(connecting Wunderlich and Huddart Parks)

Horses seem to like this trail, recovering quickly from their climb and trotting at an easy pace almost the entire distance . . . How quiet it is, and beautiful . . . it makes you wish you knew something more about botany.

— Lew Reed

REASONS TO GO: A "get away from it all" trail, very lightly traveled . . . Solitude doesn't mean loneliness here because there's so much to see and to imagine on this richly endowed link between two great San Mateo County Parks . . . The peace and quiet of the lush, fern-bordered trail set your mind free to wonder about its past . . . the loggers who used portions of the trail in the 1880s and the horsemen who extended the trail to join the two ranches which were to become County parks . . . Dramatic changes in vegetation and species of trees remind you that this is an area of changing climate and terrain . . . deer and flowers punctuate the rich green tapestry of forest that surrounds you . . . occasionally there's a break in the trees and blue sky brightens your path.

SPECIAL FEATURES: Because of this trail a magnificent loop is possible offering many hours and miles of scenic riding without the necessity of permits and keys . . . Sky-high views of Palo Alto and Stanford . . . Wildflowers, madrone and redwood line the trail . . . a quiet path except for an occasional buzz from the traffic on Skyline Blvd,. an interruption quickly forgotten as deer bound across the trail and up a fern-covered bank . . .

LOCATION: Adjacent to Skyline Blvd. (Hwy. 35) above Woodside, maintained by San Mateo County Parks and Recreation. Trail is accessible from either Wunderlich or Huddart Park. Each Park is

about two miles from the center of the town of Woodside. Wunderlich is reached by taking Woodside Road west from Hwy. 280 to 4040 Woodside Road, turning right into the parking lot . . . Driveway entrance is easy to miss, so go slowly. Huddart is reached by traveling west on Woodside Rd. to Kings Mountain Rd. which is narrow and winding for about three miles, to the Park entrance.

WHERE TO PARK: Entering from Wunderlich: Entrance to parking lot and Park are one and the same . . . There are sturdy hitching posts, water and hoses available for your use . . . also a well maintained outdoor toilet . . . On weekdays the space easily accommodates six or more trailers but weekend parking is becoming a problem. Entering from Huddart Park the ranger at the gate will collect a $2 parking fee per vehicle and direct you to equestrian parking.

TRAIL FEATURES: Skyline Trail is a beautiful five-mile trail in itself but it is most appreciated when used as a link to the trail systems of two Parks . . . Between the two Parks the trail is basically level and single file in width . . . it's a safe and enjoyable route offering heavenly hours and many miles of uninterrupted riding! For a great all-day ride have a friend drop you off at Wunderlich and then park your trailer at Huddart . . . a nice friend like that should be treated to dinner at one of Woodside's

excellent restaurants . . . or at least a barbecue using Huddart's great facilities!

Lew's recommendation for a perfect day on the Peninsula: "For a ride of some 23 miles (or longer if you explore more Park trails) start at Wunderlich Park on Alambique Trail which takes off right behind the large map bulletin board. Continue on up to the Crossroads and pick up Skyline Trail which is the middle trail to the right. Skyline will wind its way up to the top of the Park nearly reaching Skyline Blvd. (Hwy. 35) and leave the Park where it crosses Bear Gulch Rd. Cross Bear Gulch Rd. (look to the right for the trail crossing) and follow the trail paralleling Skyline Blvd. until it crosses Kings Mountain Rd. Cross the road and follow the trail along the edge of a private driveway into Huddart Park . . . Skyline Trail branches at a T junction with the Chinquapin Trail to the right (down) and the Skyline Trail to the left (up). You'll have to make a decision here as there are three good routes through Huddart Park to the desired exit. The recommended ride for your first trip is to turn left at the junction and follow the Skyline Trail to its intersection with Richard's Road Trail as designated on the map. At the end of Richard's Road Trail you are out of the Park and on roadside trails until you reenter Wunderlich Park. As you come out of Huddart Park you'll be on Greer Rd. Go right on Greer (a narrow residential street) to King's Mountain Rd. Turn left on King's Mountain. At historic Woodside Store turn right on Tripp and go right on

Woodside Rd. At junction of Woodside Rd. with Tripp Rd. there's a driveway to the right. Go up the driveway about 20 ft. The Trail is on the left. Follow trail to Bear Gulch Rd. and continue up Bear Gulch to locked gate. Take ramp on the left and you're back in Wunderlich. Completing this route as designed by Lew Reed means that without the hassle of gates and keys you've been able to ride through two gorgeous parks and along the entire Skyline Trail . . . length of ride is approximately six hours depending on the extent of your side trips and lunch break! "Your horse will have had a real workout," says Lew, "but neither of you will be over-tired and you will have had a wonderful day."

A variation of this ride might include a short side trip to the Upper Meadows in Wunderlich where you'll find a picnic table and nearby trees and rails for tying. Within Huddart Park you might try heading down toward the Archery Range and on to the bottom of Greer Rd.

ACCOMODATIONS: Day use only.

FEES: No parking fee at Wunderlich . . . $2 trailer parking fee at Huddart.

PARK SERVICES: Beautifully maintained trails and a very accommodating County Parks system operating in a way that makes you feel welcome! Rangers appreciate your reports on trail conditions and are very prompt in clearing trails . . . Parks have ranger patrol on foot and in radio-equipped trucks.

WEATHER: Trail is open and passable all year round. The Skyline Trail is on a mountain ridge so don't be surprised by foggy weather . . . take a jacket! This is an especially pleasant trail when the rest of the world seems hot and smoggy.

PARK RULES: Open year-round from 8 a.m. to dark . . . . All animals and natural features are pro-tected . . . No smoking on trails, do not bring dog . . . No campfires are allowed.

CAUTION: Very few trail hazards . . . other trail users are mainly hikers but there have been some problems here with mountain bikes . . . Poison oak flourishes in this area but the trails are wide enough for it to be easily avoided.

Nancy Stuart

25

PESCADERO CREEK COUNTY PARK
(Jack Brook Horse Camp)

One of the best horse camps in existence . . . The place to really enjoy your horse in a peaceful, beautiful atmosphere . . .

— Lew Reed

Advance planning is a key ingredient in the success of your horse camping trip.

REASONS TO GO: A magnificent trail system with plenty of distance for long, leisurely rides . . . Over 6,000 acres linked with trails which climb over 1300 feet . . . you'll have an "on top of the world" feeling riding along Butano Ridge with glimpses of the Pacific Ocean in the distance . . . Trails lined with a tremendous variety of trees and ferns . . . grassy areas blanketed with wildflowers and the sight of thriving wildlife inevitably deepen your love of nature and the horse that gives you access to so much beauty . . .

SPECIAL FEATURES: From a horseman's point of view the most special thing about this Park is the Jack Brook Horse Camp with its indelible aura of beauty and hospitality . . . As you enjoy "first class" overnight horse camping take a few minutes to appreciate the cooperation and backbreaking labor of San Mateo County horsemen who built the camp — the Mounted Patrol of San Mateo County, the Los Viajeros, the San Mateo County Horsemen, and the Shack Riders . . . the efforts of these groups in tandem with San Mateo County Parks and Recreation Department epitomize the effectiveness of cooperation between Park managers and dedicated volunteers.

LOCATION: Located within the Sam McDonald County Park, a segment of the Pescadero Creek County Park system . . . on Pescadero Rd. in San Mateo County near the communities of La Honda and Pescadero . . . A 40-minute trailer trip from the

Town of Woodside or 20 minutes from the junction of Hwy. 84 and Hwy. 35 at Skylonda.

Hwy. 84 and Pescadero Rd. are both paved and easily traveled by car and trailer, but from Hwy. 280 to Skyline Blvd. (35) it is uphill and winding and from Skyline to La Honda on Hwy. 84 it is downhill and winding, so it is still slow going in some areas.

WHERE TO PARK: For **day use** drive to the large Sam McDonald Park parking area at 9500 Pescadero Creek Rd. There is no special area designated for horse trailers but to date there has not been a problem of over-crowding. For **overnight use** of the Jack Brook Horse Camp by individuals or groups, reservations must be made in advance with the Park. Phone: (415) 363-4021 or write to: Jack Brook Horse Camp, County Government Center, 590 Hamilton St., Redwood City, CA 94063. For trail information phone: (415) 747-0403 or write to Sam McDonald Park, Pescadero Creek County Park, 13435 Pescadero Rd., La Honda, CA, 94020.

ACCOMMODATIONS: Overnight facilities at the Jack Brook Horse Camp include an open kitchen, fire pits, hot showers, and a barn with a corral and paddocks. **Make your reservations early** as use of the camp for horses is limited to the dry season between April 15 and November 15. For **day use** water is available at the parking lot but bring your own bucket for watering horses . . . Clean restrooms at the ranger station.

TRAIL FEATURES: Bring well-conditioned horses for these rigorous trails and plan on a full day's riding — but an overnight stay is even better! Trails are well maintained and generally well marked, but don't set out for a day's ride without the beautifully detailed map provided by the Park and a review of up-to-date trail conditions supplied by the rangers . . . In addition to the new, machine-built trails and narrow, forest trails a lot of ground can be covered on old logging roads and former ranch roads . . . the latter offer safe and easy side-by-side riding, but expect some dust!

Good shelter for the horses is a luxurious feature of the Jack Brook Horsemen's Camp.

For **day use** of Pescadero Creek Trails Lew suggests starting at the back corner of the Sam McDonald parking area, crossing Pescadero Rd. and entering the well-marked trail leading to the Horse Camp. You'll be on a deeply shaded forest trail which will take you past the Horse Camp to the junction of Towne Trail and Bear Ridge Trail. Take Bear Ridge Trail to the left and follow it all the way downhill toward the Honor Camp . . . You will see a large "Horse Trail" sign which directs you to a bypass around the Honor Camp and onto a blacktop road . . . turn left, cross the bridge and pick up the Tarwater Loop Trail . . . take this trail to the left, up the hill to the point where it again crosses blacktop. Continue past the trailhead parking area until you reach a junction with the newly constructed Canyon Trail. This leads back to Bear Ridge Trail. By bearing right you end up on the Towne Trail leading back to your trailer at the ranger station. This suggested route allows about five and a half hours for a 15-mile trip.

For a shorter ride on the Tarwater Loop Trail drive westerly from Alpine Rd. from Hwy. 35 to the junction with Camp Pomponio Rd. known as Tarwater Trailhead. This parking area accommodates about six vehicles with horse trailers . . . A five-mile loop trail is possible from this point . . . allow about three hours to really enjoy a trail which starts out at the location of an old ranch (the blacksmith shop still stands), runs along a pear orchard and open grass areas, travels down into the canyon and along Shingle Mill Creek.

Ranch roads for carriage driving and enough distance for competitive rides!

FEES: No charge for day-use parking. Fees for overnight use of the horse camp are $3 per person per night for groups up to 10. Groups larger than 10 are charged $25 per group, plus $2 per person per night.

PARK SERVICES: A beautifully illustrated and detailed map available through the Park office . . . Friendly and accommodating rangers patrol the Park using trucks and motor bikes . . . rangers generally available at the Sam McDonald Ranger Station on Pescadero Creek Rd.

PARK RULES: Horses must stay on designated trails . . . no dogs allowed . . . all wildlife, plants and natural features are protected . . . no cutting and gathering of wood . . . camping and picnicking are permitted only in designated areas.

WEATHER: The Park is open year-round but some trails are subject to closure in the rainy season . . . check with rangers for current trail conditions. In the event of closures there is still at least 20 miles of riding on service roads which are open year-round . . . Park can be cold, windy and wet . . . always ride with a light jacket or windbreaker . . . even in summer months forest trails are cool and dark very early in the evening.

 CAUTION: There's not much to discourage you in this Park with its thoughtfully, beautifully maintained trails . . . San Mateo County Parks Department and involved San Mateo County horsemen (not to mention Mother Nature!) have gone to great lengths to make your ride pleasant and memorable . . . it's up to you to come prepared with a horse adequately conditioned for some of the steep trails.

SAN FRANCISCO WATER DEPARTMENT RIDGE TRAIL (permit required)

Excellent all-weather trails for horsemen
who appreciate high open space vistas . . .
I never tire of riding here . . .

— Lew Reed

REASONS TO GO: Magnificent views of San Francisco Bay from safe, wide trails . . . Overlook the entire length of Crystal Springs Lakes from Sawyer Ridge . . . Monitor the hubbub of San Francisco International Airport from the serenity of Portola Ridge . . . on clear days impressive views across the Bay to Hayward and Mt. Diablo . . . Wide, fairly level trails promote quiet, relaxed riding with abundant opportunities for birdwatching and glimpses of wildlife . . . Approximately 20 miles of trail that are easy to reach and in great shape year-round open to all riders . . . **Groups may apply for special permission** to ride 10 additional miles along Fifield Ridge and Spring Valley Ridge . . . from these ridges the Pacific Ocean is seen far out enough to spot an occasional ship! . . . Views of Lake Pilarcitos nestled in a valley inspires dreams of staying forever in open country . . .

SPECIAL FEATURES: Access to Sweeney Ridge and the Portola Bay Discovery site . . . if all the open space makes you lonely, follow the trail to the Coastside Corral in Pacifica and meet up with some fellow riders! Treat this land with care as the entire 23,000 acres is not only a game refuge but also watershed land providing San Francisco's water supply . . . Sightings of rabbits, bobcats, coyotes, and a spiraling hawk almost guaranteed!

LOCATION: In northern San Mateo County on high ridges above Crystal Springs Lakes, Hillsborough, San Mateo, Burlingame, Millbrae, San Bruno, and South San Francisco. 25-minute drive from Woodside and 10 minutes from Black Mountain Road off-ramp on I-280.

TRAIL FEATURES: Trails were originally the routes used by rangers on horseback, but in recent years they have been graveled for vehicle patrol . . . Only dirt surface trail is Portola Ridge . . . Wide trails for easy side-by-side riding with no single file paths . . . All routes are well maintained and suitable for novice horsemen . . . Trails are not signed (except where horses are not permitted) but it's almost impossible to get lost if you remember that the Bay is on your right going north and the hills are on your left . . . Steady uphill grade for about a mile from the parking area takes you to Sawyer Ridge.

Trail boss Lew Reed describes the various routes in detail: "Turning right on Sawyer Ridge leads to a road junction and a cement block building providing clean drinking water and toilet facilities . . . Future plans call for tie rail and horse trough. Continue north on this route to Portola Ridge and go as far as you can till you see a road to your left (west). Here is an opportunity to make a side trip off S.F. Water Department lands onto Sweeney Ridge through the equestrian gate. Or you might swing left just past the gate and follow a path down to Coastside Corral in Pacifica. **With a group that has permission** you may stay on Water Department lands and head westerly till you come to Spring Valley Ridge which leads you back toward the south past Lake Pilarcitos on the right to a five-point junction . . . For the **individual rider** the recommended route is to enter the gate at top of Millbrae Avenue, follow the paving down across the dam to equestrian gate on the right, and up the road to the cement block building — from here you may make a figure 8 loop or a circle loop either to

the right or left, coming ultimately back to the cement block building and back to your trailer.

For group rides: "an alternate to Spring Valley Ridge is Fifield Ridge paralleling it. Take the middle road to the left and the trail will lead you back to the original starting point on Sawyer Ridge. The above ride is about 17 miles long. For a shorter ride cut across from the five-point junction back to the cement building on Sawyer Ridge for an hour-and-a-half ride. The cutoff is paved and is the first route to the left at the five-point junction.

"Basic thing to remember is that the trail system is laid out like the figure 8. Riding the large circle will take about four and a half hours, riding the smaller circle will reduce the ride to one and a half hours. Add an extra hour to ride to the Bay Discovery site and an extra hour to ride to Coastside Corral" . . . **Favorite conditioning trails for endurance riders, group riders, and possible carriage drives.**

A southward view from the San Francisco Water Department lands.

WHERE TO PARK: Groups take Black Mountain Rd. cutoff from I-280, turning west under the freeway to Golf Course Road. Go north past the clubhouse through the parking area. You will come to a gate which seems to indicate the road is closed, but go through the gate (after opening it, of course! I say that because I've known some pretty determined horsemen!) There will be a road on your left across the golf course. Follow the road westerly to the bottom of the hill to the ranger's residence. Just outside his gate there is a telephone pole, here bear left down the lane to the vehicle gate. Cross Sawyer Camp Road, pass through one more gate, across the dam and at last you are in the group parking area at the beginning of the trail. Sounds complicated, but the ride is worth it and you'll return again and again! Above arrangements are adequate for at least 40 trailers. Apply four weeks in advance to: San Francisco Water Department, 1000 El Camino Real, Millbrae, CA 94030. No fee. Applicants will have to seek special permission to utilize picnic areas located at Sawyer Camp Ranger Station and Lake Pilarcitos Ranger Station. We are advised that management of these areas is presently undergoing change. **Individuals:** Improved parking areas for individual riders are being considered, but at present individuals desiring to ride the Ridge trails will have to share Millbrae Avenue underpass of I-280 with other trail users . . . a definite problem on the weekends.

ACCOMMODATIONS: Day use only. No camping and no overnight . . . Several chemical toilets located along the trail . . . There's drinking water for you but none for your horse at the pre-

sent time . . . **Remember that these trails are available by permit only both to individuals and to groups.** Please protect this privilege by honoring all regulations.

FEES: None.
Permit is mandatory and strictly enforced. Application for key and permit is made by writing to S.F. Water Department, P.O. Box 730, 1000 El Camino Real, Millbrae, CA 94030. Applications must be cosigned by a judge, sheriff, police chief or mayor or officer of a local Horsemen's Association. A 1″ x 1″ photo and a stamped, self-addressed envelope must accompany application. The effort to maintain a permit is very well spent, resulting in many miles of pleasurable year-round riding. A group permit will also require a copy of the group's insurance policy naming the Water Department as a coinsured.

SERVICES: Friendly, helpful ranger patrol by San Francisco Water Department and California Fish and Game.

RULES: Camping, fishing, bathing, hunting, trapping, carrying or use of firearms, and dogs are prohibited. This is a preserve area, so any disturbance of plant life is not allowed. Groups should leave their horses and vehicles at the group parking area and walk or shuttle with only one car to the picnic area. There are no trails to Lake Pilarcitos, and trespass is strictly forbidden. Water District officials advise that the general purpose of the entire area is water control and management and not really recreational. Equestrians enjoy a special privilege in the area not to be abused.

WEATHER: Ridge trails are only about two miles inland from Pacific Ocean, so always carry a jacket or windbreaker . . . Rarely has the trail been closed because of heavy rains . . . Trail is in good condition even after storms.

 CAUTION: Trail rules are strictly enforced, which makes for very safe riding as long as you are on the right side of the law!

Entrance to Filoli is through stone pillars at Cañada and Edgewood roads.

Cañada Rd. entrance to Edgewood County Park.

Terrain varies from wide open spaces to shady, forested areas perfect for a summer picnic.

SAN FRANCISCO WATER DEPARTMENT
FILOLI TRAIL (permit required)

Year-round pleasure riding on shady, forested trails . . .
Happy memories return when you think back to the old days
when every summer the paddocks of the Filoli estate were filled
with gorgeous mares and their frisky colts . . .

— Lew Reed

REASONS TO GO: Year-round riding at its best . . . shady in hot weather, dry trails in wet weather . . . easy access to beautiful, tree-lined trails and grassy meadows filled with wild flowers.

SPECIAL FEATURES: Loop trail leads to the back of the Pulgas Water Temple which is hospitable enough to provide a watering trough . . . access to the wild flower mecca, Edgewood Park . . . Indian digs operated by Cañada College and College of San Mateo are seen just to the right of the trail while riding north, and also north of the stable area . . . Also a State Game Refuge with abundant birdlife.

LOCATION: In San Mateo County three miles north of Hwy. 84 and west of Cañada Rd. in Woodside. It is about 45 minutes by horseback from Hwy. 84 and Cañada Rd. and 10 minutes by vehicle. Access is also just five minutes by vehicle from the I-280-Edgewood Rd. junction.

WHERE TO PARK: Entrance at Edgewood Rd. and Cañada can be reached by traveling north on Cañada from Hwy. 84 or south on Cañada from Hwy. 92. Entrance is also reached by traveling west on Edgewood Rd. from I-280. Equestrian entrance is just inside the two stone pillars on the west side of Cañada Rd. The equestrian gate is right there. Use your key and you're on the trail! Trailers frequently park at intersection of Cañada Rd. and Runnymede and follow Cañada's roadside trail to the entrance, or park along Cañada Rd. near Edgewood. Group parking might be obtained by special permission

from Woodside Stables on Cañada Rd. ¾ mile north of Hwy. 84. Phone (415) 851-9976.

TRAIL FEATURES: Water District trails leading through Filoli are level and well marked on posts with a horseshoe and arrow. A round trip within this area would take three hours going at a leisurely pace. The trails are actually service roads for the Water Department . . . wide, graveled, and well maintained. (Lew recommends adding variety to your ride by turning onto a loop trail that leads to the back of the Pulgas Water Temple and out to Cañada Rd. . . . On the main trail, about a mile north of the cut-off to the Water Temple, is a large grassy area that is a favorite picnic spot of the San Mateo County Horsemen . . . ample room to tie horses to the trees.

An additional loop trail utilizes the trails of San Mateo's Edgewood Park. A road crossing is involved here but it can be safely done (using caution) and early spring wildflowers will reward your effort. Cross Cañada Rd. south of Edgewood Rd. and follow the constructed trail along the fence line. This will lead you to the I-280 underpass and into Edgewood Park. This is a county park and no keys or permits are required . . . It offers one long loop trail that takes about one hour to complete and one of the best wildflower displays in all of the Bay Area. A new county golf course is slated for this area, but the trail system has been designed to accommodate it.

Lew's recommended day ride through Filoli:

"Start in Woodside, parking along Cañada Rd. Ride the Cañada Rd. trail, crossing into Edgewood Park, near the powerline towers . . . make a loop through Edgewood, then head out to the Edgewood-Cañada Rd. entrance into the Water District lands. Stop for lunch at the picnic area (Lew never leads a ride that doesn't stop for a good lunch!) and return via the Water Temple. Return to your vehicles on the county trail alongside Cañada Rd. . . . a great way to spend about five hours!"

ACCOMMODATIONS: Day use only. If you forget your picnic lunch just hang in there, because there are great restaurants nearby in the beautiful little town of Woodside . . . Watering trough at San Francisco Pulgas Temple (terminus of the Hetch Hetchy water pipe originating in the reservoirs some 200 miles away in the Sierra) . . . Chemical toilets adequately spaced along the trail system.

FEES: None. Permit to ride here is required as described in detail in previous section. Application should be made to San Francisco Water Department, P.O. Box 730, 1000 El Camino Real, Millbrae, CA 94030.

SERVICES: Rangers are friendly, courteous, and happy to give additional information on the area. They patrol in vehicles and are equipped with radios.

RULES: This San Francisco watershed furnishes public drinking water, and any pollution is closely monitored. It is imperative that horses stay on the designated trails and away from the banks of the lakes. This is also a State Game Refuge, so the usual rules regarding hunting, trapping, dogs, firearms, and the disturbance of vegetation apply.

 CAUTION: Hard to find safer trails anywhere! Our only warning is that all horses should be well shod because of the graveled trails.

31

TRAIL PATRONS

San Mateo County Parks

SINCE THE ESTABLISHMENT of its first park in 1924, San Mateo County Memorial Park, the County has had 61 years of recreational and trails experience through their management of 20 facilities on more than 14,000 acres. Under the administration of Director David Christie, office staff and rangers satisfy a full scope of recreational needs to over 2,000,000 park visitors annually. The County is noted for its smooth operation and excellent planning in conjunction with the five-member Parks and Recreation Commission and the all-volunteer Trail Advisory Committee. Policy is set by the Commission subject to the approval of the County Supervisors.

In addition to parks the County also maintains some of the area's roadside trails, the most notable example being the trail from Hwy. 92 which travels along Cañada Rd., Whiskey Hill Rd., Sandhill Rd. and Portola Rd. to the Portola Valley town limits. Within the San Francisco Water Department they supervise the Sheep Camp Rd. trail from the Pulgas Water Temple to Ralston Ave. in Belmont. The concept of a linear park is demonstrated in the County's Sawyer Camp Road Park, which is a paved area approximately 40 feet wide and 7 miles long. Use of the linear park is greatly diversified, attracting hikers, runners, horsemen, roller skaters, and skate board enthusiasts! A County innovation was the closing of Cañada Rd. from Edgewood Rd. to Hwy. 92 two Sundays per month, making it available to equestrians, bikers, hikers, and runners.

The Parks and Recreation Commission meets on the first Thursday of each month at 1 p.m. in the Board of Supervisors chambers in Redwood City. Citizens are welcome to address the Commission on specific agenda items. General information and maps are available at 590 Hamilton St., Redwood City, CA 94063. Phone: (415) 363-4020.

San Mateo County has established a reputation for an excellent trail system through years of hard work and productive interaction with the public. Your continued involvement as a trail user is invited.

San Mateo County Trail Users

SAN MATEO COUNTY is blessed with many trail systems. In addition to County park trails, roadside trails, and the horse camp operated by San Mateo County, the Towns of Woodside and Portola Valley provide miles of roadside trails. The Woodside Trail Club provides a private-key, off-road trail system of permissive trails and manages the off-road dedicated trails by contract with the Town of Woodside. Also, San Francisco Water Department has miles of trails throughout its 26,000 acres.

Horse access to these systems did not just occur because of good fortune. The trails we enjoy today are the result of years of dedicated efforts by many horsemen groups who are committed to trail riding, and who have made a substantial contribution to trail building projects with donations of physical labor and money. While not all horsemen groups are equally dependent on trails, it is the sum total of the equestrian related activities that provides the proper atmosphere for community support of the entire trail system. And the job is not finished. More planning, more trail exploration, more public input and constant monitoring — all are necessary to supplement the system as new areas open up and established areas are reorganized. The horsemen groups listed below welcome your continued involvement.

San Mateo County Horsemen's Association
P.O. Box 620092
Woodside, CA 94062

Los Viajeros Riding Club
P.O. Box 620171
Woodside, CA 94062

Happy Hoofers
P.O. Box 620072
Woodside, CA 94062

Woodside Trail Club
P.O. Box 620152
Woodside, CA 94062

Mounted Patrol of San Mateo County
521 Kings Mountain Rd.
Woodside, CA 94062

Los Altos Hunt Pony Club
5000 Woodside Rd.
Woodside, CA 94062

Woodside Pony Club
District Commissioner Carol Fisch
675 Mountain Home Rd.
Woodside, CA 94062

Junior Riders — a free riding program open to all youth residents of Woodside Fire District. For information contact San Mateo County Horsemen's Association.

TRAIL PATRONS
Horsemen Associations

Horses and trails are a sure-fire combination, so it's not surprising that some of the most dedicated trail activists are those who can clean a hoof with one hand and clear a trail with the other! But let's face it. If horse clubs were all work and no fun there wouldn't be so many of them. The following is a partial list of horse clubs and trail groups active in the Peninsula and San Jose areas. They all welcome you. Check one out soon and you're on your way to enjoying the camaraderie of a trail ride.

Castle Rock Horsemen's Association, Garrod Farms, 22600 Mt. Eden Rd., Saratoga 95070.

Coe Park Mounted Patrol, 9395 Kern Ave., Gilroy, 95020.

Los Altos Hills Horsemen's Association, P.O. Box 425, Los Altos Hills, 94022.

Los Altos Trails Club, P.O. Box 1329, Los Altos, 94022.

Los Gatos Horsemen's Association, P.O. Box 561, Los Gatos, 95030.

Palo Alto Horsemen for Trail Preservation, 3127 David Ave., Palo Alto, 94303.

San Martin Horsemen's Association, P.O. Box 275, San Martin, 95046.

Santa Clara County Horsemen's Association, P.O. Box 20124, San Jose, 95160.

Santa Cruz County Horsemen's Association, P.O. Box 1014, Santa Cruz, 95061.

Summit Riders Horsemen's Association, 24705 Miller Hill Rd., Los Gatos, 95030.

In addition, two recently formed trail groups actively involve riders in the development of multiuse trails:

Carmel Valley Trails, P.O. Box 1636, Carmel Valley, 93924.

Trail Information and Volunteer Center, 2253 Park Blvd., Palo Alto, 94306. A Trail Crew Leadership Training program is one of the achievements of this well organized group, which operates in association with the Sempervirens Fund.

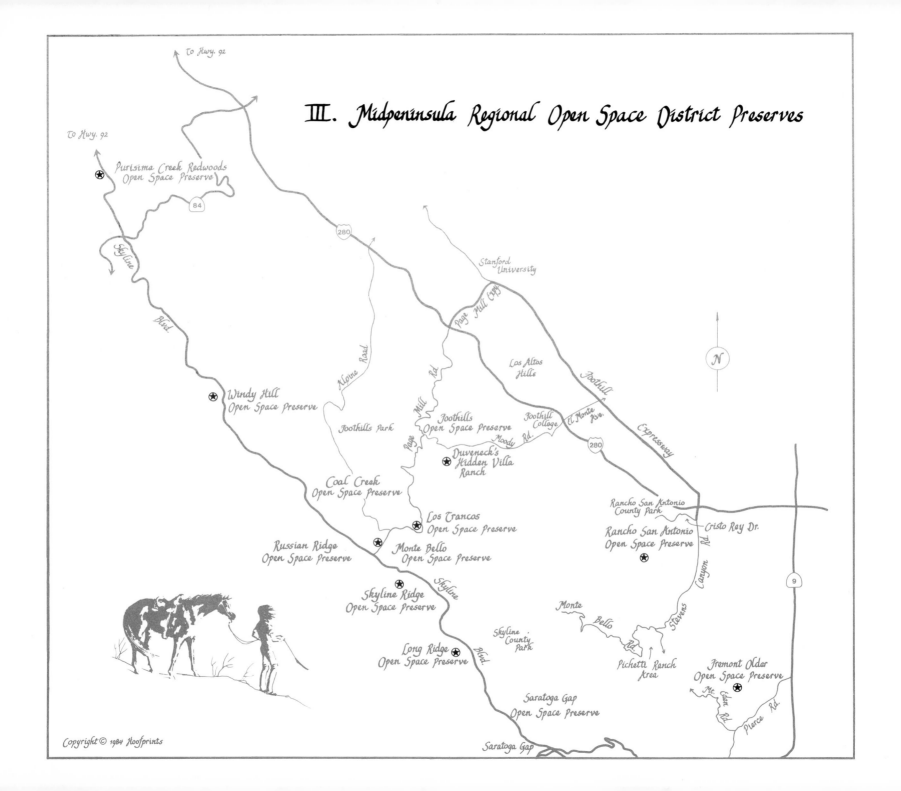

III. *Midpeninsula Regional Open Space District Preserves*

To Hwy. 92

To Hwy. 92

Purisima Creek Redwoods
Open Space Preserve

84

Skyline

280

Stanford
University

Page Mill Expy.

Blvd.

Los Altos
Hills

Foothill

Windy Hill
Open Space Preserve

Alpine Road

Page Mill Rd.

Foothills Park

Foothills
Open Space Preserve

Foothill
College

El Monte Ave.

Expressway

Page Mill Rd.

Moody Rd.

280

N

Coal Creek
Open Space Preserve

Duveneck's
Hidden Villa
Ranch

Rancho San Antonio
County Park

Los Trancos
Open Space Preserve

Rancho San Antonio
Open Space Preserve

Cristo Rey Dr.

Russian Ridge
Open Space Preserve

Monte Bello
Open Space Preserve

Canyon Rd.

9

Skyline Ridge
Open Space Preserve

Skyline

Monte

Bello

Stevens

Rd.

Long Ridge
Open Space Preserve

Blvd.

Skyline
County
Park

Pichetti Ranch
Area

Fremont Older
Open Space Preserve

Mt. Eden Rd.

Pierce Rd.

Saratoga Gap
Open Space Preserve

Saratoga Gap

Carolyn Lekberg conditioning her young Arab, Spirit, on Peninsula trails.

Dedication to a high quality trail system is demonstrated in the planning being done by a special committee of the Midpeninsula Trails Council. (Left to right) Del Woods, MROSD planner, Carolyn Lekberg, MTC president, Lewis Reed and Sylvia Ferguson.

CAROLYN LEKBERG is a rider who loves to run — not only with a horse but also on her own two feet. Avid participation in the American Endurance Ride Competition and her commitment to the Trail Trotters keeps this already busy school teacher on the move.

"Running is an absolutely fantastic way for the rider to keep in shape, to be fair about demanding the same physical stamina of himself that he demands of his horse," says Carolyn.

A well conditioned runner riding a well conditioned horse is a natural for competing in the increasingly popular Levi Ride and Tie Events. (Two people per team alternate running and riding using the same horse in relay fashion.) Carolyn has competed in three Ride and Tie events and finds them the most exciting rides of all, especially when they feature over 150 teams lined up for "shotgun" starts reminiscent of the land rush days! She recalls stories of the first Brown's Ride and Tie in Almaden where out of 40 riders lined up at the start only four were still mounted when the bucking and dust subsided.

"The triathlon event with one runner, one rider, one bicyclist composing a team (let's not forget the horse!) is yet another way people can combine the enjoyment of running and riding. I'm always looking for new ways to enjoy my horse. There are lots of exciting things to do with your horse if you'll just get out there and investigate."

Is this the admonition of a carefree sports enthusiast with nothing but time on her hands? Hardly. Both professionally and in her private life the petite, dark-haired woman is laden with the kind of responsibilities that send other human beings to hideouts in the hills or at least as far as the local therapist. For eight years the Sunnyvale resident has taught special education classes for handicapped and gifted children in the public schools. As a mother she is a single parent working to support herself and a teenage daughter with college expenses looming on the horizon like an ominous cloud. Given all these cares she seems to be having an enormous amount of fun.

Rather than claim her responsibilities as an exemption from community involvement and athletic pursuits, she is an eager participant in both. Just spend five minutes with Carolyn and you find yourself getting caught up in her energetic support of:

Trail Trotters: "You don't have to be a great speedster to really enjoy this group. Runners at all levels of experience meet at Rancho San Antonio Park and hit the trail at their own pace. It's great fun. Join us!"

Endurance riding: "The greatest sport! You develop a real partnership with your horse and a real love for the terrific people you meet. They seem more like a family than a group of competitors. Best of all, the ride takes you along the most gorgeous trails you can imagine."

Midpeninsula Regional Open Space District: "Thanks to the District the Peninsula now has a most magnificent trail system, and access to the trails is being improved all the time. The District is very open to use issues, and especially in working with Del Woods and David Hansen (District planner and manager, respectively) I've found people very receptive, with many suggestions of their own for improving access to trails."

Midpeninsula Trails Council: "I feel very good about what the Trail Council has been able to accomplish in working with the MROSD. I think our success is that we've come to be viewed as a help in resolving trail issues. Also we've broadened our geographical base since the Council was first formed 4 years ago, and we're making sure that local trail issues are being addressed. I think we've been able to demonstrate that volunteers are a valuable resource mainly because we have a strong core group vigorously committed to the Council. A sense of crisis about trails has made us cohesive. As president of the Council for the past two years I really value what I've learned about organizing people to accomplish something. It's been easy to make friends in this group because we have a common cause."

Peninsula Carriage Club: "These people have given me tremendous help in training my horse to pull a cart. Carriage driving is a reviving art. With life getting so fast in our high-tech society it's no wonder that more and more people are getting a sense of accomplishment and pleasure from something as basic as hitching up a horse and going out for a Sunday drive!"

Accomplishment and pleasure are evident in the activities of this respected, well liked teacher whose personal trademarks are sincere enthusiasm and a love of learning. Carolyn's quick sense of humor and vibrant laugh indicate a person having a tremendous amount of fun with life. Where does all the energy come from?

"Another teacher once asked me how I could tolerate teaching all the time and still maintain a cheerful attitude. I said, 'That's simple. I have a horse!' It's true. Horses refresh me and allow me to go back to school with a renewed outlook on life. They take me away from the rest of my life and give me a new perspective. Then I go back to my daily routine with more zest. It isn't easy to work caring for a horse into my schedule as a teacher, but I've made it work because I'm having so much fun."

Horses have had an impact on Carolyn's life since her childhood days in Illinois. She was a city girl but her parents owned a small farm and her uncle lived just across the road.

"We used to spend our summers there," Carolyn recalls, "and our favorite thing to do was ride the old draft horse our uncle kept as a pet. She was very gentle, a good horse for a kid to grow up with. When I graduated from Northern Illinois University I thought back to the happy summers on horseback and got inspired to take some riding lessons at the local stable. Eventually I owned my own horse, a Quarter Horse. I started out as a western rider, then went on to hunting and jumping, but nothing I learned in a lesson situation has taught me so much about horses as endurance riding. One endurance ride will do more for your skills as a horseman than anything else I can think of. You just can't log all those miles in the saddle and not learn something."

When Carolyn moved from Illinois to California she sold her horse to her sister for one dollar, and today her first horse is retired on her uncle's farm. "I went without a horse for a few years after we

Jack Wells

Carolyn relaxing with her horse friends after a full day as a classroom teacher.

came out here but I always envied everyone I saw trail riding and I started dreaming of horse ownership again," she recalls.

"One of the teachers where I worked owned horses, and told me one day she needed to lighten her herd. She modestly described a little untrained, brown horse that she would give me! I went out to look at him and found something a lot more special than she described. He was a nice-looking strawberry roan Appaloosa with a perfect blanket, a star, and a white sock. There was nothing wrong with him. It was just that he was four years old and hadn't been trained. He had been standing out in a pasture all his life so nothing had happened to spoil his disposition. I claimed him immediately and named him John, which in the Bible means 'God's gracious gift.'"

With no horse training experience behind her, Carolyn accepted the challenge of training a horse in true school teacher form — she bought a book. Armed with her native optimism and desire to learn, she set out to teach her horse. Carolyn credits the success of the experience to the horse's disposition rather than her ability as a trainer.

37

"Training was a completely new experience for me. I found it to be an awful lot of fun because we were both learning something all the time. John was a good horse to learn from because he didn't have any personality quirks that would cause me great harm. He wasn't hyper and dangerous but more inclined to be stubborn, and there's a lot a horseman can learn in coping with that kind of disposition. The lesson I learned from John was to be assertive when I had to be, to demand obedience unless the horse is frightened. He turned out to be an excellent trail horse and I'm very proud of the fact that I've taught him everything he knows. Of course, all of his faults I have to blame on myself! He was my first endurance horse, too, so we've had a lot of firsts together!"

Success with John gave Carolyn the confidence to tackle the training of a completely different kind of horse. While John has been equal to the task of 50-mile endurance rides ("in 700 miles of competition we've never been pulled or had a problem with lameness") Carolyn has set her sights on 100-mile rides and bought an Arab named Spirit to do the job.

"Spirit is aptly named," says Carolyn. "He came to me green broke and he's taught me all new lessons about horse training. He's a spooky horse, much

Susan, the other half of the mother-daughter team which has taught John to be a harness horse.

more timid about life than John was. I've had to learn to be very gentle. On a steep grade or on rough terrain he has a tendency to panic, to charge through obstacles instead of picking his way carefully as John would. I have to be very sure to maintain control of him because he really relies on his rider to get him through tough spots. With the right handling he has a good, pleasant personality, very vivacious and eager for the trail. Even with the challenges I feel very safe on him because his personality hasn't soured."

Not only has Spirit brought new adventure, but also Carolyn feels that buying Spirit was the best investment she could have made in promoting family happiness. Now as a two-horse family, mother and daughter ride together. "Having her own horse is a nice reward for Susan who has been the sole member of my 'crew' on many endurance rides," Carolyn says with pride. "We're also a team in training John to pull a carriage. Since I'm a teacher I'm fortunate to have my summer months free, but with Susan headed for college I need to fill up my summers in a practical, income-producing way, hopefully with a horse! Enter John the carriage horse. No sooner had he graduated from basic training than be was the star of a wedding, transporting bride and groom! Soon he'll be handling wine tours, even parades. There's some doubt that he was fully aware of all the work that Susan and I had planned for him but, so far, he's being very cooperative. I think his attitude is good because we took our time in training him. He spent plenty of time standing between the shafts getting used to the idea. Also, he may sense that putting him to work is one way of keeping him in the family!"

The economic benefits of a horse "broke to drive" won't be known for some time. Although, horses and new business ventures are fraught with uncertainty, bet on Carolyn Lekberg's enthusiasm and skill as a teacher to produce another success!

TRAIL PATRON:
Midpeninsula Trails Council

IF YOU'RE looking for new trails and you don't mind a little action, fun, and friendship thrown in for good measure, you can't do better than join the Midpeninsula Trails Council. Organized in 1980 after the closure of a favorite horse trail, today the Council is a dynamic agent for trail users on the San Francisco Peninsula. Although the original impetus for the organization came from dedicated horse owners deeply concerned about declining access to trail areas, MTC's success is a tribute to the shared interests of all trail users. Some four years after the founding of MTC the membership includes not only 13 horsemen's organizations, but also 15 individual members, 2 running clubs, 3 hiking clubs, representatives from the San Mateo County and Santa Clara County Parks and Recreation Departments, Midpeninsula Regional Open Space District, Sierra Club, and neighboring trail councils.

Inspired by the concept that "good trails connect; so do good trail-using organizations," the Council serves as a focal point for communication among trail users by means of well attended monthly meetings and a bimonthly newsletter. "Trail Links" is a high-quality publication which merits the attention it receives from county supervisors and parks commissioners as well as individuals seeking new trails.

In addition to special projects involving trail work parties, field trips to public lands, and seminars featuring guest speakers, MTC gives top priority to working closely with the Midpeninsula Regional Open Space District. Trail corridors and access points to District lands have been developed with the input of MTC members who regularly attend District meetings and participate with staff in on-site studies leading to the developing of use and management plans for each of the District's Open Space Preserves. The good working relationship which exists between the District's professional planners and their trail-using constituents is a key element in the Council's effectiveness in promoting access to District lands.

"We try to be a help to any agency we're dealing with, not just a special interest group showing up to demand something or to point out weaknesssess," says MTC president Carolyn Lekberg as one explanation for the Council's success. "It's hard work, but very exciting to work with a public agency like MROSD which is farsighted in its planning and still responsive to the public needs at

Carolyn Caddes

Looking toward the East Bay from a mid-Peninsula hillside.

hand. Working with the District and the Council has not only brought some new trails into my life but also many new friends. If a trail council is needed in your area, don't hesitate to start one!"

MTC meets regularly on the first Monday of each month in the MROSD conference room, 375 Distel Circle, Los Altos, CA. Visitors and new members are welcome at all meetings. To receive the newsletter, "Trail Links," send $15 to MTC, P.O. Box 872, Los Altos, CA 94022.

Monte Bello Open Space District rangers put the finishing touches on the new parking lot.

Equestrian stile at the entrance to the Monte Bello trail system.

Photos: Charlotte MacDonald, MROSD

Well marked trails are a special Monte Bello feature.

MONTE BELLO OPEN SPACE PRESERVE
(Saratoga Gap and Coal Creek)

My most favorite place in all of California! Ride Canyon Trail once and you'll be back again and again . . .

— Carolyn Lekberg

REASONS TO GO: 2,634 acres of superlative scenery ranging from the summit of Black Mountain (2,800') to the cool evergreen forest of Stevens Creek Canyon . . . a feeling of infinity on the grassy slopes of Monte Bello Ridge . . . a vital link to popular Hidden Villa Ranch, Skyline County Park, and the neighboring District Preserves of Coal Creek, Saratoga Gap, and Skyline Ridge.

SPECIAL FEATURES: Unlimited vistas from the ocean to the Bay . . . bask in the clean air of open country as you view the intensely developed Valley floor below . . . Riders who also like to hike will appreciate the docent-led walks (once a month) which inspire an informed gratefulness for the land . . Self-guided Stevens Creek Nature Trail can be enjoyed by family members on foot while riders explore trails through the Stevens Creek watershed and the picturesque setting of ponds along the Canyon Trail . . . an open space jewel in the Bay Area.

LOCATION: Monte Bello Open Space Preserve (the District's largest Preserve) is located at Page Mill Road and Skyline Blvd. about 14 miles from the town of Woodside, via Skyline Blvd. The Preserve is located primarily in Santa Clara County and encompasses the entire Stevens Creek watershed, forming a backdrop for the communities of Palo Alto, Los Altos and Cupertino.

Although the Preserve is only five miles from Foothill College in Los Altos Hills, via Page Mill Road, **this access is not recommended for trailer pulling.** Better access for horse trailers from the north is to take Hwy. 92 to Skyline Blvd. Travel south on Skyline Blvd. 20 miles to Page Mill Rd. Turn left and drive one and a half miles to Monte Bello parking area. Coming from the south travel on Hwy. 9 from Saratoga up to Skyline Blvd. Turn right and go 7 miles to Page Mill Rd., turn right and go 1.5 miles to Monte Bello parking area.

WHERE TO PARK: A large gravel parking lot is located on the south side of Page Mill Rd., 5 miles west of its intersection with Hwy. 280 and 1 mile east of Skyline Blvd. A special parking area is available to equestrians and other group users by phoning the Midpeninsula Trails Council, (408) 737-2763, or the District office, (415) 965-4717. Upon request the combination to the locked parking area known as the permit parking area will be given . . . parking is located one half mile east of Skyline Blvd. on the south side of Page Mill Rd.

TRAIL FEATURES: "Riding Canyon Trail is the ultimate trail riding experience," says Carolyn . . . it's a beautiful, restful seven-and-a-half-mile ride leading to Stevens Creek and Saratoga Gap . . . tranquil ponds and bright streams mark the way . . . There are plenty of nice level areas for cantering, but take your time to enjoy the wide variety of vegetation of this peaceful environment . . . Canyon Trail is linked to Longridge Preserve by the Grizzly Flat Trail through Skyline County Park . . . The only trail you can't enjoy entirely on horseback in this Preserve is the Stevens Creek Nature Trail, a three-mile, self-guided interpretive trail originating at the Page Mill Rd. parking area . . . A suggested short ride is to start at the permit parking area, pick up the trail heading south, and return via the Canyon Trail . . . Another good short ride is to follow Canyon Trail up to Black Mountain and then back to the parking area via Monte Bello Rd. . . . For an all-day ride head for Saratoga Gap and return on the same trail.

ACCOMMODATIONS: Day use only. Restroom at Monte Bello parking area. An outstanding feature of Monte Bello Preserve is the opportunity for wine-tasting on horseback! Phone ahead to Sherril Wineries (415) 851-1932 or Ridge Wineries (415) 867-3233.

FEES: None.

PRESERVE SERVICES: Area is well patrolled . . . Friendly and knowledgeable rangers add to the enjoyment of your ride.

WEATHER: Well maintained trails inspire good year-round riding . . . The ridge top can be both windy and foggy so dress accordingly.

 CAUTION: Watch for bikes on trails . . . This is a very popular Preserve with all trail users so use your best trail etiquette.

Photos: Charolette MacDonald, MROSD

42

Fence line to the right borders Page Mill Rd. but horsemen will appreciate the District's map to guide them through nearby shaded woods and canyons.

LOS TRANCOS
OPEN SPACE PRESERVE

Cross-country riding for the exploring, adventurous rider . . . new trail connections in the works!

— Carolyn Lekberg

REASONS TO GO: 274 acres offering a pleasant combination of rolling grassland knolls and cool, shaded woods . . . great place for a relaxing exploratory ride topped off with a picnic! . . . Dazzling displays of wildflowers from spring through summer. . . . Inspiring views of Santa Clara Valley and Skyline Ridge.

SPECIAL FEATURES: Beautiful grassy knolls for picnicking . . . panoramic view ranging from the skyscrapers of San Francisco to the prominence of Mt. Diablo across the Bay. . . . Return on foot for a self-guided trail along the San Andreas Fault zone featuring a fascinating display and explanation of earthquake phenomena. . . . Go home rejoicing that horses are claimed to be excellent earthquake warning devices!

LOCATION: On Page Mill Rd. five miles from road intersection with I-280. Adjacent communities are Palo Alto and Los Altos Hills. **Trailer access from Page Mill Rd. is very winding and difficult.** Better access for horse trailers from the north is to take Hwy. 92 to Skyline Blvd. Travel south on Skyline Blvd. 20 miles to Page Mill Rd. Turn left and drive one and a half miles to Monte Bello parking area. Coming from the south travel on Hwy. 9 from Saratoga up to Skyline Blvd. Turn right and go 7 miles to Page Mill Rd., turn right and go 1.5 miles to Monte Bello parking area. To enter Los Trancos trail system leave Monte Bello parking area following fence line along Page Mill Rd. to equestrian stile at entrance to Canyon Trail. Then cross Page Mill Rd. being

extremely careful of auto traffic at this crossing. Special arrangements for group parking can be made by phoning the Midpeninsula Trails Council, (408) 737-2763, or the District Office, (415) 965-4717.

TRAIL FEATURES: Meadow and canyon trails in many combinations of fire roads, single-file trails, machine-made trails giving riders approximately a 10-mile round trip ride. . . . Additional Preserve mileage is open to hikers only, but you won't feel shortchanged as you experience the varied beauty of the terrain and the dense meadows of wildflowers. . . . Best of all, trails are linked to the Monte Bello trail system and more connections are proposed to the Arastra property in Palo Alto. Proposals now under study for a regional trail system inspire gratitude for the planning efforts of the Midpeninsula Regional Open Space District. . . . At this point the only trail signing for horsemen is one sign pointing through a clump of trees. Otherwise, you're on your own, so take the map provided by the District. Recommended route for an all-day ride is to ride the connecting trail to the Monte Bello Open Space Preserve which leads to more hours of riding in adjoining Preserves . . . a real tribute to regional planning!

WHERE TO PARK: Both the Monte Bello Open Space parking area and the Los Trancos Open Space Preserve parking area are open to horse trailers but are heavily used for auto parking, especially on weekends. To assure yourself a place to park phone the District office for a special parking permit for the equestrian parking area which is

one mile south of Skyline on Page Mill. The district will provide you with the combination to the locked pipe gate which marks the permit area . . . an especially nice facility for group use. Phone (415) 965-4717.

ACCOMMODATIONS: Day use only. Restrooms at the Monte Bello parking area . . . Water for horses in creek along horse trail.

FEES: None.

PRESERVE SERVICES: Map available on site at Los Trancos parking lot and at District Office, (415) 965-4717, 375 Distel Circle, Los Altos, CA 94022. Friendly, available ranger patrol. . . . Docent-led hikes every Sunday at 2 p.m. will only lead to greater enjoyment of a future trail ride. Reservations are not necessary.

PRESERVE RULES: Open dawn to dusk. All natural resources are protected. No dogs, firearms, fishing, fires, or camping are permitted.

WEATHER: Open year-round . . . vivid green scenery of spring and winter changes to a golden, tawny panorama in the summer and fall . . . hard to pick a favorite time to ride, it's all so beautiful.

 CAUTION: Good ranger patrol keeps motorcycles and bikes off the trails, but crossing Page Mill Rd., watch out! In a few spots the trail parallels Page Mill Rd. and 10-speed bikes whizzing down the road can be disquieting to your horse. . . . Trail is elusive so be sure to take a map.

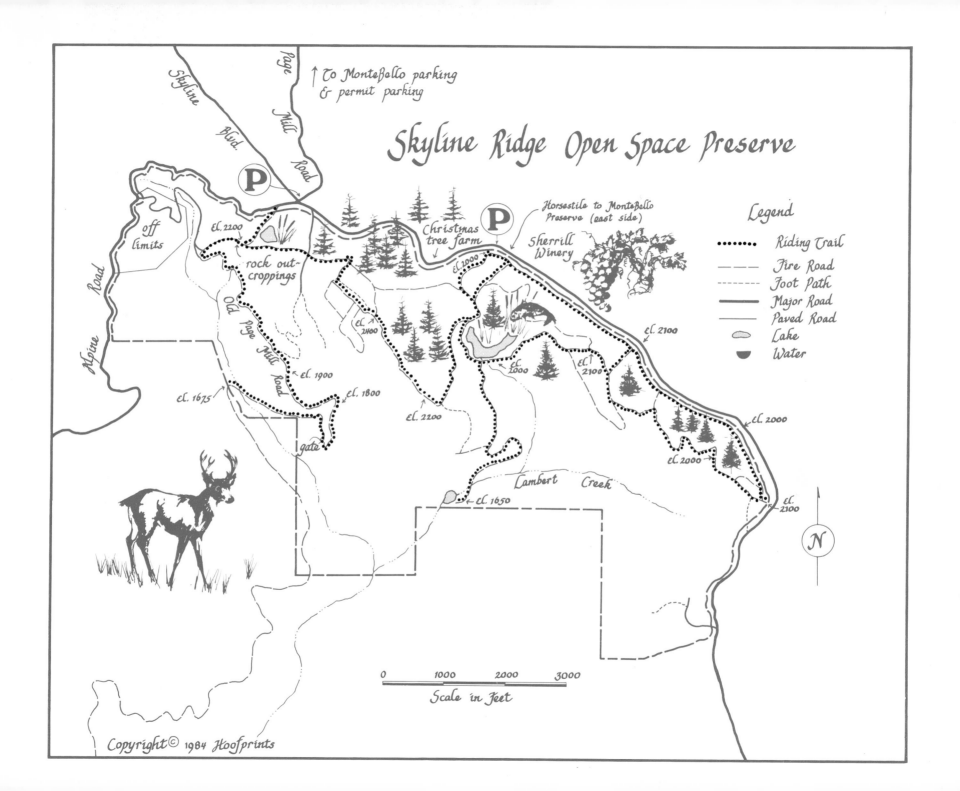

Skyline Ridge Open Space Preserve

↑ To MonteBello parking & permit parking

Skyline Blvd.

Page Mill Road

Alpine Road

Old Page Mill Road

P

P

off limits

rock out-croppings

El. 2200

El. 2400

El. 1900

El. 1675

El. 1800

El. 2200

gate

Christmas tree farm

Horsestile to MonteBello Preserve (east side)

Sherrill Winery

El. 1000

El. 1000

El. 2100

El. 2100

El. 2000

El. 2000

El. 1650

Lambert Creek

El. 2100

N

Legend

∙∙∙∙∙∙∙	Riding Trail
– – –	Fire Road
- - - -	Foot Path
———	Major Road
———	Paved Road
◯	Lake
◗	Water

0   1000   2000   3000

Scale in Feet

SKYLINE RIDGE OPEN SPACE PRESERVE

Expect some exciting changes here while this new Preserve is being developed for public use . . . in the meantime there's a tremendous variety of trails to enjoy . . .

— Carolyn Lekberg

Looking southeast with Alpine Rd. in foreground.

REASONS TO GO: 944 acres of exceptionally varied landscape ranging from open ridgetops to quiet wooded trails lined by dense, evergreen forests . . . Scenic highlights are two sparkling reservoirs and a Christmas tree farm!

SPECIAL FEATURES: Beautiful areas for picnicking on the hilltops and near the reservoir . . . Expansive views of Monte Bello to the east and the Pacific Ocean to the west . . . Plans are under consideration for a rental stable and overnight camp for horsemen . . . many exciting possibilities exist in this Preserve because of its location as the center of 7,500 acres of public land . . . The MROSD is providing many opportunities for public input, so don't miss out!

LOCATION: In the Santa Cruz Mountains at the intersection of Skyline Blvd., Alpine Rd., and Page Mill Rd. Centrally located between other Midpeninsula Regional Open Space District Preserves, including Monte Bello, Longridge, and Los Trancos.

WHERE TO PARK: Coming from the north take Hwy. 92 to Skyline and follow Skyline about 20 miles south to Page Mill Rd. . . . Easy trailering conditions via Skyline Blvd. to the large gravelled Monte Bello parking area on Page Mill Rd. (five miles west of Page Mill intersection with Hwy. 280 and one mile east of Skyline Blvd.) . . . Traveling from the south on Hwy. 9 is slow going . . . Alternate parking is available in the locked permit parking area by arrangement with the Midpeninsula Trails Council, (408) 737-2763, or the District Office, (415) 965-4717. In addition there's room for five trailers in a large pull-out on the east side of Skyline Blvd. across from the Christmas tree farm. From this point an equestrian/hiking stile links the Preserve with the trails of the Monte Bello area.

TRAIL FEATURES: Fireroads, old logging roads, and roads through the tree farm provide 10-plus miles of moderate climbing on quiet, timber-lined trails, excellently maintained . . . Great connections with other District Preserves, Monte Bello, Coal Creek, Los Trancos, and Longridge . . . **Potential here for competitive trail events and carriage driving** . . . stay tuned to the planning process through the Midpeninsula Trails Council . . . they welcome your involvement, (408) 737-2763.

ACCOMMODATIONS: No amenities for horses in the parking area at the present time but proposals are on the drawing board for improved equestrian staging areas within the Preserve . . . Water for horses is available at the barn near the entrance. Weekend parking can be a problem except for the generous permit parking area which is usually available.

FEES: None.

PRESERVE SERVICES: Open Space District office offers a free topo map . . . stop in at MROSD office, 375 Distel Circle, Los Altos, CA 94022, or phone (415) 965-4717 . . . Preserve has resident ranger . . . a visitors' center is being considered as a special feature of this Preserve.

PRESERVE RULES: Day use only . . . visitors to the Preserve are asked not to disturb the privacy of the ranch buildings area, as the property is currently leased as a private home.

WEATHER: Trails are well maintained and a joy to ride all year long, particularly if you're exhilarated by wind and fog!

CAUTION: Don't worry too much about unmarked trails . . . you have a good map to guide you . . . but if you want to throw all caution aside and explore, this is a good place to do it! Just remember to use Skyline as your marker . . . Bicycles are allowed here, so watch for blind curves.

45

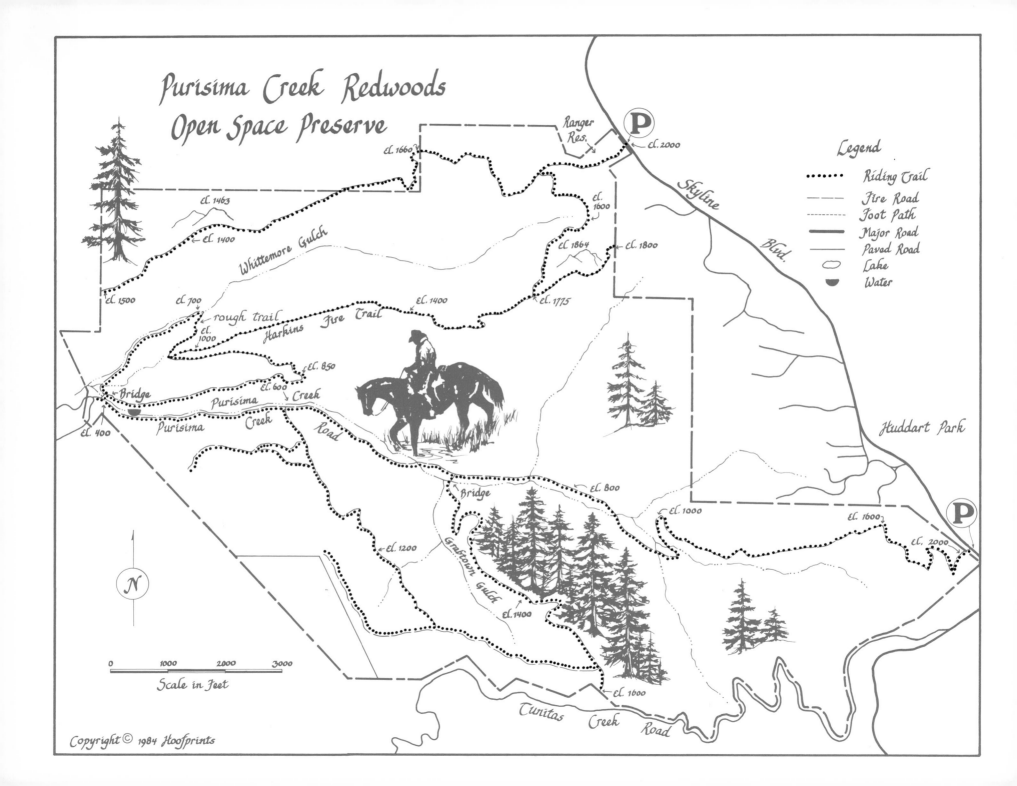

Purisima Creek Redwoods
Open Space Preserve

P El. 2000

Ranger Res.

El. 1660

El. 1600

El. 1463

El. 1400

Whittemore Gulch

El. 1864

El. 1800

El. 1500

El. 700

rough trail

El. 1000

El. 1400

El. 1775

Harkins Fire Trail

El. 850

Bridge

El. 600

Purisima Creek

El. 400

Purisima Creek Road

Skyline Blvd.

Huddart Park

Bridge

El. 800

El. 1000

El. 1600

P

El. 2000

El. 1200

Grabtown Gulch

El. 1400

El. 1600

Tunitas Creek Road

Legend

· · · · · Riding Trail
– – – – Fire Road
········ Foot Path
━━━━ Major Road
══════ Paved Road
◯ Lake
▱ Water

N

0   1000   2000   3000
Scale in Feet

Copyright © 1984 Hoofprints

PURISIMA CREEK REDWOODS OPEN SPACE PRESERVE

A brand new Preserve . . . wild and wonderful, but still plenty of old logging roads for safe, easy riding . . .

— Carolyn Lekberg

REASONS TO GO: Easy-to-reach access to the western slopes of the Santa Cruz Mountains. . . . A second growth redwood forest is only one feature of this richly diverse 2,500-acre Preserve. . . . The largest single acquisition ever made by the District, it adjoins the 849-acre Whittemore Gulch Redwoods Open Space area and borders on Huddart County Park . . . all this adds up to un-limited enjoyment for horse and rider! Wild-flowers, berries, and ferns border the trail with a bonus of breathtaking views in all directions, in-cluding an overlook of Half Moon Bay!

SPECIAL FEATURES: Purisima Canyon is a cool, moist retreat through the Purisima Creek watershed giving riders and hikers a refreshing route along the western side of the Santa Cruz Mountains . . . A year-round stream and summer fog are vital to the existence of the lofty redwoods monitoring the entire route of an old logging road. . . . Relive history on horseback as you recall that back in the 1850s pack animals were necessary to the logging operation here.

LOCATION: In the unincorporated area of San Mateo County on the ocean side of Skyline Blvd. 4.5 miles south of Hwy. 92. . . . From Saratoga Gap 23 miles north of Hwy. 9. For trailer pulling Hwy. 92 and Hwy. 9 are okay, but access is very winding and steep from Page Mill Rd., La Honda Rd., and Kings Mountain Rd.

WHERE TO PARK: Horse trailers and autos share a common parking area at the northeastern corner of the Preserve along Skyline Blvd. Entrance to the parking area is four and a half miles south of the intersection of Hwy. 92 and Skyline Blvd. Enter the parking area 200 feet south of the Vista Del Mar Restaurant. The trail takes off from the southwest corner of the lot. In the 10–12-car parking area there is generally ample room for a few trailers, but for group equestrian use a special permit will be granted to park in a separate area. For permission phone (415) 965-4717 or write to Midpeninsula Regional Open Space District, 375 Distel Circle, Suite D-1, Los Altos, CA 94022.

Another place to stage is at a large pull-out along Skyline Blvd. across from Huddart Park. This pull-out is six and a half miles from Hwy. 92 or two miles south of the parking area near the Vista Del Mar Restaurant as described above.

TRAIL FEATURES: 15 miles of trail a rider would classify as moderate to steep. . . . This is a wonderful, new acquisition so, as we go to press, trails would be described as "wild" in some areas with definite challenges for both rider and hiker. . . . This doesn't detract, however, from the great possibilities here both for interior trails and future connections to adjacent Preserves and San Mateo County's Huddart Park. Logging activities have promoted an extensive network of roads and trails which are well defined, although not yet named and maintained as trails . . . Novice riders can comfortably begin to explore the area with a ride from the parking area out to several lookout points and back . . . In the near future a longer ride will be possible by riding a loop down to Purisima Rd. at the western edge of the Preserve and back to the parking area . . . 2,500 acres of open space land with public access expands into a magnificent total of over 24,000 acres when you consider connections between this property and San Francisco's Crystal Springs Watershed Game Refuge, Hassler Open Space Preserve, and Edge-wood and Huddart County Parks!

ACCOMMODATIONS: None in the Preserve at this time, but reservations can be made at nearby privately owned stables. Fellow horsemen at Woodside Equestrian Showplace and Avila Stables welcome your phone call for additional trail information or overnight accommodations. Avila Stables owned by Mike and Cher Avila, Rte. 1, Box 313 J, Half Moon Bay, CA 94019. Phone: (415) 726-3322. Stable is located on Purisima Creek Rd. which is four miles south of Hwy. 92 on Hwy. 1. . . . Woodside Equestrian Showplace is located on Skyline Blvd., 0.6 miles north of the Pre-serve parking area. Euclid Patin is the owner and invites you to phone at (415) 851-4170 or write: 12670 Skyline Blvd., Woodside, CA 94062.

FEES: None.

PRESERVE RULES: Open dawn to dusk. Please use the map provided so that you do not trespass on adjacent private property.

PRESERVE SERVICES: Zeroxed copies of topo maps available at the MROSD office, 375 Distel Circle, Suite D-1, Los Altos, CA 94022. Phone: (415) 965-4717. Planning is under way for a descriptive brochure which will be available at the main entrance . . . Resident ranger.

WEATHER: Preserve is open year-round and there is enough variety in trails and terrain to pro-vide good all-weather riding . . . you're likely to encounter summer fog and some of the most beautiful areas are cool and shaded . . . don't forget your jacket!

 CAUTION: This new Preserve invites adventure and exploring . . . stay close to your map unless you are fearless about getting lost! . . . It's disconcerting, to say the least, to hear occasional gun shots but this situation will be improved as ranger patrol of the area is in-creased . . . as always in the Bay Area, watch for poi-son oak!

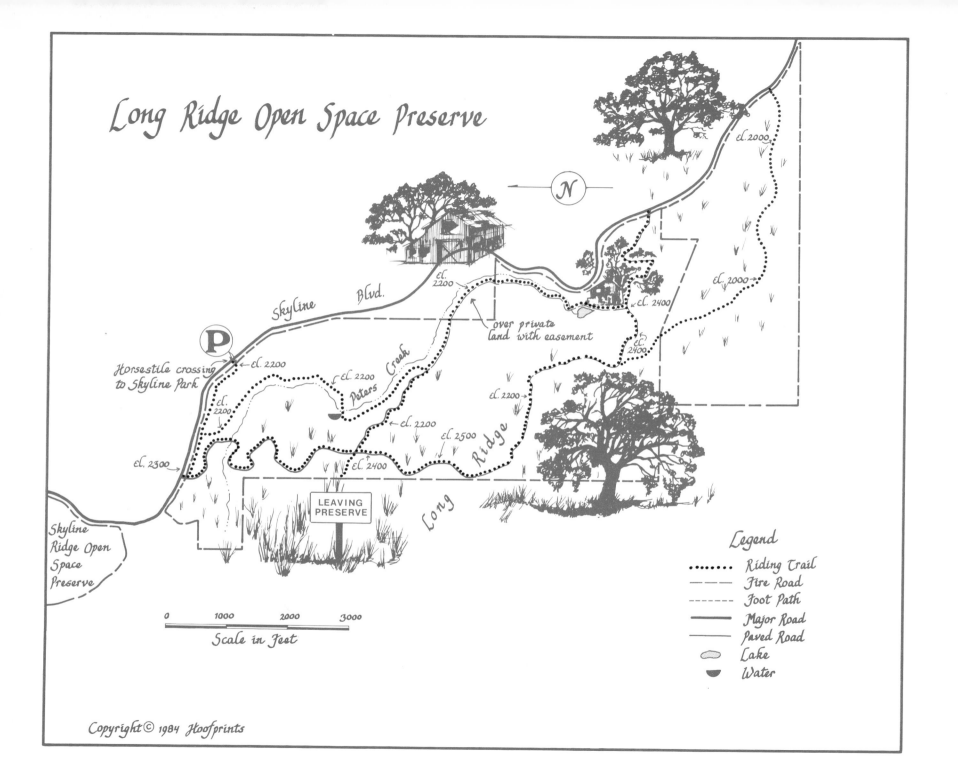

Long Ridge Open Space Preserve

N

Skyline Blvd.

el. 2200

el. 2000

el. 2000

el. 2400

over private
land with easement

el. 2400

el. 2400

P

Horsestile crossing
to Skyline Park

← el. 2200

el. 2200

Peters Creek

el. 2200

el. 2200

el. 2200

el. 2200

el. 2500

el. 2400

Long Ridge

el. 2300

LEAVING
PRESERVE

Skyline
Ridge Open
Space
Preserve

| 0 | 1000 | 2000 | 3000 |

Scale in Feet

Legend

.... Riding Trail
– – – Fire Road
- - - - Foot Path
——— Major Road
——— Paved Road
⬭ Lake
◠ Water

LONGRIDGE OPEN SPACE PRESERVE

A quiet, little-used Preserve where you ride with the feeling of climbing up to heaven! . . .

— Carolyn Lekberg

The serenity of Longridge punctuated by bounding wildlife.

REASONS TO GO: Discover an "undiscovered" Preserve! . . . 360-degree views of Montebello Ridge to the east and Butano Ridge to the west . . . quiet riding on wide trails with spectacular views toward the ocean and Big Basin State Park . . . marvelous potential here for connecting with other Open Space Preserves . . . definitely worth the time and effort to hitch up the rig and get there.

SPECIAL FEATURES: 787 acres of open land bountiful with its vistas and grassy, knolltop picnic areas (all natural, of course!) . . . Neighbors are Devil's Canyon and Skyline Ridge Open Space Preserve to the north, with Saratoga Gap Open Space Preserve to the south . . . Expansive openness dotted with oak, madrone, Douglas fir, wildflowers, and grazing cattle.

LOCATION: On the ocean side of Skyline Blvd. three and a half miles north of Saratoga Gap (intersection of Skyline Blvd. (Hwy. 35 and Hwy. 9) . . . Preserve is intersected by boundary lines of unincorporated San Mateo and Santa Cruz Counties . . . Coming from the north easy to reach by taking Hwy. 92 and traveling down Skyline Blvd. . . . Coming from the town of Saratoga it's a long, slow pull up Hwy. 9, but the road is wide and easily managed.

WHERE TO PARK: At Grizzly Flat Parking area, Skyline County Park . . . Three and a half miles from "Saratoga Gap" there is a large pull-out on both the east and west sides of Skyline Blvd. which will accommodate three trailer rigs each. Watch for parking area between road markers

numbered .13 and .43. You know you've arrived when you see a split rail wooden fence on the east side of Skyline Blvd. Directly across the street from the east pullout is a horse stile marking the entrance to the Preserve. Crossing Sklyine Blvd. to reach the Preserve is **very hazardous** because of speeding autos and motorcycles . . . use caution. Plans are under consideration which will correct this situation, such as a major staging area at Skyline Ridge only a half mile away. . . . Weekend parking can be a problem, so plan to arrive early to guarantee yourself a space.

TRAIL FEATURES: This is an "undeveloped" Preserve with little maintenance and no marking on its 10 miles of trails as of June, 1984 . . . this isn't a drawback but a genuine pleasure as you explore along cattle trails and the beautiful, wide trails on the ridge top! The mention of a ridge top tells you that there will be some steep up and down hill work (great for conditioning!) but there is plenty of easy riding along the ridge top as your reward . . . One short road used for resident access cuts through the property, but you rarely meet a car . . . For an all-day ride connect with other Preserves via the Grizzly Flat trail or ride to the top of the ridge and circle the property . . . For a shorter ride follow the lower loop near Skyline Blvd. . . . Thanks to a good map provided by horsewoman artist Deborah Young, and to intermittent noise from Skyline Blvd., you can enjoy an exploratory ride without fear of getting lost.

ACCOMMODATIONS: None . . . small pond and creek for watering horses. A great picnic area

for riders is near the old cattle corral along the trail at the south end of the Preserve.

PRESERVE SERVICES: Ranger patrol.

FEES: None.

PRESERVE RULES: Day use only . . . No dogs, firearms, or camping . . . No fishing in the reservoir, as it is privately owned.

WEATHER: Wildflowers destine this Preserve to be a favorite springtime ride, but there's good riding the rest of the year, too, because of access to jeep-road-width trails.

 CAUTION: Use great care in crossing Skyline Blvd. if you park at Grizzly Flat . . . The main trail from the north of the Preserve is a combination of pavement and gravel for 1.3 mile. Horses should be shod . . . Although there are shoulders along the paved roadside, take care that your horse doesn't slip if he wanders onto pavement . . . "Don't let the word 'road' dismay you," says Carolyn. "I've ridden in this Preserve an entire day and met one car. It's a gorgeous place. Don't miss it!"

49

RANCHO SAN ANTONIO OPEN SPACE PRESERVE

The most popular and heavily used of all the District's properties . . . great trails for conditioning with loop trails giving variety and magnificent views of Santa Clara Valley . . .

— Carolyn Lekberg

Wide trails and easy riding for Linda Cooper and Pat Meredith at the entrance to the Rancho San Antonio Preserve.

REASONS TO GO: Nearly 1,000 acres of open land in the heart of the Bay Area . . . easy access from urban communities of Los Altos and Cupertino into a well maintained trail system linking wooded areas, grassy ridges, canyons, and creeks . . . bountiful wildlife and a pleasing variety of trails make this a most enjoyable ride.

SPECIAL FEATURES: The popularity of this Preserve with riders makes it easy to visualize its history as a cattle ranch dating back to the 1800s. The Perham family maintained the ranch use until purchase of the land by the Midpeninsula Regional Open Space District in 1977. Originally it was the neighborliness of the ranch owners which encouraged the status of the area as a favorite destination for trail riders. In recent times the popularity of the trails has increased due to public ownership of the land and the provision of generous parking areas giving easy access to the Preserve. . . . Adjacent to the trail system is Deer Hollow Farm (not open to horses) . . . glimpses of the picturesque farmyard will inspire you to return on foot with your children or animal lovers of any age! Although access to the Farm isn't allowed on horseback, the trail system gives you ample opportunity to see a variety of wild animals including coyote, bobcat, and deer . . . even a mountain lion has been spotted! (Author's note: I've had a bobcat pad along the trail behind me for about a quarter mile, keeping a respectful distance but

close enough to explain why the Sierra Club conducts their African Safari trips on horseback — you can get closer to the wildlife!)

LOCATION: Just west of I-280 in the foothills of Los Altos and Cupertino. The community of Los Altos Hills with its beautiful, thoughtfully preserved system of trails is also a next door neighbor.

TRAIL FEATURES: Ten-plus miles of varied and excellently maintained trails. . . . The District's 1984 addition of 375 acres greatly improves the trail linkage and the variety of terrain available to the public . . . on the drawing board are many more miles of trail by connecting the original Preserve with Duveneck's Windmill Pasture and the Monte Bello Open Space Preserve. . . . Machine built trails have been added to the original horse trails and fire roads. . . . Steep trails for great conditioning rides and wide PG&E access trails for easy side-by-side riding. . . . The top of Wildcat Loop Trail will give you views of Deer Hollow Farm set among original farm buildings preserving the

ranch history of the land . . . Wide, shady trails along Permanente Creek . . . Wildcat Loop Trail (originating with the Rogue Valley Trail near High Meadow Stable) is narrow and steep but still a pleasant trip to the ridge top, offering terrific views of Santa Clara Valley and the reward of a vivid green or golden meadow (depending on the time of year) for your picnic. . . . A less crowded and wider route to the top is the PG&E fire road which takes off from the parking area.

WHERE TO PARK: Equestrian parking is generously provided and maintained by Santa Clara County at the Rancho San Antonio County Park adjacent to the Preserve entrance. Take Foothill Blvd. south from I-280, turn immediately right on Cristo Rey Drive, and continue about one mile to the first lot on the left as you enter the Park. The conditions for trailer pulling are excellent and the designated equestrian area (a nice gravel surface) easily handles 10 rigs with plenty of room to turn around. Weekend parking can be crowded so plan to get there early.

50

ACCOMMODATIONS: Day use only. Restrooms and drinking water at the adjacent auto parking lot area . . . Water for horses in the creek near the parking lot and along the trail up the PG&E road. High Meadow Stables has always been generous with water and friendly advice to horsemen "passing through", but under the new ownership of the District the fate of the stable is uncertain.

PRESERVE SERVICES: Midpeninsula Regional Open Space District (415-965-4717) provides a map at District headquarters, 375 Distel Circle, Los Altos, CA 94022. Preserve is well patrolled with a ranger in residence and additional vehicle and foot patrol. . . . There are many places to picnic although no formal picnic sites are provided. . . . For maximum enjoyment of the area you're riding take a preride trip on foot! The District will provide, upon request, an excellent program of docent-led Discovery Walks on Saturdays leaving from the Preserve entrance. . . . Deer Hollow Farm, leased and maintained by the City of Mountain View, offers a wide range of environmental programs. For more information phone (415) 966-6331.

FEES: None.

PRESERVE RULES: Preserve is open from dawn to dusk. No dogs or firearms are allowed . . . all natural resources are protected. Bicycles are allowed on a few designated bicycle trails only.

WEATHER: Trail riding is good here year-round but occasionally a trail or two might be closed after a heavy rain.

CAUTION: You won't get lonesome in this Preserve . . . not only riders love it, but hikers and joggers as well, so ride with care and consideration. . . . Portions of Wildcat Loop Trail are steep and narrow and shared with joggers. Passing points can be hazardous unless both rider and runner use caution and consideration. . . . Rattlesnakes and poison oak are part of the native charm of the place. . . . Several wooden bridges for you to test your horse-training skills.

A Preserve landmark is the Maryknoll Missionary Home easily visible from Hwy. 280.

Many thanks to the Santa Clara County Parks Department for the generous sized equestrian parking area at the entrance to the trail system.

WINDY HILL OPEN SPACE PRESERVE

A beautiful example of what volunteers can accomplish . . .

— Carolyn Lekberg

REASONS TO GO: 651 acres . . . scenic mountain backdrop to town of Portola Valley . . . variety of recreational experiences . . . part of an expansive grassland hilltop from Skyline Ridge to Valley floor . . . Windy Hill can be seen throughout Midpeninsula area . . . oak and Douglas fir forests . . . terrific loop trail! From top of 1,900-foot Windy Hill an exceptional view of the Pacific Ocean to the west and the Bay Area to the east.

SPECIAL FEATURES: One of the few formal picnic areas in District Open Space Preserves. . . . Culmination of efforts of 98 volunteers known as the Windy Hill Trails Task Force whose members contributed 1,000 man hours for trail building and through the Peninsula Open Space Trust raised over $65,000 . . . volunteers continue to maintain the trail . . . Atop Windy Hill non-motorized model airplane gliders dot the sky . . . great place for kite flying, too, so hang on to your horse! . . . Good restaurants nearby on Skyline Blvd.

LOCATION: Portola Valley in San Mateo County. . . . Two good access routes for horse trailers: One is up Hwy. 9 from town of Saratoga to Skyline Blvd., right on Skyline and travel 13 miles north to parking area. . . . The other is up the mountain on Hwy. 92 to Skyline Blvd., left on Skyline and travel 14 miles south to parking area.

TRAIL FEATURES: 7.2 mile loop trail with about 3 miles of additional trail . . . maintenance of trail is excellent, well signed with wooden trail signs . . . great conditioning trails are Hamms Gulch and Razorback Trail which are up and down the mountainside . . . Eagle Trail and Lost Trail are easy trails to catch your breath on. . . . Machine-made trails with a 10% grade, although a

52

Contrast the peace and solitude enjoyed by this lone rider at the base of Windy Hill with the group effort being organized in the photo below. Beautiful trails and work parties . . . "you can't have one without the other!"

photos: Sheldon Woodward, POST

Carol Ivie, POST

Rangers, horsemen and hikers compare notes after a day's work on the trail.

little steeper in a few spots . . . Razorback Trail is narrow, a gorgeous wooded trail winding down the steep hillside . . . Eagle Trail winds along Corte Madera Creek and Hamms Gulch trail is wooded with terrific views of the valley and grassy hillsides . . . view from top of Windy Hill is exciting and on windy days possibly a little too exciting for your horse! If so, head for Razorback, Hamms Gulch and Eagle Trails which are sheltered from the wind. The loop ride is excellent for all levels of riders . . . when conditioning your horse the ride can be done in a brisk time of an hour and a half . . . for an all day ride just walk the trail, have a picnic, and explore feeder trails.

WHERE TO PARK: Recommended parking is at the three large pull-outs on either side of Skyline Blvd. at the north end of the Preserve close to the picnic area. . . . No horse trailer parking available at the picnic area. . . . If you've parked on the west side of Skyline be very careful when crossing the road. . . . Horse stile is in the plan but at time of printing just walk around the fence to enter the Preserve. Follow the fence line southerly to the

picnic area where the trail is signed.

A second entrance to the Preserve is 3 miles from Page Mill Rd. and about 16 miles south of 92 at the South Gate entrance. The South Gate entrance is designated by a brown pipe gate and gives you immediate access to the Loop Trail. Access for local riders from the valley floor (no trailers) is on Alpine Rd. Enter around large green gate at 5020 Alpine Rd.

ACCOMMODATIONS: Day use. Open dawn to dusk. . . . Three picnic tables at the picnic area on Skyline . . . lots of trees for tying horses, and hitching posts are scheduled for the future . . . Corte Madera Creek runs year round and watering horses here is no problem. . . . Carry your own drinking water.

FEES: None.

PRESERVE SERVICES: Ranger patrol of parking areas, and equestrian patrol a future possibility . . . Excellent maps which include mileages are available from Midpeninsula Regional Open Space District, 375 Distel Circle, Suite D1, Los Altos, CA

94022, (415) 965-4717 or on site at the picnic area . . . they're free! For a docent-led hike or other programs phone (415) 965-4742.

PRESERVE SERVICES: All natural resources are protected . . . leave plants, rocks, animals undisturbed . . . no guns, shooting, fires, bicycles allowed . . . dogs allowed on leash in certain areas with a special "dog map" available at the picnic area.

WEATHER: Don't miss spring here . . . spring wildflowers are breathtaking . . . park is open year round but be conservative about riding here in the rainy season as trails are susceptible to damage. . . . Windy Hill deserves its name, especially in the spring, but you can always find shelter along Razorback, Hamms Gulch, and Eagle Trails . . . Fog may drift in so a light jacket is in order.

 CAUTIONS: Watch for kite-flying, model gliders on Windy Hill if you pass that way . . . Illegal bike use on the trail can be a problem . . . Motorcycles and fast traffic on Skyline Blvd. so watch carefully when you cross.

Charlotte MacDonald, MROSD

Santa Clara Valley history can be captured in a single view as you ride along orchard trails with an overlook of Silicon Valley and the East Bay beyond.

Carolyn Caddes

54

FREMONT OLDER OPEN SPACE PRESERVE

Horsemen feel right at home here . . . riding through the hay fields with Garrod Ranch nearby . . .

— Carolyn Lekberg

REASONS TO GO: 734 acres of grassland, shady walnut orchards, chaparral, open hay fields, Seven Springs Canyon, and ridge-top riding. . . . If that isn't enough to entice you there is also an expansive view of Santa Clara Valley with the East Bay hills as a backdrop!

SPECIAL FEATURES: You can take a horseless friend out on the trails thanks to nearby Garrod Ranch Stables and Stevens Creek Ranch. . . . According to the District, equestrian use is the major activity of this Preserve so you can usually count on company and friendly advice out on the trail. The horseman you meet is likely to be a member of the Castle Rock Horsemen's Association which not only enjoys the trails but also works with the District in maintaining them. . . . After a hot summer day's ride nearby Stevens Creek Reservoir offers refreshing breezes and the pleasures of boating, fishing, and windsurfing! . . . The view from Hunter's Point gives you the fun of picking out Valley landmarks while rejoicing that you're out on a trail and not caught in the traffic below. . . . Vineyards and hayfields give you a feeling for the history of the Preserve as a working ranch, the home of William Pfeffer in the 1870s. The Pfeffer Cabernet grape is still used in today's fine Cabernet wines. . . . The District named the Preserve after Fremont Older and his wife, Cora, who owned a portion of the ranch for 60 years. The preservation of the Older home, "Woodhills", is a tribute to the historical significance of Older, a prominent San Francisco newspaper editor whose opposition to graft in local government made him a respected

community leader. "Woodhills" is opened to the public once a year by its residents, Mort and Elaine Levine. The home was restored under a special arrangement with the Midpeninsula Regional Open Space District and is now listed in the National Registry of Historic Places.

LOCATION: Santa Clara County in the hills of Saratoga and Cupertino. The main entrance to the Preserve is on Prospect Rd. which is reached by taking I-280 to Hwy. 9 to Prospect, then left two miles to parking area. Because of limited size this area is not usually desirable for trailer parking. Preferred parking is described below.

WHERE TO PARK: Equestrian parking available **by reservation** at Garrod Stables, 22600 Mt. Eden Rd., Saratoga, CA 95070. Take Hwy. 9 to Pierce Rd., Pierce Rd. to Mt. Eden Rd., and then one and one half miles on Mt. Eden to Garrod's. Be sure to call ahead for reservations, (408) 867-9527.

TRAIL FEATURES: Ten miles of trail with additional riding in adjoining Stevens Creek County Park. . . . Mostly wide fire trails and some narrow hillside trails traversing gently rolling hills . . . terrain varies from flat to moderately steep . . . good conditioning trails as well as good terrain for novice horses and riders. . . . A good, short ride is to leave from Garrod Stables, ride out to the hay fields, pick up the Seven Springs Loop Trail, and back. . . . For a longer ride head to Stevens Creek Reservoir and ride back through the hay fields and

along the Seven Springs Loop Trail. . . . Trails are well marked with wooden trail signs indicating destinations and mileages. . . . The Seven Springs Trail goes through beautiful hayfields up to Hunter's Point, then down through a walnut grove along a quiet stream . . . all this peace and beauty only a few minutes away from city life! **Carriage drives are possible here** by arrangement with Garrod Stables . . . Strongly recommended that trail be preridden for suitability for carriage drive.

ACCOMMODATIONS: Day use only in the Preserve but possible overnight boarding at Garrod Stables, (408) 867-9527, and Stevens Creek Ranch, (408) 996-RIDE. Water for horses and refreshments for humans at Garrod Stables. . . . No camping allowed but there are many motels in the area available to you (assuming you've boarded your horse elsewhere!) Phone and restrooms also available at Garrod's.

FEES: None.

PRESERVE SERVICES: Maps are available at the MPROSD office and at the Preserve entrance, at Prospect Rd., but not at Garrod Stables. An informative brochure is also available at the District office, 375 Distel Circle, Los Altos, CA 94022. Phone (415) 965-4717. . . . Trails are well maintained by the District with help from volunteers and are well patrolled by friendly, helpful rangers.

PRESERVE RULES: Dogs are allowed on leash in dog area — map available at Prospect entrance and District Office. . . . No firearms, no camping or fires. . . . All natural resources are protected.

WEATHER: Good riding any time of year but heavy horse use in rainy weather makes some areas boggy. . . . Storm damage may require the temporary closure of some trails to horse use.

 CAUTION: Snakes and poison oak, of course! . . . Avoid boggy areas in wet weather . . . bikes (may be hazardous to your health) are allowed here, and heavy use by cyclists is common.

55

TRAIL PATRONS
The Garrod Family

Horses and men at work baling hay in 1917 on an 80-acre parcel now part of the Fremont Older Open Space Preserve (courtesy of the Garrod family album).

I N 1894 David and Sophia Garrod joined Ralph Creffield, Sophia's brother, in a partnership which purchased 110 acres from the Mt. Eden Orchard and Vineyard Company in the hills northwest of Saratoga. Soon the partnership was split and the land divided between the Garrods and Creffields. The David Garrods and their children, R.V., Harold and Mary, retained 65 acres. A barn, still standing, was built in 1902.

The Garrods acquired adjacent land as it came up for sale until there was a total of 242 acres, some of which was planted in apricots and prunes. Eucalyptus seedlings, raised by Sophia Garrod, were planted on the non-crop land.

R.V. Garrod left the Garrod Farms to his children, Richard, Vince and Louise, who sold 118 acres of non-crop land to the Midpeninsula Regional Open Space District in 1980 as an addition to the Fremont Older Open Space Preserve.

The Garrod Farms Stables, established in 1962, are presently managed by Jan Garrod, a fourth-generation member of the family. Many of the Stables' original trails are now part of the Fremont Older Open Space Preserve, where they are used regularly by equestrians.

Text courtesy of California History Center, De Anza College.

Three generations of Garrod family members fill the shade of an old oak tree.

THE GARROD family albums are probably your best introduction to Fremont Older Open Space Preserve. The family group photo on the opposite page is recent, but the remaining photographs are 1960s vintage and much earlier. The best part of viewing them is that in the 1980s they still depict the activities of the Garrod family — ranching, riding, stable management, and an unofficial welcoming committee for those entering Fremont Older Open Space Preserve. What the photos do not depict are the many hours of volunteer work given by Vince Garrod and his family to ensure the preservation of open land for public enjoyment. Vince is a board member of the Peninsula Open Space Trust. Garrod family history is closely linked with the history of Santa Clara County, and in 1984 was a featured exhibit of the California History Center.

This isn't a trail class — just the Garrod children, 20 years ago, fetching the mail for their mother. Hundreds of people riding the trails today got their horsemanship training at "Garrods."

The Vince Garrod family saddles up in celebration of the newly built covered arena.

TRAIL PATRONS
Peninsula Open Space Trust

TODAY'S TRAILBLAZERS need to know more than machetes and a sense of direction. Long before they clear a path they must overcome political and financial barriers more forbidding than a thicket of poison oak. One successful approach is to allow private conservation organizations to finance and supervise the building of trails on public land.

Peninsula Open Space Trust (POST), a private, nonprofit land conservancy with offices in Menlo Park, is dedicated to preserving land for open space uses in the three counties of the San Francisco Peninsula. Founded in 1977, POST has combined private and public resources for a number of mutually desirable projects — acquiring parkland, preserving wildlife habitat, protecting scenic areas, providing mitigation lands to offset bayland development, and constructing recreational facilities.

Windy Hill Trail, an 8.4-mile loop in Portola Valley, is an excellent example of what can be accomplished through such public-private partnerships. The trail was built on public land belonging to the Midpeninsula Regional Open Space District (MROSD), which is a tax-supported public agency. The land has special importance for POST because the original parcel of 536 acres was a gift to POST. In 1981 POST sold the land to MROSD at less than market value. Since then additional gifts and purchases have increased Windy Hill Open Space Preserve to 651 acres.

Opening Windy Hill to the public for hiking, riding, and picnicking had been a primary goal of POST since 1979 when the initial gift of land was made, but before any kind of development could take place all interested parties had to be consulted and involved. They included the POST trustees and advisory council, the MROSD directors, the Portola Valley Town Council, and Peninsula citizens.

POST developed a plan to build much of the trail by hand with volunteer labor. Additional help in planning and constructing the trail came from MROSD staff. Machine work and materials brought the trail budget to $50,000. Robert V. Brown, a POST advisory council member and a resident of Portola Valley, led the fund-raising committee. Simultaneously Jane Ames and Bo Gimbal, Portola Valley residents with trail-building experience, organized a task force to do hand labor.

Success beyond the most hopeful expectations was the result. Less than a year after all the necessary approvals had been granted, a celebration was held to mark the opening of the trail. In August 1983 recognition was given to donors of the original gift of land as well as to more than 100 volunteers who worked on the trail. POST received $55,000 in donations. With the addition of a $16,000 trust fund accumulated by Portola Valley residents over a period of years, POST found itself with more than $20,000 over budget. The extra money has been placed in an endowment fund to pay for repairs or improvements to the Trail.

"As urbanization of the Peninsula becomes more intense, people grow more appreciative of open spaces close to home," observes Rosemary Young, president of POST's Board of Trustees. Young sees the Trail project as an important model for the kind of public-private partnerships necessary to achieve results in this era of growing public need and dwindling government money.

Private organizations can build trails on public land elsewhere provided there is adequate citizen involvement. Community support for Windy Hill Trail was extraordinary. Portola Valley has a long history of appreciation for rural beauty. A trail network for Windy Hill and adjacent hillsides has long been part of the Town's general plan. Part of the credit for success of the project must go to the land itself, conspicuous and lovely, with a wide variety of natural features. A series of ridges within the preserve form a major visual backdrop for the Peninsula. The highest portions of the property are seen by more than a million people every day.

As a land conservancy, POST works to preserve land for open space uses in addition to recreation. Farms and forests, scenic areas, and special habitats also need protection. Unlike park districts, POST does not hold land but instead transfers it to other agencies after appropriate legal protections are placed on the land. It is part of the POST philosophy that not all land with high open space value needs to be in public ownership.

"The high cost of owning and maintaining land argues in favor of leaving it in private hands whenever possible," explains Robert Augsburger, POST's executive director. "One of POST's functions is to work with interested land owners in exploring mutually beneficial techniques for keeping land open."

— Ann Duwe, POST

TRAIL PATRON

Midpeninsula Regional Open Space District

GRASSY MEADOWS to picnic in, wooded trails to explore, windy hilltops to fly kites from: these are just a few of the recreational possibilities available to you on the open space preserves of the Midpeninsula Regional Open Space District.

Established in 1972 as a tax-supported public agency by midpeninsula voters, the MROSD has acquired 17,470 acres of scenic and recreational lands in the foothills and baylands of Santa Clara and San Mateo Counties. The land is contained in 19 open space preserves managed by the District for the use and enjoyment of the public — and for the preservation of the natural environment.

These close-to-home wilderness areas are visited regularly by hikers, picnickers, joggers, equestrians, photographers, birdwatchers, and groups of school children — as well as by people of all ages who simply wish to renew their feelings of kinship with the land. The preserves also provide a safe habitat for the midpeninsula's original natives: the plant and animal communities that once lived here undisturbed.

All the preserves are open without fee to the public from dawn to dusk 365 days of the year, but none of them are developed "parks" in the usual sense of having ballfields, barbecue pits, or even trash cans. The most highly-developed preserves boast gravel parking lots, rest rooms, well-marked trail systems, and detailed site brochures. The least developed of the preserves are identified only by small MROSD boundary plaques, but their unmarked roads and trails are open to visitors.

Many of the preserves have very limited or even non-existent parking facilities. Access to these areas will be improved as the District gradually assembles the pieces of a regional greenbelt linking District lands with each other and with State and county parklands. Please read about each preserve and check the specific site map to ascertain what preserves require a call to the District office before visiting. Some may require a permit or special directions for access.

Motor vehicles, fires, or firearms are not allowed on District preserves, but there are planned future facilities for overnight camping. Dogs are generally not permitted so that wildlife can be observed under natural conditions.

Carolyn Caddes

A tranquil view at Skyline Ridge Open Space Preserve.

Each open space preserve is a remnant of our natural heritage, each has its own unique characteristics, from oak-studded hilltop to shady creekside or redwood forest. The original uses of the land are continued on some of the preserves through grazing and the cultivation of crops, while the natural and cultural history of each site has been kept intact through the preservation of early landmarks, geologic features, and historic buildings.

All of these special places are within a 30-minute drive of the urban Peninsula's center. We invite you to explore and enjoy them!

— *Charlotte MacDonald, MROSD*

IV. Santa Cruz Mountain Area

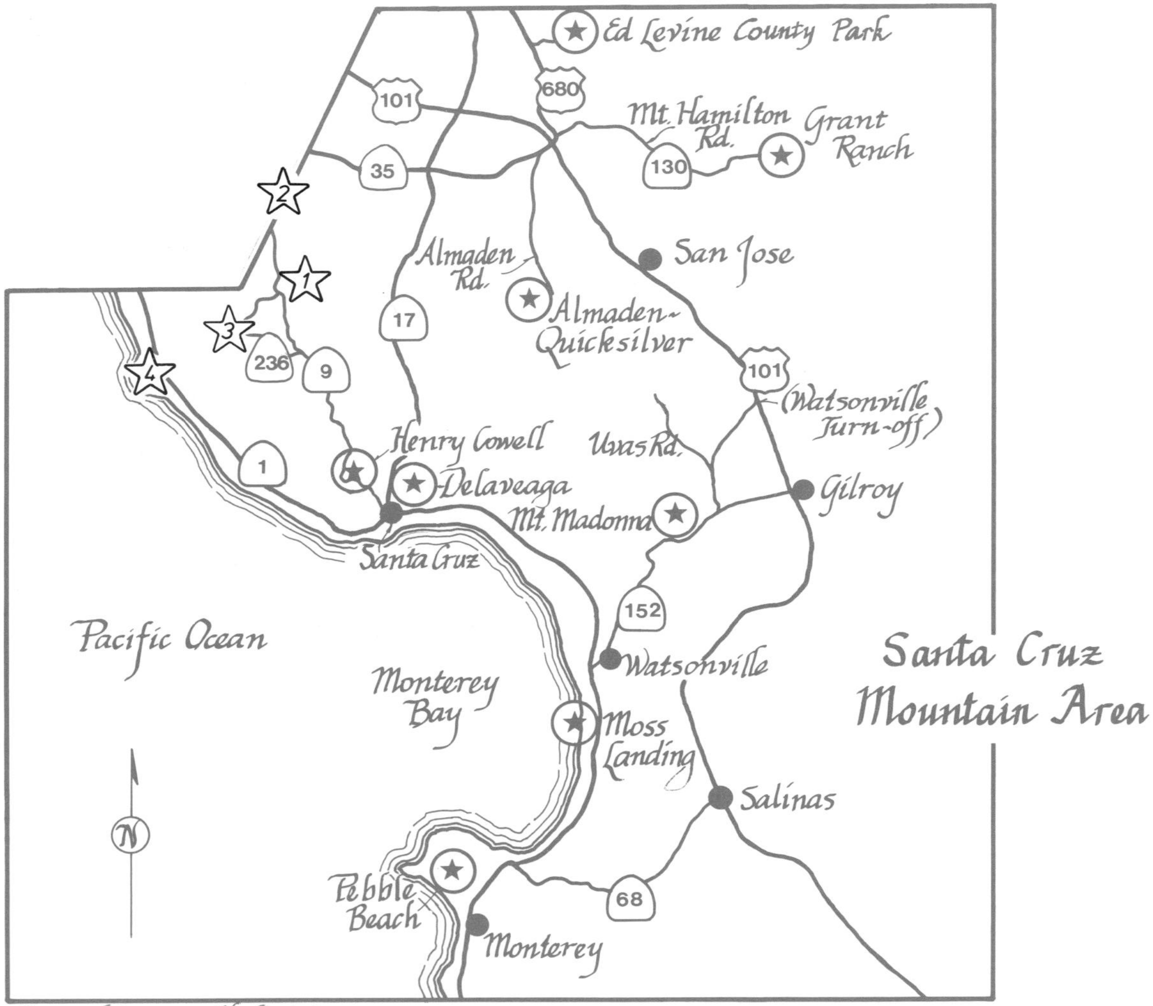

Featuring

☆ 1 Castle Rock State Park
☆ 2 Toll Road
☆ 3 Big Basin State Park
☆ 4 Skyline~to~the~Sea Trail
(Rancho del Oso)

(★) Neighboring trail areas

Santa Cruz
Mountain Area

Ed Levine County Park
Mt. Hamilton Rd.
Grant Ranch
San Jose
Almaden Rd.
Almaden~ Quicksilver
(Watsonville Turn~off)
Henry Cowell
Uvas Rd.
Delaveaga
Mt. Madonna
Gilroy
Santa Cruz
Pacific Ocean
Monterey Bay
Watsonville
Moss Landing
Salinas
Pebble Beach
Monterey

101
680
35
236
9
17
130
1
152
68

N

JULIE WESTON galloped the borrowed horse through her family's Santa Clara Valley pear orchard, headed unknowingly toward the most lasting adventure of her life. It wasn't the speed of the horse or the dodging of tree limbs that was making her heart race ahead of the animal beneath her. Adventuresome, daring, rambunctious were labels which had been securely fastened to the tall, slender Stanford student for some time, but nothing in her 20 years could match the drama before her now.

Most people live a whole lifetime without witnessing the landing of a huge helium balloon on their property. Even fewer are astride a horse in utter astonishment as a handsome, young naval officer steps forward from the craft. But truth exceeds all possible fiction when the young woman on horseback and the pilot of a 1944 balloon landing live "happily ever after" as is the case with Bob and Julie Suhr.

It may be too much to claim love at first sight since the balloon landed in 1944 and the wedding took place in 1946. But almost 40 years later Julie will tell you with gusto how fortunate she was to live precisely five miles downwind from Sunnyvale's Moffett Field Naval Air Station when Bob Suhr was in "free balloon" training!

"Bob was flying blimps during the war and had been stationed in Tillamook, Oregon, until he came to Moffett Field in 1944. The free balloon training was necessary so that if the blimp engines failed the pilots would know how to take advantage of the wind currents," explains Julie. The wind currents were certainly on target that day because Julie and Bob have shared not only a very happy marriage and four children, but also countless adventures on horseback.

"We've ridden together on four continents, a tribute to the worldwide interest in endurance riding. I can't say enough how grateful I feel to be a part of AERC (American Endurance Ride Conference). It has brought so much adventure and such a cross section of interesting, wonderful people into our lives. Bob was 50 years old when he rode a horse for the first time, and he was 57 when he competed on his first endurance ride, the toughest one of them, the Tevis Cup. He's been hooked on riding ever since."

Bob may have been slow in coming around to share Julie's love for horses, but she feels she gave him fair warning as to what she'd be like as a wife when she galloped up to him on horseback 40 years ago!

"Well, maybe not entirely a fair warning," Julie admits as she recalls the drastic action taken by her father to curtail the horse interest of the young bride. "You see, when Bob and I returned from our honeymoon I was shocked to discover that my father had torn

Endurance rider Julie Suhr at home at Marinera Ranch.

down my corrals and turned my barn into a tractor shed. 'You're a married woman now and you'll never ride a horse again' was his proclamation. I guess he felt he had to take strong measures because his prophesying hadn't worked years before when he'd said that my riding days were over now that I was a college girl! While I was away at school he had turned my two, tired old geldings out to freedom and retirement on the Mt. Hamilton range. After an idyllic childhood spent with two, gentle old horses and the freedom to ride anywhere I wanted (we felt very safe in those days!) I just couldn't accept the shock of being without horses. So contrary to my father's prediction about college girls, I just kept the barn full of borrowed horses! But as a married woman, I must have taken Dad's advice to heart because I didn't ride again for 18 years!"

Julie's horseless years were spent raising the children in the picturesque community of Saratoga. Life was too busy as a young wife and mother for horses to be missed, but one by one the children left for college and her desire to ride returned. Desire became a reality when she bought a half-Thoroughbred, half-Saddlebred which she boarded out in Almaden Valley, southwest of San Jose. For a nominal purchase price the handsome mare brought back all the pleasures of riding Julie had known since childhood and then some.

"I was content to trail ride around Almaden Valley until one day I happened to overhear a brief discussion about a one-day, 100-mile endurance ride, the Tevis Cup. The challenge of such a ride triggered something in me and on the spot I discovered a new life's ambition," recalls Julie.

The year was 1964 and the 100-mile ride from Squaw Valley to Auburn along the beautiful, rugged Western States Trail was the only endurance ride in the nation. Endurance riding was an infant sport 20 years ago (today there are over 500 rides a year throughout the U.S.), and while theories abounded on conditioning the equine athlete, there were few proven data available to trail competitors.

"Not knowing any better I trained for the toughest race of them all (still is!) by trotting round and round the Almaden Golf Course. The day of the ride I got as far as the first vet stop when the horse was pulled for being lame and having a pulse and respiration count that didn't recover in the allotted time. Even if the horse could have gone on I couldn't have made it, I was so totally exhausted," admits Julie. "Tearful, but also relieved to be pulling out, I suddenly realized I was in totally over my head and that for a grueling ride like the Tevis Cup you don't train a horse by running around a golf course!"

Julie's spunkiness quickly reasserted itself and she determined to ride a smarter ride the next year and finish the race. "I borrowed an Arabian who carried me through beautifully in 1965 and that was it. I was totally hooked and have been ever since," Julie says emphatically.

How does she explain this compulsion to test herself and her horse to the utmost?

"It's the adventure!" she says without hesitation. "I was testing myself both mentally and physically in a way I had never been tested before. It was the hardest work I had ever done (incredible statement from a woman who'd raised a large family!) and it was totally invigorating. I couldn't bear the thought of waiting a whole year for the next Tevis Cup Ride so I teamed up with the Castle Rock Horsemen's Association and founded the Castle Rock Challenge Ride in 1967. We're proud of the fact that this ride continues to be a beautiful, successful ride every year. The continued success of the ride is mainly due to the McCrary family, owners of the neighboring Big Creek Lumber Company. This family has put the ride on for years. Their support is very important to our trail system because they allow the riders to cross their private property before passing through Big Basin State Park."

The ride which was started by Julie, and is being carried on by the McCrary family, is well established as the second official endurance ride in the U.S. and the first 50-mile endurance ride. Not only did Julie found one of the most popular competitive events in the country, but she is also one of only ten people named in the past 13 years to the AERC Hall of Fame. She has successfully completed the Tevis Ride 14 times. There are only three people in the world who have

Charles Barieau

Julie and Marinera competing on the Castle Rock Challenge Ride.

completed this international event more often. In 1983 and 1984 she won the coveted Haggin Cup when her Arab, HCC Gazal was judged the Best Conditioned Horse in the Tevis competition. As of 1984 Julie has logged over 6,000 miles in endurance riding. Julie's father may have been right about young married women and riding, but how could he possibly have foreseen all the accomplishments of his daughter forty years later?

The supreme effort required in Tevis competition is enough to change anyone's life, but it could be argued that Julie's boldest act was ventured in her kitchen seated before her typewriter. With one simple letter written in October, 1965, she changed her life almost as drastically as she did by riding forward to meet the wind-borne balloon.

"I had bought a *Western Horseman* magazine at the local drugstore and read about a new breed of horse being imported into the United States from Peru. The writer of the aricle was Verne Albright (currently editor of the *Peruvian Horse World Review*) who extolled the virtues of the Peruvian Horse, carefully bred for centuries to produce an extremely gentle, naturally gaited horse with great stamina. I was presumptuous enough to write to the president of the American Association of Owners and Breeders of Peruvian Paso Horses and request the loan of a horse! (The actual proposal was that I would have the use of a horse for the next Tevis Ride, and if all went well the stamina of the Paso breed would have been proven on North American soil, a plus for North American breeders promoting the horse). As incredible as it seems I received a letter back from Association President, George Jones offering to turn my dream proposal into a reality! After her 27-day boat trip from Lima, Peru, a five-year-old roan mare named Marinera entered my life and nothing has been the same since!"

You can almost guess the successful ending of the story when you consider that the Suhr home is no longer in citified Saratoga but is now Marinera Ranch, 205 acres of Scotts Valley beauty, bounded by views of redwoods, the Pacific Ocean, and Monterey Peninsula. How one little horse could have so much impact on human lives is best told in a beautifully written series of articles by Julie and published in the *Peruvian Horse World Review*. The following are excerpts from the articles which, in their entirety, offer a wealth of information on conditioning horses in general, as well as the training of a particular breed.

(Marinera arrived in California in good health and settled into the Santa Cruz Mountains under the watchful eye of Verne Albright, whose article had originally inspired the adventure. The high-strung, ultra-smooth, sure-footed little mare was plenty tough and responded to Julie's rigorous training program with a full-speed-ahead attitude).

"When she arrived in January it was our idea that she would be returned after the Tevis Ride in July of 1966. . . We embarked on an incredibly rough training program in which I overdid everything in my enthusiasm as a rookie endurance rider. . . In retrospect I realize that I sorely abused this horse. That she survived my ignorance is remarkable. . .she gave and she gave and she gave. . . Her legs stayed clean and her muscles hardened and her nostrils enlarged for the great gulps of air required to fuel her body under my incessant demands. I learned to love her while never recognizing that somehow her spirit kept the horse going long after her body should have yelled quit. It is so easy for the uninitiated to think that if the horse wants to run it must be okay. So many endurance riders have found out the hard way that nothing is further from the truth.

"With the cooperation of Verne several pre-ride training trips to the

Bob Suhr riding Arab gelding SS Myllany in AERC Endurance competition.

64

Sierra were made to familiarize Marinera with the Tevis trail. It was considered essential to have the horse recognize the last 30 or 40 miles that on the day of the ride would be ridden in the dark.

"When the day of the pre-ride veterinarian examination arrived, Verne, Bob, Marinera, and I were by the shores of Lake Tahoe ready for the 5 a.m. start the next day. My skinny little gaited horse was not considered a likely finisher. But her indomitable spirit overcame the handicaps I heaped upon the animal, and she finished 22nd out of 92 starters and 54 finishers. It is traditional to gallop your mount around the track at the Auburn Fairgrounds at the finish of the 100 miles. I pushed her into a gallop but she felt weak, and I pulled her back. She crossed the finish line in the paso gait with brio that belied her true condition . . ."

"The criteria for the training of endurance horses has changed so much since then. Had I treated Marinera as I treat my present endurance horses she would, in my estimation, have been just about unbeatable. What this horse needed was more rest, not more miles. She needed more grain, vitamins, blood supplements, and all the good alfalfa hay she could eat. In those days we were told to make them tough, like the mustang that survives on almost nothing. But no mustang ever ran 100 miles carrying 150 to 200 pounds along the roughest trail in the West. (In the days of the Pony Express this same trail was covered using five horses to go the 100 miles.) It is because of the changes in training, particularly feeding, that modern endurance riders set new records every year. The first year that Marinera did the Tevis Cup the record for completing the ride, 16 hours and 30 minutes, was considered as unbeatable as the four-minute mile. The record is now under 12 hours. . . .

"The thought of returning Marinera upon completion of her assignment was more than I could stand. I wanted this horse with her 'brio' (her inner fire, or excitement) and her wonderfully smooth gait. Although we still lived in town Bob agreed that I should have her forever and he purchased her and gave her to me as my birthday present. Twenty years later she is still with me. Marinera Ranch and the forsaking of the comforts of city living are a constant reminder of the power one skinny little blue roan has had on the destinies of several humans."

Marinera is retired today as a most loved and honored broodmare, still full of spunk and fire at the age of 26! The second time she did the Tevis she finished 24th out of 125 horses, and placed third on the Castle Rock challenge Ride, also winning the greatly prized Best Condition award. On one 17-mile stretch she galloped the entire length without changing gait. She and Julie had accomplished their goal — they had proven beyond a doubt that Peruvian Pasos are horses of stamina, not only in their native country but also in U.S. competition. The popularity of the breed continues to grow.

The stamina of Julie and Bob Suhr on foreign soil has been proven as well with another adventure related to AERC. Julie was serving as secretary of the organization when a letter came to the organization from South Africa inviting some Americans to come and ride in a South African endurance ride! "You come and we'll provide the horses," the letter said.

"That was enough of an invitation for us," Julie recalls with enthusiasm. "So in 1980 we found ourselves in South Africa being treated to a royal time in every possible way. Our hosts welcomed us with open arms. They housed us, fed us, and flew the American flag the whole time we were on the trail. (It was a 130-mile ride, done in three days). As proof of their hospitality they even blessed the riders with a church service performed in English instead of their native Afrikaans. We were their guests for 11 days and couldn't have been treated any better. They gave us really great horses as well, a good thing, too, because it was a flat-out gallop the whole way! Because of the African horse sickness over there they don't run rides in the hot summer months, so the ride was run in the freezing winter (which happens to be July in So. Africa!). Still the country was beautiful, the high desert terrain of the Orange Free State. They run their rides like ours in terms of the speed and the vet stops, but there was one major difference about their ride — you were racing with the army! Horses are used to patrol South African borders, and endurance rides are a proving ground for army horses. Out of 87 riders about 27 were military men."

How did our American representative, the married woman whose father had predicted would never ride again, do against such competition? On a borrowed horse she finished second, just five minutes behind the winner with a time of 9 hours and 41 minutes for the distance of 130 miles.

"Yes," Julie remembers with a smile, "I guess you might say that in spite of what my Dad said I returned to riding in a big way."

And how could Bob Suhr have known when he landed in Julie's pear orchard his adventures had only just begun? "It's Bob's incredible tolerance of my horse activities that has allowed me to stretch a childhood love of horses through more decades than I care to mention," acknowledges Julie. "His support promises me a future of many more happy hours on the trail."

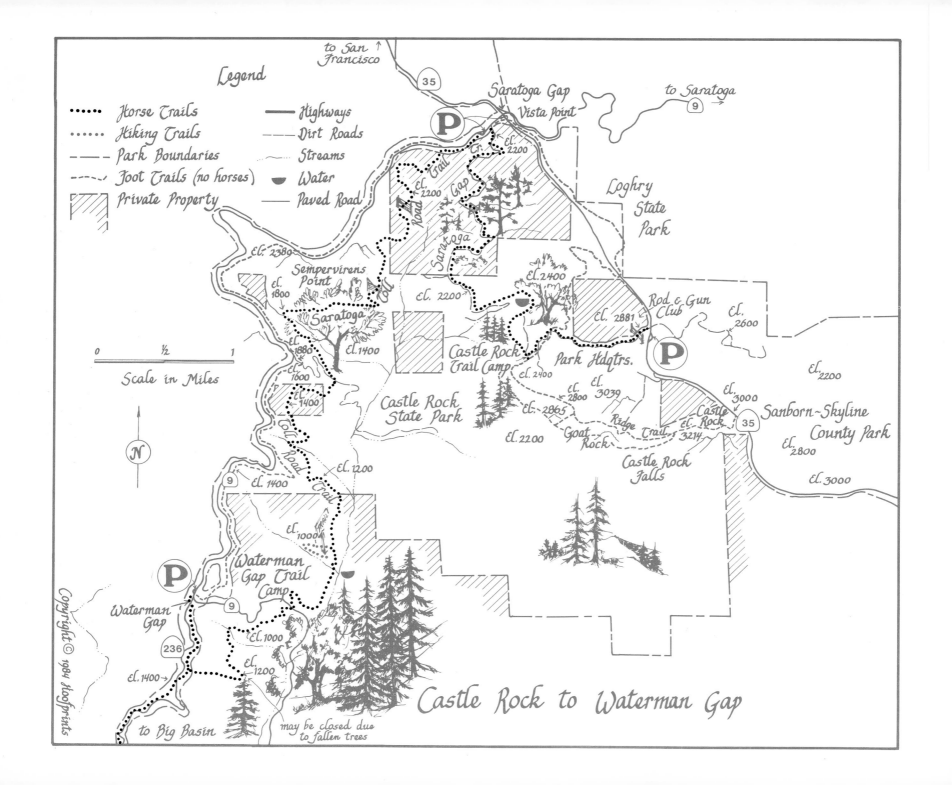

Castle Rock to Waterman Gap

CASTLE ROCK STATE PARK

Truly unsurpassed views in every direction . . .

— Julie Suhr

REASONS TO GO: Spectacular views, waterfalls, groves of oak, madrone, and Douglas fir, virgin redwoods . . . abundant wildflowers splashed across grassy meadows . . . deer, bobcats, rabbits, and a wide variety of birds share with you the vivid contrast of dense, cool woodlands and hot, dry chaparral-covered ridges . . . creeks bordered by lush ferns, gooseberries, wildflowers . . . deep canyons, watershed areas . . . 3,300 acres of park land and about 14 miles of excellent trail with about five miles open to horses . . . not much in terms of mileage, but the scenery and the access the Park provides to other trails make it well worth the trip.

SPECIAL FEATURES: Castle Rock itself! . . . a sandstone outcropping 80 feet high, frequently overrun with climbers earning a breathtaking view of San Francisco Bay to the north and the ocean to the west . . . can be viewed from Toll Road by horsemen . . . only seven miles from the lovely community of Saratoga, home of the Castle Rock Horsemen's Association, original sponsors of the Castle Rock Challenge Ride (oldest 50-mile endurance ride in the U.S.).

LOCATION: In Santa Cruz County seven miles west of Saratoga via Hwy. 9 at intersection with Hwy. 35 (Saratoga Gap) . . . Easy access from San Francisco area on Hwy. 35. Good conditions for trailer pulling, although coming from Saratoga on Hwy. 9 the road is "twisty." Access is on wide, well paved road, and Skyline Blvd. has little traffic except for weekend motorcycles, according to Julie . . . Park Rangers add that it's best to avoid typical rush-hour commute traffic during the week . . . In summer months you may find the highway saddled with fog, so take it easy.

Charles Barieau

Endurance riders take time out from the rigorous riding of the Castle Rock Challenge Ride to enjoy their lunch break.

67

Riding toward Saratoga Gap along Hwy. 9 the trail takes off to the right . . . never fear, it's less than 50 yards of roadside riding.

Rider entrance to Park from Rod and Gun Club looks very narrow but Julie made it through with a saddled Peruvian Paso!

TRAIL FEATURES: Approximately five miles of well maintained and well marked trails with access to portions of the Skyline-to-the-Sea Trail, Big Basin State Park, and the Saratoga Toll Road . . . As you leave the Saratoga Gap parking area the first one and a half miles is pavement, but it is very well worn by horses so it's not too slick . . . there's little traffic. Beyond the pavement you are on dirt trail through both wooded and open areas with striking views of the San Lorenzo watershed and the ocean beyond . . . **Suggested routes for beginners or for short rides:** Enter the trail system from the Saratoga Gap area and ride toward Castle Rock Trail Camp or start at Rod and Gun Club access point and ride as far as you and your horse are comfortable headed toward Saratoga Gap . . . remember that on your return trip the last few miles will be uphill . . . For an all-day ride the 10 miles round trip from Castle Rock to Saratoga Gap will be too short, but additional beautiful mileage can be gained by connecting with the Toll Road en route to Big Basin State Park.

WHERE TO PARK: Most popular spot used to be well known Saratoga Gap which is the intersection of Hwy. 9 and Hwy. 35 . . . now very limited parking here is made even more difficult by heavy motorcycle traffic on the weekends . . . (Some riders still risk it for the sake of the refreshment wagon which stops here on the weekends!) **There are alternate areas if Saratoga Gap looks too crowded:** Follow Hwy. 9 west 50 yards or so past Saratoga Gap to a wide turnout on the left . . . there's room for about 10 trailers . . . lead horse back to entrance of trail system OR approximately one and a quarter miles south of Saratoga Gap on the east side of Hwy. 35 is a pull-out area suitable for two trailers. Ride on road shoulder (or lead your horse) 100 yards north to the entrance of the Los Altos Rod and Gun Club. Chain link gate has equestrian entrance on the right. Entrance is OK for horses on the slim side, but a heavy horse might have problems at this narrow entrance. From the Rod and Gun Club follow the dirt road one and a half miles into Castle Rock Camp area and pick up a lovely marked trail which takes you to Saratoga Gap.

ACCOMMODATIONS: Day use only for horsemen . . . Midway on five-mile trail there's good water for horses.

FEES: None.

PARK SERVICES: Friendly rangers welcome a call before your ride to check trail conditions (408-867-2952) . . . best time to reach them by phone is between 1 and 2 p.m.

PARK RULES: Horses are to stay on marked horse trail . . . The trails are open from dawn to dusk every day except during a "red flag" fire alert. No dogs or firearms are allowed on the trails. Campfires are not allowed, as the threat of forest fires is serious.

WEATHER: Park is open year-round and the trail holds up well after a rain . . . "Anytime is a favorite time to ride here," says Julie . . . Fog can sneak up on you here, so you'll be glad you brought a jacket.

 CAUTION: Carry your own drinking water . . . Stay on the trails to avoid poison oak.

Scenes from Castle Rock State Park — photos by Alexander Lowry

Toll Road in the early 1900s when it was a means of livelihood for Santa Cruz Mountain residents. Note the bells on the two lead horses. They were to warn Toll Road travelers of heavily laden wagons coming 'round the bend!

TOLL ROAD

A gem of Western heritage preserved here... dating back to 1871 this was a vital link for oxen-powered lumber wagons and the stagecoach line between Santa Clara and Santa Cruz... easy riding and marvelous beauty!...
— Julie Suhr

REASONS TO GO: Miles of gorgeous views of the San Lorenzo Valley watershed... riding along miles of tree-trimmed mountain ridges... Oxen required a gentle grade, so this is a great area for novice horses and riders.

SPECIAL FEATURES: Ride with a sense of history... visualize the lumber wagons, the hopeful settlers, the rumbling stagecoaches whose tracks are buried deep beneath your horse's hooves... In 1890 the Toll Road changed character when it became a free public highway deeded to Santa Cruz County and maintained as a public road through the 1920s... Today it is a public trail and the historic name remains. Thanks to the Sempervirens "Trail Day" volunteers we can still enjoy its beauty as a riding and hiking trail.

LOCATION: In Santa Cruz County one and a half hours south of San Francisco, linking Castle Rock and Big Basin State Parks.

WHERE TO PARK: In wide turn-out area along Hwy. 9, 100 yards west of Saratoga Gap Vista Point (intersection of Hwy. 9 and Hwy. 35). The trail is well marked at entrance to the trail system.

TRAIL FEATURES: Nine miles of incredibly lovely trail with no obstacles that even an unconditioned horse cannot easily maneuver... Very gradual slope consisting of trail and fireroad... In some spots trail is narrow but is basically a wide-vehicle-width fire road... Not very well marked but almost impossible to lose your way. A couple of intersections need better marking, but if you

The Toll Road today, a public riding and hiking trail.

Photo courtesy of Sempervirens Fund

remember to choose the trail that goes neither up nor down you'll have no problem... Connects with Castle Rock Trail and in the near future will connect with Skyline-to-the-Sea Trail below Waterman Gap.

ACCOMMODATIONS: Day use only.

FEES: None.

PARK SERVICES: Closest services are at Castle Rock State Park.

WEATHER: Good year-round riding, although trail is sometimes closed after a storm due to downed trees... "red alert" fire conditions may also force closure, so it's strongly recommended that you phone ahead to confirm access: Castle Rock Park ranger's office (408) 867-2952, Saratoga Gap Fire Station, Department of Forestry (408) 867-3625.

PARK RULES: No smoking on the trail. No dogs allowed.

CAUTION: Fog rolls in, so come dressed for cool weather... Because of a lack of water on the trail not recommended for a full day's ride in summer heat.

71

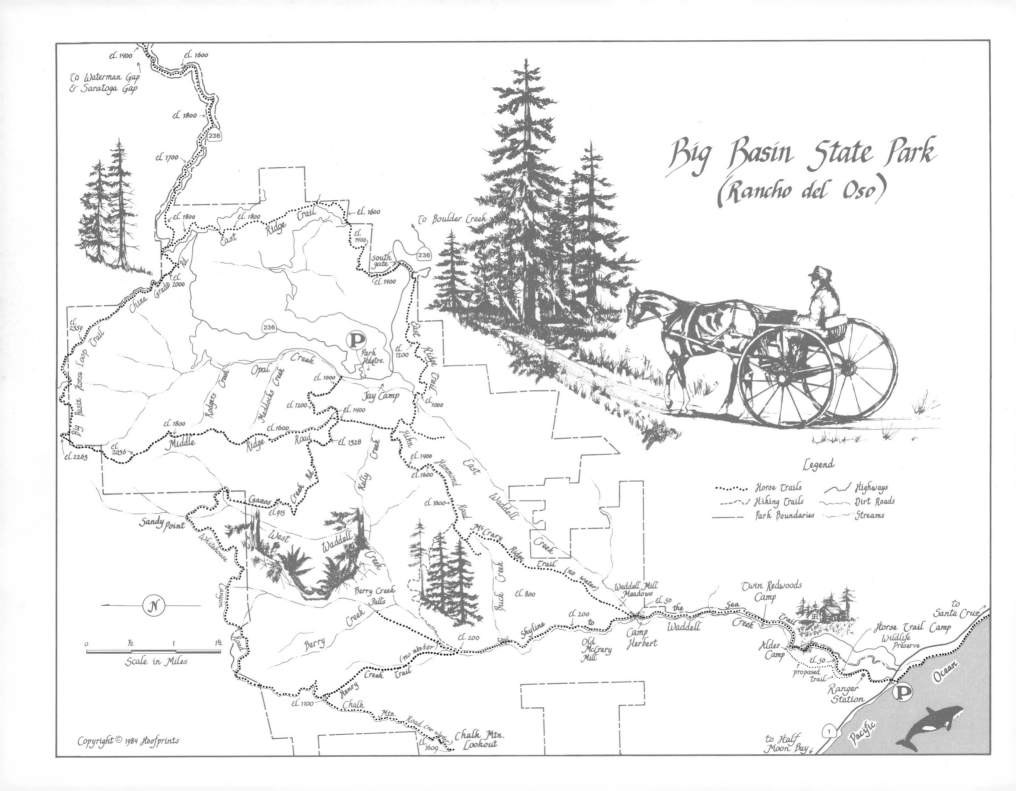

Big Basin State Park
(Rancho del Oso)

To Waterman Gap & Saratoga Gap

el. 1400
el. 1600
el. 1800
236
el. 1700
el. 1800
el. 1800
East Ridge Trail
el. 1600
el. 1400
south gate
236
el. 1400
To Boulder Creek

el. 2000
China Grade Rd.
el. 2350
Big Basin Horse Loop Trail
236
Opal Creek
Rodgers Creek
Maddocks Creek
Creek
P Park Hdqtrs.
el. 1200
East Ridge Trail
el. 1000
Jay Camp
el. 1000

el. 1800
el. 1200
el. 1400
el. 2036
Middle Ridge Road
el. 1600
el. 1528
Kelly Creek
John
el. 1400
el. 1600
Hammond Road
Waddell Creek
el. 2265
Creek Rd.
Gazos el. 915
Sandy Point
Whitehouse Canyon
West Waddell Creek
el. 1600
McCrary Ridge Creek Trail (no water)
Berry Creek Falls
Buck Creek
el. 800
Waddell Mill Meadows
el. 50
Twin Redwoods Camp
to Santa Cruz
Shyline
el. 200 to Old McCrary Mill
Camp Herbert
the Waddell
Sea Creek
Horse Trail Camp Wildlife Preserve
Berry Creek Trail (no water)
el. 200
Alder Camp
el. 50
proposed trail
Road
Henry Creek Trail
el. 1100
Chalk Mtn. Road (no water)
Ranger Station
P
Ocean
el. 1609
Chalk Mtn. Lookout
to Half Moon Bay
1
Pacific Ocean

Legend

- ••••••• Horse Trails
- – – – – Hiking Trails
- –––––– Park Boundaries
- ∿∿∿ Highways
- ‗ ‗ ‗ Dirt Roads
- ∿∿∿ Streams

N

| 0 | ½ | 1 | 1½ |

Scale in Miles

BIG BASIN STATE PARK

All the miles you want and all the beauty you can imagine . . .

— Julie Suhr

REASONS TO GO: Exquisitely beautiful trails through dark, mysterious redwood groves and across mountain ridges with a panorama of ocean and pounding surf . . . The largest park in the Santa Cruz mountains . . . a symphony of redwoods, madrone, waterfalls, knob-cone pine, and chaparral . . . magnificent lookout point from Chalk Mountain.

SPECIAL FEATURES: Awe-inspiring coastal redwoods (Sequoia *sempervirens*), some over 2,000 years old and towering as high as 300 feet with 15-foot diameters . . . Springs, waterfalls, and creek giving refreshment to over 150 species of birds and a magnificent variety of trees and wildflowers . . . An area of historical interest as the site of major logging operations in the 1800s . . . Home of the Sempervirens Fund, the guardian angels of Big Basin and Castle Rock State Parks.

LOCATION: In Santa Cruz County, 25 miles from the town of Saratoga, 18 miles from Saratoga Gap (intersection of Hwy. 9 and Hwy. 35), 23 miles from Santa Cruz or 9 miles from Boulder Creek on Hwy. 236. Recommended access for trailers is through the town of Boulder Creek to Hwy. 236, 9 miles to Park entrance or at junction of Hwys. 236 and 9 at Waterman Gap.

WHERE TO PARK: Enter at Big Basin State Park Headquarters and ranger at entrance will give directions. The parking area has no amenities for horses such as water troughs and tie rails, so Julie recommends bringing along a bucket and getting water at Park Headquarters . . . Canteens can be filled here too! Horses can also be watered at creek crossings, and there is usually water for humans at the campsites. Weekend parking during the busy summer tourist season can be a problem, but during the rest of the year the parking area is generous enough for easy maneuvering.

Go slowly on this curve as there's a nice parking area only a few yards ahead on the right.

From Park Headquarters you may enter the trail system on Gazos Creek Rd. which will take you approximately six miles to Sandy Point Fire Station (not inhabited) and farther on to the Chalk Ridges . . . A second choice at the Middle Ridge and Gazos Creek Rd. intersection is to make a quick left around a steel gate down Middle Ridge Fire Rd. to Hihn Hammond Rd. where you have the choice of going left to East Ridge Trail or right to McCrary Ridge Trail, down a steep hill to Canyon Trail, and on to the sea through Rancho del Oso! (Never fear . . . you have a good map and the trails are well marked!)

ACCOMMODATIONS: Day use only for horses . . . The State Park has a grocery store (open Easter through October) and a nature museum, the latter of little interest to horses, but you'll appreciate the cold drinks sold there . . . Clean restrooms are in the camping area.

TRAIL FEATURES: Over 35 miles of trail with access for trail riders getting better all the time. Gazos Creek Rd. to Chalk Mountain via Sandy Point and White House Canyon Rd. is a 12-mile ride, Park Headquarters to Sandy Point 6 miles, Sandy Point to Chalk Ridge 6 miles. Both routes are on well maintained and well marked fire roads . . . For level riding you'll enjoy Gazos Creek Rd., but for building up endurance try the steep trails along Chalk Ridge . . . For a full day's ride head to Chalk Mountain and back (24 miles).

East Ridge Trail: a five-mile moderately difficult wooded trail with some fireroad . . . From Park headquarters ride to junction of Gazos Creek Rd. and Middle Ridge Trail. Turn left and go another mile to junction with Hihn Hammond Rd. Turn left again and go approximately one mile to East Ridge Trail . . . a lovely trail, narrow but not difficult . . . Travel on the East Ridge Trail five miles to China

Fast moving endurance riders looking for ribbons to guide them on Big Basin trails.

Grade crossing and three quarters of a mile further to Hwy. 236. At this junction you have the choice of continuing across Hwy. 236 and picking up the China Grade Loop which again becomes Middle Ridge Trail and returns to Park Headquarters (a nice half-day ride), OR you can turn right immediately before crossing 236 and go north toward Waterman Gap on the Skyline-to-the-Sea Trail. (Note: horses are not allowed on all parts of the Skyline-to-the-Sea Trail, but are allowed from the China Grade junction to the Toll Road or up to Waterman Gap . . . four and one half miles.)

To ride from Park Headquarters to the ocean take Hihn Hammond Rd. west to McCrary Ridge Trail, which is a steep drop to Canyon Trail along Waddell Creek, which leads to the ocean . . . 11 beautiful miles.

74

FEES: Day use fee is $2 per vehicle and $1 per horse.

PARK SERVICES: Visitors' Center which features nature walks and evening campfire shows in the summer months beginning in June . . . rangers on duty encourage you to phone ahead for trail information, (408) 338-6132 . . . An excellent map (detailed in history, flora, and fauna) is available for $1.00 from the Sempervirens Fund, Box 1141, Los Altos, CA 94022.

PARK RULES: No smoking on the trails, and please leave your dogs at home . . . no firearms and no fishing temporarily, until streams are revitalized after two severe winters.

WEATHER: Good riding year-round as a rule,

but severe storms do bring down trees occasionally and trails are closed . . . Take the precaution of phoning ahead to be certain of trail conditions . . . Except for the hottest summer days you'll ride along shady trails, very grateful that you remembered to bring your jacket!

 CAUTION: Remember to bring a bucket for watering your horse in the Park Headquarters area . . . remember that there is no water on the steep McCrary Ridge Trail and Henry Creek Trail, both are very dry and rocky . . . horses utilizing these trails should be trail sure and in excellent condition . . . Rangers report the increased use of mountain bikes on the fireroads . . . stay alert!

Cal Yeats

Al Lowry

A lot of hard work on the trail precedes pleasure riding. Top right: Trail Days volunteers. Bottom right: The McCrary family trail crew. Their generosity with family-owned lands enhances the mileage of endurance rides utilizing Big Basin trails.

Los Altos Trails Club enjoying Waddell Beach.

SKYLINE-TO-THE-SEA TRAIL
(from Rancho del Oso)

My favorite trail . . . beach, trees, wide-open areas for cantering . . . it has it all!

— Julie Suhr

REASONS TO GO: Extraordinary beauty is ordinary here . . . dense forests, mountain ranges, steep valleys, ocean views . . . Marshlands and exotic birds in the Theodore Hoover Wildlife Preserve at the mouth of Waddell Creek and Hwy. 1

SPECIAL FEATURES: All-weather trails with pleasant creek crossings . . . easy riding with little change in elevation . . . wildflowers in abundance . . . beach riding . . . open meadows, wooded glens, dark forests cushioned with lush undergrowth . . . Rancho del Oso, 2,000-acre unit of Big Basin State Park . . . fishing and swimming in Waddell Creek . . . picnic on the beach!

LOCATION: Santa Cruz County (Big Basin Redwoods State Park and Rancho del Oso) . . . 17 miles north of Santa Cruz and about 35 minutes south of Half Moon Bay on Hwy. 1 . . . Easy conditions for trailer pulling.

WHERE TO PARK: On ocean side of Hwy. 1 park at Waddell Beach across from the Big Basin Redwoods State Park sign . . . Weekend parking can be crowded here but still adequate due to wide shoulders on the road for overflow traffic . . . Unload horses here and lead them across Hwy. 1 to Rancho del Oso gate. Go around the gate. This is the start of the Canyon Trail portion of the Skyline-to-the-Sea route which will connect you with the Big Basin Redwoods State Park. Go up the road past the ranger's office and continue east . . . a special treat for sea lovers is riding several miles along the beach traveling south from the parking area!

TRAIL FEATURES: Canyon Trail travels six beautiful miles inland from the sea along Waddell Creek . . . feel the freedom of open meadows and the majesty of giant redwoods . . . enough creek crossings to keep your trusty trail horse in top form . . . Canyon Trail is basically flat, but feeder trails (McCrary Ridge Trail and Henry Creek) taking off for higher elevations offer magnificent views . . . Feeder trails are steep and rocky with no water at upper elevations, so horses should be in good condition . . . Canyon Trail itself is mild and easy and invites a brisk canter . . . Trails are excellently maintained and well marked. Connect with the Chalk Ridges via Henry Creek Trail, about two miles long . . . rocky and steep but well worth the trouble for the view! Take Waddell Beach Trail for a brisk ride along the ocean . . . spectacular surf and whale watching from the saddle! McCrary Ridge trail . . . only three miles long **but very steep** and gorgeous all the way . . . **a 1,500-foot rise** in just two miles! For a spectacular 20-mile round trip ride from Waddell Beach to Hihn Hammond Rd. via McCrary Ridge Trail and on to Park Headquarters (note map). **Carriage trail driving possible on Skyline-to-the-Sea Trail with special permission from the ranger** (408) 425-1218.

ACCOMMODATIONS: Day use, plus the good news is that a new horse trail camp is now completed which makes overnight trips possible. For further information concerning fees and facilities for new trail camp phone (408) 425-1218. At the Waddell Beach parking area there are no tie rails or other amenities at present but there is plenty of water for horses in Waddell Creek.

FEES: None for day use.

PARK SERVICES: Visitor Center at Rancho del Oso . . . friendly, helpful rangers happy to greet you at their office one half mile inland from beach . . . Posted maps of the area at Rancho del Oso.

PARK RULES: No dogs, no firearms, and please no smoking on the trails. Fish and Game regulations apply regarding fishing in the creek.

WEATHER: Canyon Trail segment of the Skyline-to-the-Sea Trail is open year-round, rain or shine . . . can be slippery after a rain, but basically flat and easy going . . . On any given day you can experience foggy dampness near the ocean, giving way to summer heat as you ride inland.

CAUTION: Summer riding can be very hot at higher elevations with no water for many miles . . . Use the Henry Creek Trail connection and the McCrary Ridge Trail with well conditioned animals . . . Feeder trails are rocky, requiring shod horses . . . Precise location and depth of Waddell Creek crossings will vary from year to year . . . Note signing at Waddell Creek Bridge for safest creek crossing. Day use parking on ocean side of Hwy. 1 can mean sharing the parking lot with wind surfers, hang gliders, etc. Brisk ocean breezes here so hang onto your horse!

*Two very different
kinds of rest
stops along the
Skyline-to-the-
Sea trail.*

Tony Look

Hwy. 1 and Waddell Beach are in the foreground in this aerial photo of Rancho del Oso and Big Basin.

John Rodoni, pioneer teamster, with the second largest load of lumber hauled out of the Santa Cruz mountains, 11,306 board feet. The same team and driver later hauled a record-breaking 18,025 board feet. Horse and ox teams were used by Hubbard and Carmichael for 22 years. According to the files of the Saratoga Historical Museum, they were very proud of the horses and oxen which they raised for the milling operation. Neil Carmichael "drove his own ox teams and his wonderful voice could be heard miles away" as the team traveled through the mountains.

The run from the mill to the lumber yard in San Jose was done in one day. The return trip was made the next day and the loading up process began again.

*Thanks to the generosity of the Saratoga Historical Foundation you can ride through the Santa Cruz mountains with a sense of history! The following excerpt is from their book, **Saratoga's First Hundred Years,** by Florence Cunningham. The Hubbard referred to is my husband's great-grandfather so our interest in these mountain roads, today used as trails, goes way back!*

. . . the first men to do extensive cutting in this vast stand of redwood were Thomas Hubbard and Dan and Neil Carmichael at their mill on Oil Creek, an upper tributary of the Pescadero on the Santa Cruz side of the Saratoga Summit. Their lumber, most of it brought up from the steep-sided canyon by a mile-long cable was all hauled out through Saratoga . . . For years, Hubbard and Carmichael's large wagons with trailers, their seven-horse teams guided by skilled drivers, were a familiar sight as they went swinging down Lumber Street and on down Saratoga Avenue.

One old-timer recalls, "You couldn't tell what color the horses or men were in the summertime, they were so covered with dust by the time they reached Saratoga."

Teamsters took great pride in selecting harmonious bells which perched above the hames of the leaders in the team. Teamster Emile Barnard was credited with the most euphonious set of bells in the area. Their ringing warned other teams coming in the opposite direction so they could turn off the narrow road onto the occasional wide places. Local residents could hear the silver-toned bells long before the wagons came into sight . . . Some of the teams were owned by the lumber company, and the drivers were paid by the month including room and board. Those who owned their own teams and wagons were paid by the thousand feet of lumber they hauled . . .

By 1911, all the available timber had been cut, and the Hubbard and Carmichael Mill closed . . . Now no longer were heard the rich, melodic bells announcing the ponderous wagons coming around the mountain causing many a youngster to run to see it pass, and to hope that when he grew up, he too, could be a teamster. Even to adults the wagons had a strong fascination that the biggest, fastest, noisiest modern lumber truck can never have . . .

Reminiscing about her childhood days, Eva Lipscomb Cunningham said, "We would hear the sound of bells and soon a seven-horse team pulling a big lumber wagon loaded with redwood came into view. It was a thrilling sight to see and hear. The driver expertly handled the numerous reins, the strong handsome horses trotted easily along the street, their manes tossing, the bells on the lead horses jingling merrily . . . some of the Swiss or Italian drivers, especially on their homeward journey and feeling quite happy, would sing snatches of Italian opera or folk songs. As some of them had quite good voices their singing, mingling with the jingling bells made pleasant music as they passed along."

*text and photos courtesy of **Saratoga Historical Museum***

20450 Saratoga-Los Gatos Road.
Open Wednesday through Sunday 1-4 p.m.
Phone 867-4311

TRAIL PATRON
Sempervirens Fund

Sempervirens Fund is the nonprofit land conservation organization dedicated to completing Big Basin Redwoods and Castle Rock State Parks. The Fund acquires parcels of land which become available for sale, and then, with its monies matched by the State of California, deeds the land to the State for the two parks.

Taking its purpose from the original Sempervirens Club, founded in 1900 to save Big Basin from the loggers' saws, Sempervirens Fund reformed in 1968 to save Mount McAbee, near the heart of the Basin, from further logging.

The establishment of the Sempervirens Club took place at the turn of the century when photographer Andrew P. Hill, angered at being ordered off redwood-forested land while photographing the ancient coast redwood, *Sequoia sempervirens,* decided these magnificent giant trees should be saved for posterity. Thus began the movement toward the formation of California's first state park, Big Basin Redwoods.

Since Sempervirens Fund reorganized in 1968, more than 3,000 acres have been added to the two Santa Cruz Mountains parks through the Fund's efforts and with the help of the State of California and Save-the-Redwood League.

Currently, Sempervirens, under the continuing leadership of Claude A. (Tony) Look, is campaigning to raise funds toward such purchases as Hickory Oak Ridge, a 298-acre skyline area adjoining the Big Basin corridor and providing valuable trail links between the Skyline-to-the-Sea Trail and the Midpeninsula Regional Open Space District's Longridge Preserve.

Sempervirens also is raising funds for the construction of a bridge over Waddell Creek which will allow hikers to traverse the Skyline-to-the-Sea Trail without crossing private acreage.

The next project will be a large purchase of redwood land located on the north watershed side of Big Basin.

Since 1969, when a group of volunteers aided by Sempervirens Fund drew up the first plan for a system of trails to link San Mateo, Santa Clara, and Santa Cruz Counties, more than 80 miles of trails have been built. Volunteers have contributed thousands of hours of labor to construct and maintain these trails.

Sempervirens Fund supports these volunteer efforts by negotiating for land which provides trail links, by securing funds from donors both for the land and for trail construction, and through publication of calendar events and news stories.

courtesy of Sempervirens Fund

Volunteers hard at work during Sempervirens Trail Days.

82

U.S. CAVALRY'S PLAN FOR CONDITIONING

reprinted from United States Cavalry Manual 1944, Cavalry School, Fort Riley, Kansas.

Conditioning schedule — (1) When it is desired to condition horses for a particular use it is necessary that a well conceived plan and schedule of work be prepared. The nature of the plan and schedule will be determined by many influencing factors which must be carefully considered. Granting that the objective in training is the same for both, it is hardly probably that two different groups of horses will begin this conditioning period on an entirely equal basis. Each will present a separate problem. For this reason it is not feasible to outline in detail a standard schedule of conditioning work which can be indiscriminately applied. Even the plan and schedule prepared at the beginning of a conditioning period for a specific group of horses must be elastic so that it may be modified to suit the actual progress of conditioning. More, less, or different work may be desirable — the needs cannot always be foreseen.

(2) The following is a suggested 9-week schedule aimed at fitting the horses of an average troop of cavalry for march, maneuver, or other forms of field service. It is assumed that the horses are mature, seasoned, and doing average garrison duty which is approximately the equivalent of the work prescribed in the first week of the schedule. The animals are at what might be called the garrison level of condition. The amount and kind of feed and the methods of feeding will be varied as necessary to best meet the requirements of the individual horse and the group as a whole.

1st Week: Two hours' work daily, all at the walk except one 5-minute trot period each hour; stripped saddles.

2nd Week: Two hours' work daily, all at the walk except one 7-minute trot period each hour; stripped saddles.

3rd Week: Two and one-half hours' work daily, all at the walk except one 7-minute trot period each hour; up and down gentle slopes; stripped saddles.

4th Week: Two and one-half hours' work daily, all at the walk except two 7-minute trot periods each hour; rolling country; saddles packed to carry one-half normal weight.

5th Week: Three hours' work daily, all at the walk except two 7-minute trot periods each hour; rolling country; saddles packed to carry one-half normal load.

6th Week: Same as 5th week, except carry full pack. Include a slow gallop of one mile every other day to improve wind.

7th Week: Three hours' work daily, all at the walk except three 7-minute trot periods each hour and a slow gallop of one mile every other day for wind; full pack; use one day to march 18 miles in 3 hours.

8th Week: Same as 7th week, except use one day to march 25 miles in about 5 hours; and include two gallops (12 mph) of one mile each, with a 10-minute walk between, every other day.

9th Week: Two and one-half hours' work daily, all at the walk except two or three 7-minute trot periods each hour; full pack; gallop same as 8th week.

Throughout this schedule reduce the work to about half of the usual amount on Saturdays. The horses should be turned loose in the corral for a part of the day, grazed for a half hour or more, or exercised in hand for about 20 minutes on Sundays. Do not forget that it is important that the regulation gaits be maintained at all times while marching or exercising. A 5- or 10-minute halt should be made each hour to rest the animals and readjust equipment.

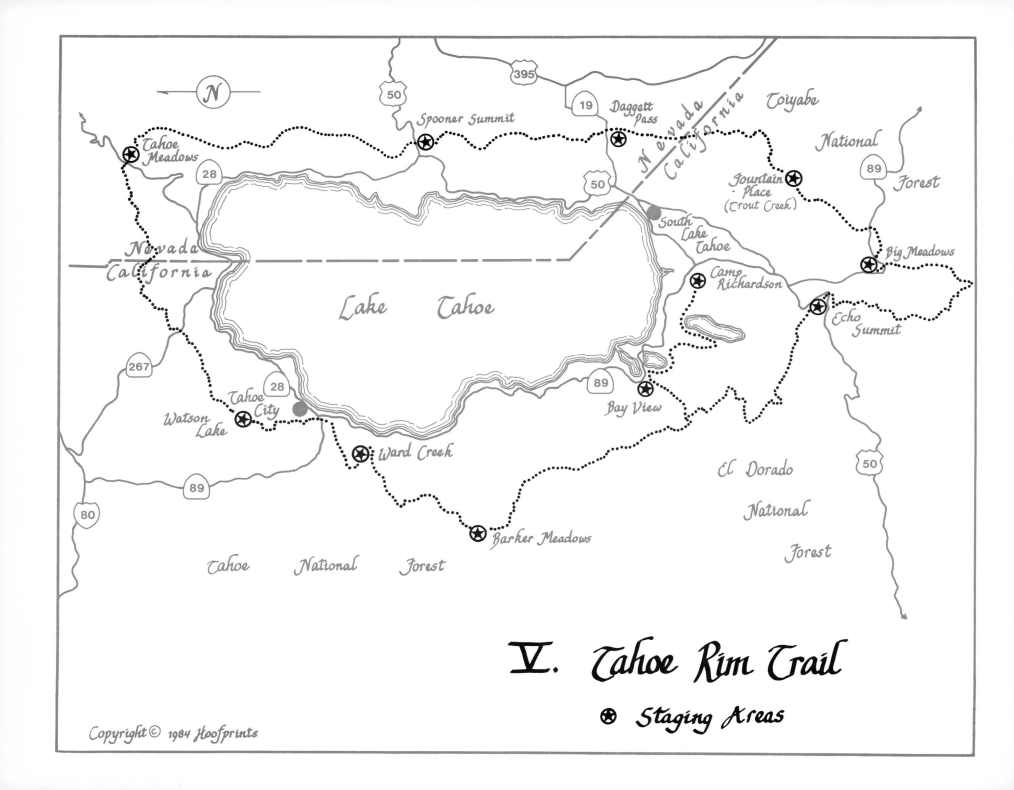

Tom Upton

85

George Cardinet gripped the reins linking him to the frightened, whirling horse as both man and animal shuddered against the onslaught of a sudden Sierra storm. Quietly spoken assurances to calm the horse were futile, instantly lost as lightning exploded against a darkened mid-day sky. Both man and horse scrambled for footing as avalanches of water crashed down the mountain, turning trails into rivers. The violence of the storm — an unjust thrashing which alternated between sheets of rain and the rapid fire of hail, the possibility of being struck by lightning or of losing his horse on the highest point of the mountain — all this was far more adventure than the adventurer had bargained for, especially in July! Certainly it didn't seem a just reward for a man peacefully exploring a route through the Sierra above Lake Tahoe with the purpose of establishing a trail system for public use.

"It was a very humbling experience," recalls the Concord horseman two years later, now surrounded by the security and comfort of his white frame home built in the 1800s. "I've been in lots of storms before but I'd never experienced anything like being on the side of a mountain at 10,000 feet with no way to protect ourselves . . . We were just out there, taking it, struggling to get down off the ridge, worried that we'd get struck by lightning."

George's worries were shared not only by his bay Arab gelding, but also by his trail companions, East Bay horseman Bruce Lee and endurance rider Tom Sherwood of Carson City. In 1982 Tom, along with Pat Fitzgerald, had helped scout out the Capitol to Capitol Trail (the 1982 ride led by Cardinet from Sacramento to Carson City). Again, Tom was lending his expertise to the Tahoe Rim Trail project when suddenly the serene, blue Sierra sky blackened and unleashed a watery rampage.

"It was a frightful experience for all of us, regardless of the years we'd all spent at different times riding in the mountains. Considering all the commotion, the horses stayed amazingly calm. The only thing that seemed to really put them in a frenzy was the hail hitting them on the ears. They'd spin around and shake their heads, but when you think of how frightening the storm was, especially for young horses, they were really quite good," says George.

"I'd go out of my way to avoid a storm like that anytime, but it didn't detract from the sense of accomplishment we had when ultimately our ride helped to determine the actual Rim Trail route. There will be variations and refinements of the route for years to come, but generally speaking it will be the same. Our pre-ride led to the actual Rim Trail Exploratory ride a month later which served a

definite purpose as far as the U.S. Forest Service is concerned. They adopted some of our recommendations for route and staging areas. The whole Rim Trail project is turning into a great success, for hikers as well as horsemen. I wouldn't have missed being in on the planning of it, storm or no storm."

That's not a surprising attitude from a man who seeks adventure with a zest as natural and constant as a horse seeking oats. His role as a business and community leader in the East Bay interwoven with more than sixty years of horsemanship, plus a natural talent for planning and "follow through," have assured him a life filled with the pioneering experiences he craves. Whether your point of contact with George has been in his role as president of the Cardinet Candy Company (now retired), as a past president of the California State Horsemen's Association, a founder of NATRC as well as the East Bay Trails Council, a founder along with Nancy Dupont of the Heritage Trails Fund, or as a leader of the Bicentennial ride from Mexico to San Francisco celebrating the De Anza expedition (George rode the De Anza route from San Diego to San Francisco dressed in full Spanish regalia and on a white horse!), if you know George you've experienced two things — his irrepressible sense of adventure (and desire to include you!) and his tenacity in achieving his goals.

George Cardinet gets set for some heavy duty work on the trail while his horse grazes peacefully on the hillside.

Heritage Trails Fund

What kind of stamina must a person possess to have been actively involved since 1941 in the politics of preserving trails? Even his wife Margaret who's been married to him for fifty years can't explain it! With laughter they both agree that George is just naturally tenacious.

"Well, I do like to hang in there! . . . But my wife flatly refuses to go to anymore trail meetings, anytime, anywhere! Seriously, a great deal of political organization is required to secure legislation favorable to horsemen. It sometimes means a fight, but not always. Generally there is very good rapport among user groups and all agencies involved in park development and maintenance. This has been particularly true of the East Bay Area Trails Council. But first the organization has to be there to support this cooperation which is necessary among trail users. I guess my stamina, as you call it, comes from my strong belief that horsemen have to be politically oriented to preserve their sport. Besides I've had a lot of fun along the way!"

Besides the fun he's enjoyed on horseback in wilderness settings, George refers to the countless friendships that have been formed as a result of reciprocating the help he's been given on his own trail projects.

"All trail systems are interrelated," explains George. "A trail problem in one area has a direct bearing on others. If horsemen are unsuccessful in preserving their access to trails in one community it sets a precedent that threatens trail use in another community. It only makes sense for all of us to help each other out and not be concerned with only our own little stretch of trail. Good friendships as well as good trails get built this way. It's easy to get discouraged about long-term planning. But short term successes, plus the sheer joy of exploring new trails, keep you going."

George's successes as a trails advocate have been considerable by anyone's standards. They bring to mind the words of the late Charles Griner, Captain of the Mounted Patrol of San Mateo County, in an interview in 1980: "I can't ride down a trail without thinking of the tremendous sacrifice of someone's time and effort that has provided each trail we ride on."

Even a little awareness of the constant, ongoing battle to preserve trails for horse use means you can't ride a mile of trail anywhere in California without gratitude to George Cardinet. His dedication can be traced back to the 1940s when he served as secretary for a subcommittee of Governor Warren's Commission on Reconstruction and Reemployment in California following World War II. He has served as chairman of the California State Horsemen's Legislative Committee for all but three years since 1946, and is a member of the

George in the lead with the Tahoe Rim Trail riders working their way up toward a panoramic view of Lake Tahoe.

Executive Committee of the National Trails Council. His trail accomplishments in recent years include:

— vigorous support of the park dedication ordinance established by the City of Walnut Creek, a measure which he believes has made the single most important contribution to trail right-of-way in the Bay Area. Similar ordinances are now being adopted outside the state of California.

— dedication of the historic Capitol to Capitol trail in 1982 linking Sacramento and Carson City via the Sierra. This was a major project for George (President Reagan sent his personal congratulations!). "Considerable portions of the trail overlap with the Tevis Cup ride and it is now possible for anyone to utilize the entire historic Capitol to Capitol route," says George, obviously gratified with the intensive use various segments of the route are getting.

— successful lobbying for the Omnibus Trails Bill and the resulting statewide workshops on the De Anza Trail which are of major importance to Californians. "Under the auspices of the National Park Service volunteers are working all along the state, from here to Mexico!" says George with enthusiasm. "We're doing all the fact-finding Congress requires to permanently establish the De Anza route as a historic trail. Based on diaries kept at the time and historical works by Professor Bolton of the University of California we know exactly where the 103 campsites were. So our job is to lay the trail on the ground, then determine what parts of the route can still be used under present-day conditions. For instance, we're pretty certain that the De Anza party rode right along what today is Ventura Blvd.! Today's traffic conditions mean we'll shift the trail for this portion of the ride to the Santa Monica Backbone Trail which is just on the ridge above, paralleling the original route from Glendale, Griffith Park, almost to Camarillo!

"The purpose of the study is to lay all this out and then to invite public comment on the proposed trail designations. The result will be a riding and hiking trail, with bike lanes in some areas."

With this wealth of experience behind him, what advice does George have for the recently inspired trail rider and activist?

"There are more trail councils today than ever so I don't want to appear critical or do an injustice to all the people actively working to preserve trails. But, generally speaking, I think there still needs to be much more participation. Too much is taken for granted. People don't stop to think of what's happened just in the short space of their own lives. In areas where there have been no open space programs, park programs, or trail systems provided for, opportunities to preserve and enjoy the land have been lost forever. I get annoyed, even angry sometimes when people don't see this and don't realize the necessity of protecting our opportunities to keep land open in our own lifetime and for future generations.

"Too many people will walk away without a fight. They'll allow situations to develop where they will be precluded from trails when with a little more initiative they could have had a trail element in their city's General Plan. People need to be more aggressive about participating in decisions that will affect them the rest of their lives, more aggressive in protecting what they really care about. I especially can't understand horsemen who don't take an active interest in land use questions. Breeders, particularly, should be looking to greater use of the horse instead of allowing horses to be phased out by zoning and other governmental policies.

"I think I started really caring about trails when as a young man I worked in San Francisco. I'd look at house after house where kids were lucky to see even a patch of bare ground. I really believe in

A big part of being a trail boss is getting people and gear organized.

George Cardinet

George is behind the camera as the group poses at Stateline Tree on the sixth day of the ride.

what we're doing now in the East Bay. Even as more buildings go up we're preserving some of the land. There's a riding and hiking trail right behind our house. Many times I'll go out and listen to the kids fantasizing that "now they're out on the trail and headed up to the mountains." In fact, they are just over their back fence and smack-dab in the middle of a subdivision with 675 homes! But I think it's great that the presence of a trail makes these dreams possible to them . . . I think it's great that kids can fantasize about exploring and mountains. It's good for them and good for all of us. We all do some fantasizing on the trails as an escape from urban pressures. Get on a horse, follow a trail, and the spirit of adventure comes alive again."

The spirit of adventure George refers to is most evident in his "exploratory rides," rides which create trails instead of following them! Trail Boss Cardinet makes it clear that before twenty-seven Tahoe Rim Trail riders could indulge in wilderness fantasies along the trail, a tremendous amount of planning had to take place. Assisted by his friend and fellow explorer, Bruce Lee, and with the help and encouragement of the U.S. Forest Service, first maps had to be researched and a general route projected in a schematic way.

"The only way to test the feasibility of the trail is to saddle up, grab your maps, and start riding," says George. "The stretches of the Rim Trail that overlap with already established PCT (Pacific Crest Trail) routes are easy, but for long stretches we were exploring deer trails or picking our own way as best we could. Many nights we slept out and cooked our own food. The Forest Service assisted as often as they could in moving our rigs around. It was pretty awkward when we had to do it on our own, but we managed. We used Camp Richardson as our headquarters, renting corrals there so we could come back in, rest the horses, and get supplies. Camping out with horses takes lots of work and planning, but I wouldn't miss the fun of it for anything! You feel a great sense of accomplishment when others join you on the trail and start caring about it like you do."

With all the fun and success George has found in the movement to preserve trails it's understandable why an occasional perilous storm doesn't deter his adventure seeking. Similarly the text which follows is loaded with warnings to the wilderness rider on the Tahoe Rim Trail, but the advice is also an invitation to saddle up and seek the adventure you're sure to find along one of the most beautiful trails on earth!

George and his bay Arab, Bel Bar Jordge, look more than eager for their next trail adventure.

Ron Riesterer, Oakland Tribune

89

"Imagine a trail that winds completely around the most spectacular lake in the United States. As you ride along this 150-mile trail you meander through areas rich in Basque history, where some of the West's first Basque sheepherders roamed with their flock through mountain meadows over 100 years ago . . . you wade through waist-high grass, large groves of aspens, through magnificent stands of red fir and ponderosa pine, and stop to drink from cool mountain streams, sweet to the taste . . . the trail wanders through old Washoe Indian hunting grounds, and . . . long-vanished game trails . . . as well as trails made by early settlers fresh from obtaining their provisions from Nevada's first settlement at Genoa. You may wander high above mysterious places with names like "Hellhole" with its many small pools and ground that shakes, rolls, and sways . . . you skirt the largest bog in the Sierra at Grass Lake . . . And most of the time you are able to view the highest and largest alpine lake in North America, Lake Tahoe. On the horizon . . . the Pine Nut Range in Nevada, the Sierra of California, the Carson Valley . . . you travel through six counties, three National Forests, and two states . . . a week and a half later, you're back where you started."

— Glenn Hampton
U.S. Forest Service Supervisor

THE TAHOE RIM TRAIL

150 miles of Sierra beauty circling Lake Tahoe . . . when completed it will be the longest trail in the Tahoe Sierra . . .

— George Cardinet

REASONS TO GO: Best explained by U.S. Forest Service Supervisor Glenn Hampton who first visualized the trail and established it as a viable project.

SPECIAL FEATURES: A wilderness experience of great beauty and adventure which you can enjoy as a ten-day ride or in ten one-day segments . . . From any access point you are no more than ten miles from various Lake Tahoe communities . . . Numerous stables and motels in the towns surrounding the Lake if you desire to add an element of comfort to your adventure!

LOCATION: Riding the rim of the Lake Tahoe Basin takes you through California and Nevada, through the counties of Placer, Eldorado, Washoe, Carson, Alpine, and Douglas . . . You will ride through portions of the Tahoe, Eldorado, and Toiyabe National Forest, as well as Lake Tahoe Nevada State Park, Burton Creek, and Tahoe State Recreation Areas.

WHERE TO PARK: The Exploratory Ride led by George Cardinet completed the entire 150 miles on horseback with support from veteran horseman Ralph Sharpless and his crew . . . Because of the experience and organization such a ride entails we have divided the ten-day ride into ten one-day rides with the various staging areas described in detail in the following chapters . . . Road conditions for pulling trailers are generally good but varied . . . Staging areas also vary in terms of size, ease of access, and amenities . . . Road crossings are required on horseback in some segments.

TRAIL FEATURES: The Tahoe Rim Trail varies from easy-to-travel fireroads to narrow, precipitous granite trails and everything in between! **In some segments you must do without a trail at all** and utilizing maps, horse sense, and prayer you will pick your way . . . don't let this discourage you because the U.S. Forest Service and the all-volunteer Lake Tahoe Rim Trail Committee are continually making improvements . . . When the trail is completed it will be a hiking, riding, and cross-country ski trail which means year-round enjoyment for all kinds of trail enthusiasts! Elevations on the trail vary from 6,222 feet to forests of pine and fir at 10,000 feet . . . On the west rim the trail is the Pacific Crest Trail . . . on the north rim from about Hwy. 89 to Tahoe Meadows and south to Tunnel Station the Rim Trail overlaps a portion of the Capitol to Capitol Trail.

ACCOMMODATIONS: It is most important to confer with the Lake Tahoe Basin Management Unit, U.S. Forest Service, on your plans to ride any segment of the trail. Supervisor Frank "Mac" Magary has kindly offered to provide information on current trail conditions and access to staging areas. Phone: (916) 544-6420. Address: LTBU, 870 Emerald Bay Road, South Lake Tahoe, CA 95705 . . . Write to: LTBMU, P.O. Box 8465, So. Lake Tahoe, 95731 . . . For some segments of the trail a Wilderness Permit is required and reservations are required in certain camping areas . . . **If you wish more information on organizing a group ten-day ride** George Cardinet has generously agreed to discuss your plans based on his own experience . . . that's quite a gesture from a horseman who's busy with trail projects all over the state! Write George Cardinet, 5301 Pine Hollow Rd., Concord, CA 94523.

FEES: As of 1985 no fees are required on any portion of the route that have been designated for public use . . . The following chapters give details on the possibility of using some private lands with permission, which necessitates arrangements being made on an individual basis.

SERVICES: An abundance of information (including Forest Service maps) is available from knowledgeable, helpful Forest Service personnel at both the Lake Tahoe Basin Management Unit and the Visitors' Center at Camp Richardson . . . The Visitor's Center is on Hwy. 89 opposite the turn-off for Fallen Leaf Lake . . . it's a worthwhile stop especially if you include it in your pre-ride planning.

RULES: For Wilderness areas refer to page 121 of this book . . . Campfire permits are required throughout the Lake Tahoe Basin.

WEATHER: Don't rule out snow in July! Generally the trail is negotiable between August and October but the Exploratory ride could not venture out until late August . . . Even then two sections of the Pacific Crest Trail on the west rim were blocked by snow . . . It's most important to check with the Lake Tahoe Basin Management Unit as you do your pre-ride planning.

CAUTION: It will only enhance your adventure if you start with a good plan . . . **It's imperative to check all trail routes and staging areas** with the Lake Tahoe Basin Management Unit *before* your ride . . . When you consider the ten-day ride segments remember that unless you intend to ride only a portion of the trail and then return to camp, you will need a "support crew" to move your rig from your starting point to the next campsite . . . The basic route of the Tahoe Rim Trail has been accurately described and mapped in this but it is continually being developed and realigned in areas . . . **Do not proceed in wilderness terrain without confirming your plans with the Forest Service** . . . In those areas where the trail crosses or skirts private property be especially diligent to secure appropriate permissions as described in each trail segment . . . **at any time and under any weather conditions take warm clothing and rain gear** . . . Blanket horses if you're staying overnight.

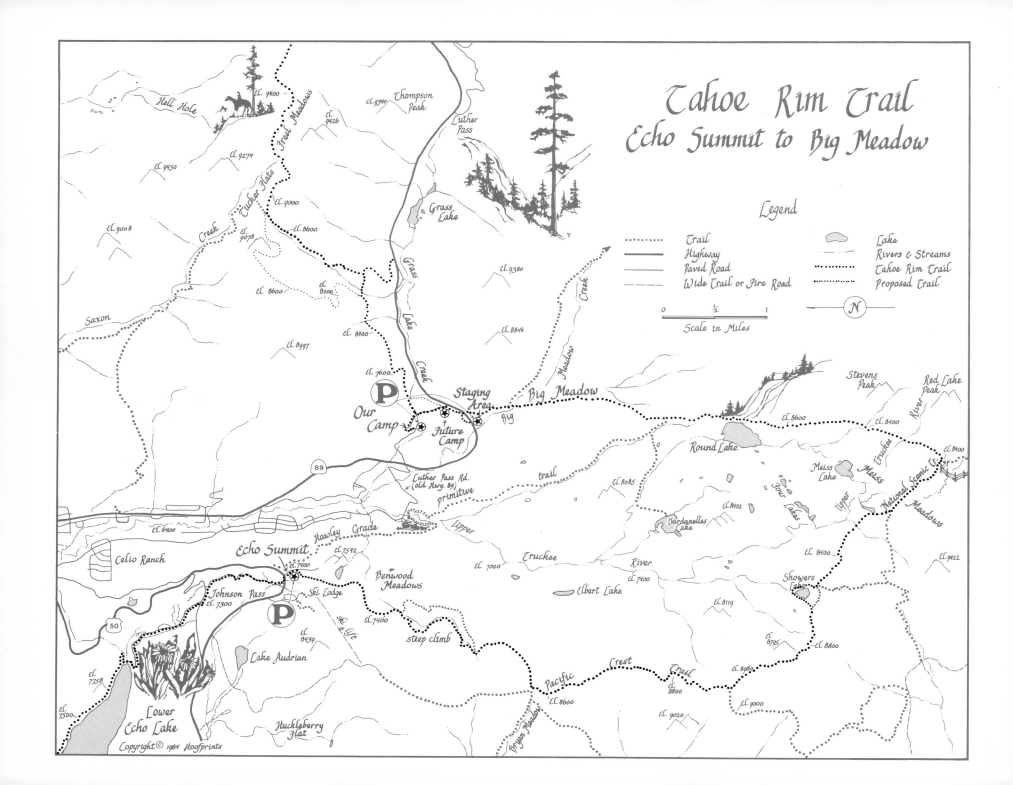

ECHO SUMMIT TO BIG MEADOW

Challenging, awe-inspiring trail through granite passes, high meadows and an eastern skyline dominated by 10,000-foot peaks . . . Trail passes one of the oldest buildings in all of the Lake Tahoe Basin, the Meiss cabin built in 1878, recently restored by Forest Service and local ranchers . . .

— George Cardinet

LOCATION: In Eldorado County, nine miles from South Lake Tahoe on Hwy. 50 at Echo Summit Ski Resort.

WHERE TO PARK: Immediately off Hwy. 50 at the entrance to Echo Summit Ski Lodge is a parking area adequate for three trailers . . . To pick up the trail, ride through Ski Lodge parking lot and enter the trail system on an easy ski trail . . . about 250 yards from the Lodge the trail plunges into the woods . . . for group rides the Echo Ski Lodge grounds are available for parking with special permission. Write to Steve Hayward, P.O. Box 8955, South Lake Tahoe, CA 95731.

ACCOMMODATIONS: Overnight boarding of horses available at Camp Richardson Stables and Cascade Stables. Excellent camping facilities nearby at Camp Richardson.

TRAIL FEATURES: 22 miles of trail . . . very rugged riding for the first one third of the ride (from Echo Summit to Showers Lake) . . . From Echo to Meiss Meadows, approximately half of the total distance, you are on the Pacific Crest Trail . . . All but brief sections of the route are single-file dirt trails . . . Pacific Crest Trail markers routed on posts at major intersections . . . Precipitous climbing out

of Benwood Meadows . . . **For novice riders the recommended route is to enter the trail system from Big Meadow Staging Area** and do the one-day ride in reverse . . . less steep climbing that way! Suggested all day ride for novice horses or horsemen would be to ride from Big Meadow to Round Lake and back. **Well conditioned horses with experienced riders** can follow the original Rim Trail route as led by George Cardinet and described in his diary.

 CAUTION: Note suggestions above for novice horses unless you are very sure of your horse's condition and experience for trail work . . . A new trail which will minimize the grade out of Benwood Meadows is being worked on but it will still be a basically rough trail for some time. Until the trail work is complete it is recommended that horses be led out of Benwood Meadows for about the first 200 feet . . . Sudden summer storms a possibility . . . should you get caught in one stay off ridges and out from trees . . . if necessary to cross snow banks, be very cautious and test for hidden holes beneath the surface . . .

CARDINET'S DIARY

Monday, August 22, day one. Twenty-seven riders departed Echo Summit Lodge on the Pacific Crest Trail going south. We traveled in groups of nine each, under the supervision of a leader and drag rider. The rules were simple: do not pass the leader or fall behind the drag, keep a horse length's distance, anticipate stops, and do not rest your horse on any unduly steep pitches.

Upon leaving Benwood Meadows one group took the so-called "new" route and the other

two groups took the traditional route. Both routes join near the summit. The new trail was quite treacherous so the riders led their horses for the first 100 yards or so. One horse went over backwards. No injuries were sustained. One mishap occurred due to rider inexperience. About three excessively steep pitches certainly warranted the seeking of an alternate route. Work on the trail could have remedied the problem. Here as elsewhere on the developed trails some clean-up and maintenance is needed.

We lunched in a vast, open park of "mule ears" under snow cornices a bit north of Showers Lake. Immediately before Showers Lake a sign indicated we should bear east from the traveled route to reach the lake. This route was not sufficiently distinct so we proceeded on the cross slope and came to the lake from the west. Here we met a hiker going from Meeks Bay to Yosemite and met an elderly couple on horseback. They were from Santa Rosa and told us they had been vacationing in this country for 25 years.

We left the Pacific Crest Trail at Meiss Meadows and followed the Big Meadow Trail to camp. As we approached Round Lake we met a party of about eight riders and a similar number of pack mules traveling south. They informed us they were 29 days out of Bishop, traveling principally on the Pacific Crest Trail. We also met a very cordial ranger on foot patrol. The destruction of the ground by erosion for about half a mile under the lava mud bluffs and pinnacles near Round Lake was the most severe I've ever seen. Camp was reached on the old Luther Pass Road north of the Big Meadow staging area. Riding time on the trail: seven and a half hours.

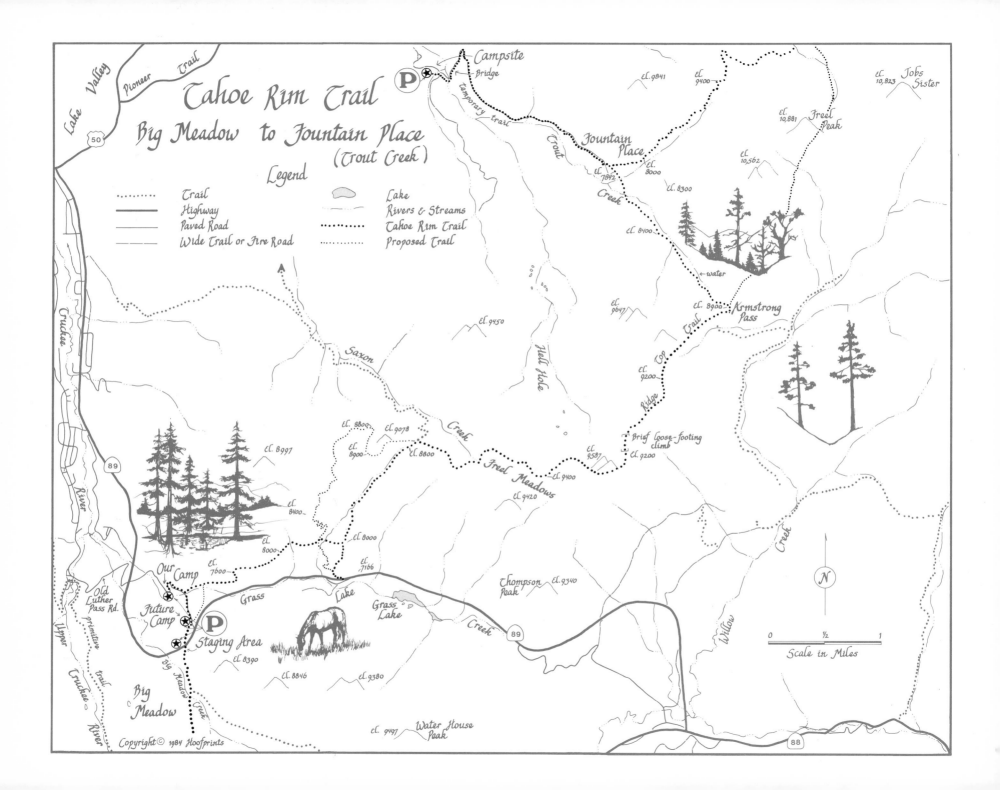

Tahoe Rim Trail

Big Meadow to Fountain Place
(Trout Creek)

Legend

....	Trail	⬭	Lake
───	Highway		Rivers & Streams
═══	Paved Road	●●●●●	Tahoe Rim Trail
═╪═╪═	Wide Trail or Fire Road	⋯⋯⋯	Proposed Trail

Lake Valley

Pioneer Trail

50

Campsite

Bridge

Temporary trail

P

Fountain Place

El. 9841

El. 9400

El. 10,823 Jobs Sister

El. 10,881 Freel Peak

El. 10,562

Trout Creek

El. 7842

El. 8000

El. 8300

El. 8400

← water

Truckee River

89

A

Saxon

El. 9450

Hell Hole

El. 9647

Ridge Top Trail

El. 9200

El. 8900 Armstrong Pass

El. 8800

El. 9078

El. 8900

El. 8800

Creek

Freel Meadows

El. 9587

El. 9200

Brief loose-footing climb

El. 8997

El. 8400

El. 8000

El. 9400

El. 9420

El. 8000

El. 8000

El. 7600

El. 7166

Willow Creek

N

Our Camp

Old Luther Pass Rd.

Future Camp

P

Thompson Peak El. 9340

Grass Lake

Grass Lake

Creek

89

Upper Truckee River

primitive trail

Big Meadow Creek

Staging Area

El. 8390

El. 8846

El. 9380

Big Meadow

El. 9497 Water House Peak

88

0   ½   1
Scale in Miles

BIG MEADOW TO FOUNTAIN PLACE
(Riding to Trout Creek Camp Area)

Primitive, unmarked country for adventurous, highly experienced wilderness riders . . . Breathtaking views in all directions . . .

— George Cardinet

Big Meadow trail head on Hwy. 89. More parking is just 100 yards up the road.

LOCATION: On Hwy. 89, seven miles south of South Lake Tahoe, five miles south of the intersection of Hwy. 89 and Hwy. 50.

WHERE TO PARK: For a day ride come in from Lake Tahoe on Hwy. 89 . . . You'll be traveling on a good, paved highway with a gentle uphill grade. Five miles from the intersection of Hwy. 50 and 89 look for Big Meadow staging area on your left. There is room here for only a couple of rigs . . . if this area is filled continue east 100 yards to Old Highway 89 (the only paved road that takes off on the left) . . . there are many wide spots for easy parking along this old, untraveled road . . . Entrance to the trailhead is not marked at this time (1985) but with the help of your map and a dose of adventure you can "pick your way" to Fountain Place and Trout Creek via Tucker Flat Trail and Freel Meadows. (It is expected that this area will be flagged and staked in 1985.)

ACCOMMODATIONS: Big Meadow staging area is being enlarged and improved for overnight use . . In the interim eight to ten rigs can be accommodated in the "overflow" area (Old Hwy. 89). This is an inviting, wooded area with a creek for watering horses and the convenience of chemical toilets. Phone ahead for reservations: Lake Tahoe Basin Management Unit (916) 544-6420, or write to P.O. 8465, South Lake Tahoe, CA 95731.

TRAIL FEATURES: 10.2 miles or 5 hours of primitive, unmarked country for the adventurous rider . . . **Definitely not a beginner's ride** if you're headed on the original Rim Trail route . . . A great beginner's ride if you head back toward Echo Summit going as far as Meiss Meadows or Round Lake . . . **Experienced riders with well conditioned horses** can enjoy a one-day ride by going as far as Freel Meadows; or make arrangements with a friend to have your rig ready and waiting for you at Trout Creek . . . Be prepared to explore . . . trails are barely visible and not marked by suburban park standards . . . Currently (1985) from Tucker Flat to Armstrong the trail is indistinguishable except for remnants of surveyor tape . . . From Freel Meadows head north and east climbing gently to the ridge . . . follow the ridge until a jumble of boulders will force you to pick your way off the ridge . . . then climb back up for spectacular views or stay at the lower elevation and enjoy a ride through timber country . . . From Armstrong to Fountain Place the trail will be easy to follow . . . Spectacular views in all directions . . . look north and west to view South Shore and all of west shore . . . look to the south for Hope Valley and peaks in the Caples Lake vicinity . . . look to the east for a spectacular panorama of Carson Pass.

CAUTION: Exploratory riding on unsigned trails! . . . But when you're ready for adventure don't let lack of signing deter you . . . the entire 5-hour route offers breathtaking views in all directions—and major improvements to the trail are under way. Work is now in progress which will make the Tucker Flat trail easier to follow . . . Trail has been realigned in some areas since Cardinet's ride . . . ultimate route will be straight across Armstrong Pass to saddle north of Freel Peak . . . **Particularly important in this trail segment to confirm route with U.S. Forest Service.**

CARDINET'S DIARY

August 23, day two on the trail. We headed for the Tucker Flat trail on a roughly selected trail keeping us to the north and east of Hwy. 89. Two old three-wire drift fences were uncovered lying beneath the pine needles. Obviously, great care should be exercised in these former grazing areas. Tucker Flat was reached without incident. Glenn Hampton (Recreation Staff Office, U.S. Forest Service) had previously advised us that a more gradual ascent was being flagged. This should be pursued or else considerable work should be done on the existing trail. It is quite strenuous at this point for the horses and would certainly be much more so for hikers.

It is quite open from Tucker Flat to Freel Meadows and the trail is indistinguishable. Numer-

A welcome rest stop in Freel Meadows.

Cardinet

Watch for these signs at the entrance to Old Hwy. 89.

ous flaggings should continue to the far end of the second Freel meadow. Lunch was held here with generous grazing for the horses. North and east of the second meadow bear scat was observed and a small cub was sighted.

The panoramic vistas that unfold in the next few miles (Hell Hole, Hope Valley, the head waters of the Mokelumne, etc.) should and do slow the pace considerably. It is a time for contemplation.

At a point in T11N, R18 E we come to a bastard section #12 (I don't know how else to read the map) at a point identified with an elevation 9587 feet, about one half mile of rocks and boulders through which flagging was discern-ible but was virtually impassable for horses. It would be an exercise in futility for a man on foot. It is possible to eventually pass through but no redeeming characteristics to warrant doing so. We dropped down a bit to where the rocks are more sparsely distributed but did have to traverse a limited area of loose, decom-posed granite. It is our opinion that the effort to stabilize this section would be minimal com-pared to the alternative. We effected the cross-ing on switchbacks.

Passing along on a descending contour from 9200 feet to about 8800 feet we reached Arm-strong Pass and then dropped down into Foun-tain Place, our camp for the night. Total riding for the day, five hours.

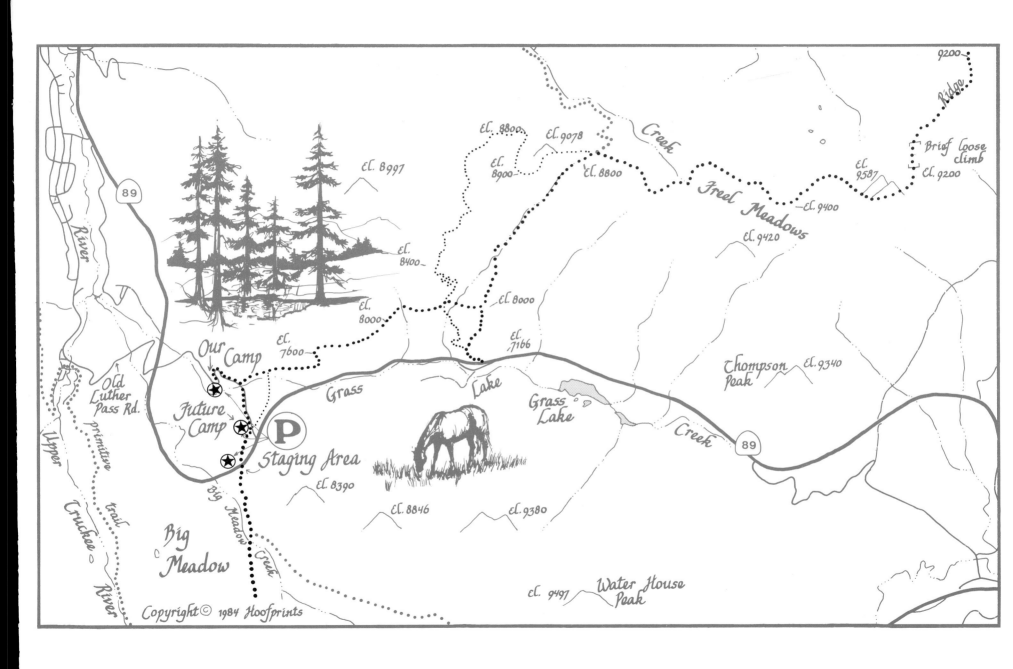

9200

Ridge

Creek

Brief loose
climb

El. 8800   El. 9078   El. 9587

El. 8997   El. 8900   El. 8800   El. 9200

El.
8400   Freel Meadows   El. 9400

El. 9420

El. 8000

El.
8000

El. 7600   El. 7166   Thompson   El. 9340
                                    Peak

Our Camp

Old
Luther
Pass Rd.   Grass   Lake   Grass   Creek   89
                                            Lake
Future
Camp

P

Staging Area

El. 8390

Big
Meadow   El. 8846   El. 9380

Big Meadow Creek

Water House   El. 9497   Peak

Copyright © 1984 Hoofprints

89

River

Upper

primitive

trail

Truckee

River

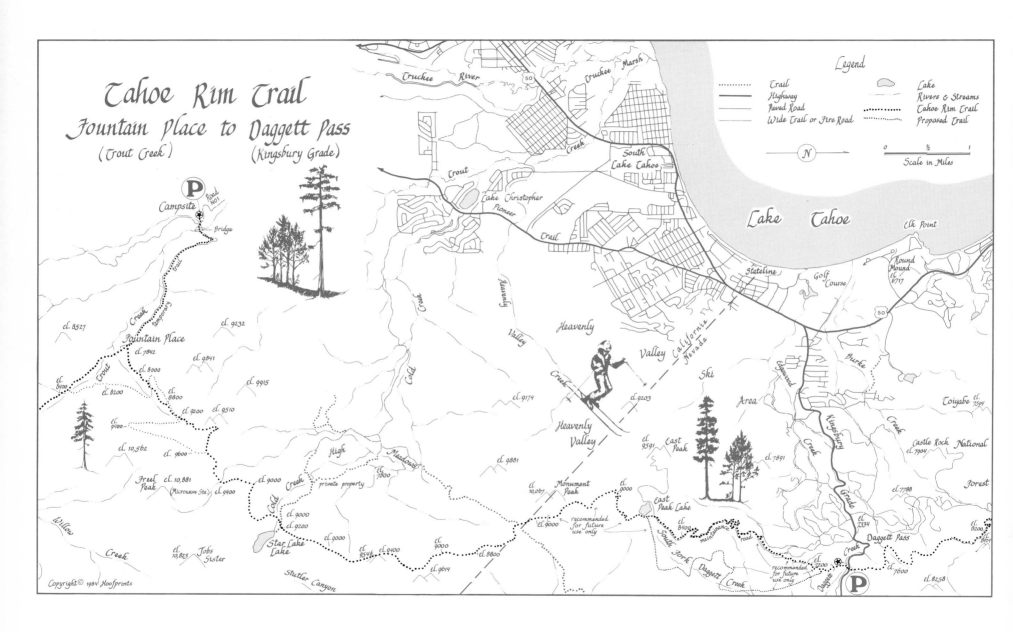

Tahoe Rim Trail
Fountain Place to Daggett Pass
(Trout Creek)   (Kingsbury Grade)

Legend

········· Trail	Lake
——— Highway	Rivers & Streams
═══ Paved Road	•—•—• Tahoe Rim Trail
━━━ Wide Trail or Fire Road	········ Proposed Trail

N

0   ½   1
Scale in Miles

Copyright © 1984 Hoofprints

Lake Tahoe

Truckee River
Truckee Marsh
South Lake Tahoe
Trout Creek
Lake Christopher
Pioneer Trail
Stateline
Golf Course
Elk Point
Round Mound el. 6717
50

Campsite
Road No.1
Bridge
P

el. 8527
Fountain Place
el. 7842
el. 9232
el. 9841
el. 8000
Trout Creek
el. 8400
el. 8200
el. 9400
el. 10,562
el. 8800
el. 9200
el. 9510
el. 9915
Cold Creek
Heavenly Valley
Heavenly
el. 9174
el. 9203
el. 9881
Freel Peak
el. 10,881
(Microwave Sta.)
el. 9400
el. 9600
el. 9000
High Meadows
Cold Creek
private property
el. 7800
Heavenly Valley
el. 9000
el. 9200
Star Lake Lake
el. 10,823
Jobs Sister
Willow Creek
el. 9000
el. 9546
el. 9400
el. 9000
el. 8800
el. 9614
Stutler Canyon
el. 10,067
Monument Peak
el. 9000
el. 9000
recommended for future use only
el. 8400
East Peak Lake
el. 9591
East Peak
el. 7891
Ski Area
California Nevada
Heavenly Valley
Edgewood Creek
Burke Creek
Kingsbury Grade
Castle Rock el. 7904
Toiyabe el. 7594
el. 7788
National Forest
maintenance road
South Fork Daggett Creek
recommended for future use only
el. 7200
Daggett Pass
el. 7334
Daggett Creek
P
el. 7600
el. 8200
el. 8258

FOUNTAIN PLACE TO DAGGETT PASS
(Riding from Trout Creek Camp Area)

A continuing panorama of Lake Tahoe . . . magnificent views of Monument Peak . . . trail is still in its exploratory stage and requires experienced riders and horses . . .
— George Cardinet

Cardinet

Wildflowers in the foreground, forest in the background — the meadow of Fountain Place is a good place to be!

LOCATION: This trail segment lies in California counties Eldorado and Alpine, and Douglas County, Nevada. To reach Trout Creek staging area take Pioneer Trail east from Hwy. 50 (at Hwy. 89) to Oneidas, a short, paved subdivision street. Turn right on Oneidas and go to the end where it becomes road 12N01 which goes along Trout Creek to Fountain Place . . . From end of Oneidas to first gate and bridge is 0.7 mile . . . Two miles further is Trout Creek. Fountain Place is unfenced, private land used for the Rim Trail Ride with the generous permission of Mr. Springmeyer of Gardnerville, Nevada . . . Public camping is directed to Trout Creek.

WHERE TO PARK: Road 12N01 is a two and three quarter mile oil and gravel fire road which is a little bumpy but in good shape. Trailer in until the road forks to the left at Trout Creek Bridge. Unload horses here and set up camp at Trout Creek. This is a variation from the actual Rim Ride which stayed overnight at Fountain Place with special permission from the private landowner.

ACCOMMODATIONS: Plans are being formulated for an improved campground to be located between Trout Creek Bridge and Fountain Place . . . Check with Forest Service for current information. Camping is now permitted in the unimproved area around Trout Creek (as described above) . . . A two mile ride up from Trout Creek takes you to the high mountain valley of Fountain Place.

TRAIL FEATURES: Very rugged riding surrounded by majestic scenery highlghting mountains, meadows, and numerous creeks . . . **This segment of trail not recommended for groups or novice riders** . . . Leaving from Fountain Place the road rapidly turns to trail as you head northeast on course with the original Rim Trail ride . . . the ultimate trail will set a new course, heading toward Armstrong Pass, then crossing the west slope of Freel Peak at about an elevation of 8800 feet to the 9800-foot elevation coming out of the saddle west of Freel Peak . . . The Rim Ride ran into a bad bog shortly after entering an aspen grove . . . to get above the bog take the steep switchback which has been cut through the aspens . . . from that point on the trail continues on loose footing and at a steep, but reasonable, grade. On improvised switchbacks you can work your way to the top of the saddle until you reach almost 10,000 feet in elevation . . . you've worked hard through steep, rugged country to get to the highest point on the ride! From Fountain Place to the top the trail is easy to distinguish, but from the saddle at about 9800 feet elevation to Star Lake and on to Heavenly Valley there is no definite trail . . . Trails around Monument Peak are partially flagged and there is some riding on jeep roads around Heavenly Valley, but the balance of the ride is unmarked.

 CAUTION: None of this trail segment is recommended for inexperienced horsemen or novice trail horses . . . The trail to Star Lake is very steep on loose rock, and the descent to Daggett Pass is on very steep switchbacks . . . Remember now, all the Rim riders made it in 1983 but they had the advantage of being led by George Cardinet! Another consideration — from Monument Peak north the trail traverses a patchwork of public and private lands . . . to avoid any difficulties with private landowners and for updated information on this very difficult terrain **it is imperative to check out your plans with the Forest Service (916) 544-6420.**

99

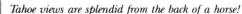

Tahoe views are splendid from the back of a horse!

Cardinet

But even without a horse (or a fishing pole) Jason Farar is having lots of fun in Trout Creek!

CARDINET'S DIARY

August 24, day three. Following the north fork of Trout Creek we followed a fair trail emerging at a saddle near the northeast corner of Section 25 T 12 N, R18 E at about 9600 elevation. The view from here of Fountain Place, Monument Peak, High Meadows, and the Lake was magnificent. The last third of this trail was straight up through loose decomposed granite and prohibitively steep. We corrected this by making a series of switchbacks slightly to the south on stable soil. Why for successive years man and beast should have exhausted themselves by going straight up through the loose footing is incomprehensible. A serious bog has developed in the first third of the trail which cast one horse and man. A rough trail was hacked out and flagged around the bog. We believe that future use of the Rim Trail will see greater use of Fountain Place, especially by groups; therefore this trail merits attention.

Our pre-ride through the area was in a blinding rain and hail storm liberally laced with lightning, making an exploration of a route around Monument Peak an impossibility. We were advised by the owner of High Meadows to go around the east side of the Peak. Because of the storm and the lateness of the day we could not find a passage, although it was obvious that a way could be cleared if time had permitted. On our pre-ride we followed the power line around the east of the Peak and descended to the foot of Kingsbury Grade. For the actual ride we took the group out of Cold Creek and transported them to the aforementioned staging area on the old Kingsbury Grade.

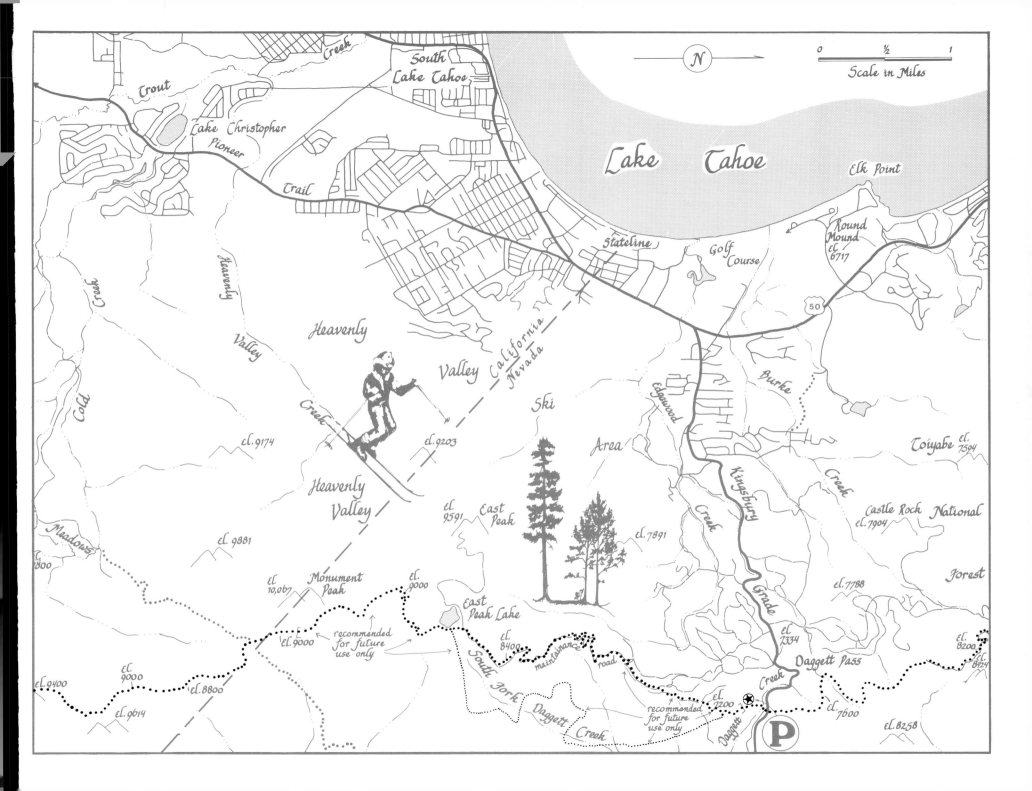

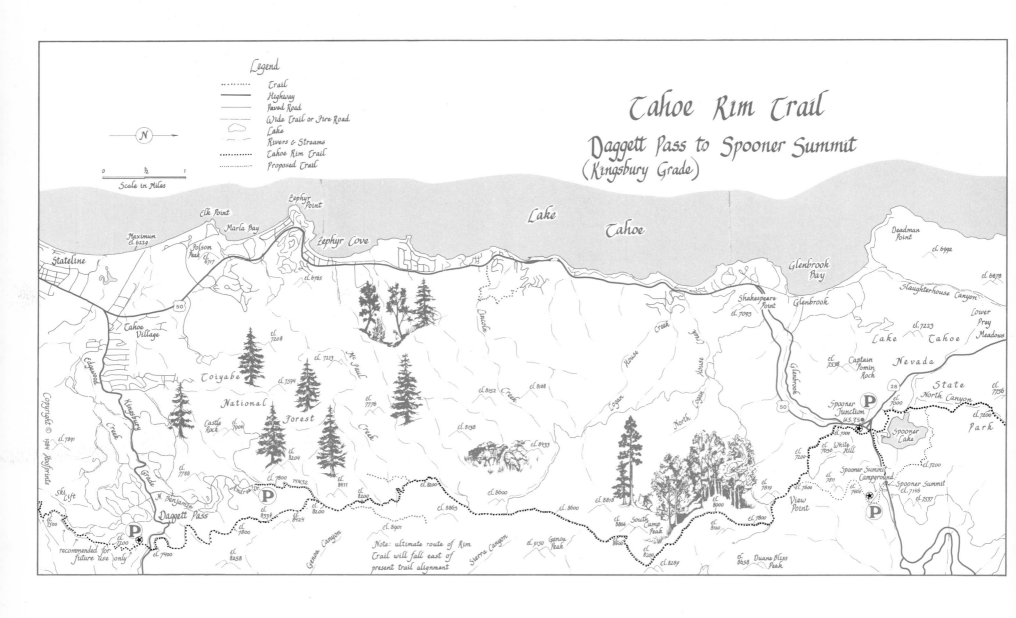

Tahoe Rim Trail

Daggett Pass to Spooner Summit
(Kingsbury Grade)

Legend

········· Trail
———— Highway
———— Paved Road
———— Wide Trail or Fire Road
Lake
Rivers & Streams
········· Tahoe Rim Trail
········· Proposed Trail

N

0   ½   1
Scale in Miles

Lake Tahoe

Zephyr Point
Elk Point
Marla Bay
Zephyr Cove
Maximum el. 6229
Folsom Peak el. 6717
Stateline
el. 6765
Tahoe Village
Deadman Point
el. 6992
Glenbrook Bay
Glenbrook
el. 6878
Slaughterhouse Canyon
Lower Prey Meadows
Lake Tahoe
Shakespeare Point el. 7093
Nevada
el. 7208
el. 7213
Toiyabe
el. 7594
McFaul
el. 7776
Lincoln Creek
Logan House Creek
North Logan House Creek
Captain Pomin Rock el. 7538
State el. 7756
North Canyon
National
Castle Rock
el. 7904
el. 8204
Forest
McFaul Creek
el. 8152
el. 8168
el. 8138
Glenbrook
Spooner Junction
U.S. 50
Park el. 7200
el. 7891
el. 7788
el. 7800 14N32
el. 8411
el. 8433
el. 7000
Spooner Lake
el. 7200
Ski Lift
N. Benjamin
Andrew Dr.
el. 8334
el. 8200
el. 8424
el. 8200
el. 8600
el. 8600
el. 8863
el. 8600
el. 8818
el. 7819
el. 8000
White Hill
el. 7650
el. 7200
el. 7600
el. 7811
Spooner Summit Campground
el. 7406
Spooner Summit el. 7146
el. 7200
Kingsbury Grade
Edgewood Creek
Daggett Pass
el. 7500
recommended for future use only
el. 7100
el. 7400
el. 8258
el. 7800
el. 8901
Genoa Canyon
Note: ultimate route of Rim Trail will fall east of present trail alignment
Sierra Canyon
el. 9150 Genoa Peak
el. 8289
el. 8866 South Camp Peak
el. 8600
el. 8200
el. 8100
el. 7800
View Point
el. 8458 Duane Bliss Peak
el. 7537

DAGGETT PASS TO SPOONER SUMMIT

Spectacular views of Lake Tahoe, Carson, Eagle and Washoe Valleys.

— George Cardinet

LOCATION: Entire route is in Douglas County, Nevada. Easy, paved highway access to either end of this trail segment . . . To reach Daggett Pass staging area turn right on Kingsbury Grade less than a mile east of Stateline . . . From the bottom of Kingsbury Grade to the Daggett Pass staging area is approximately five miles . . . Six tenths of a mile east of the summit of Daggett Pass the Old Kingsbury Grade Hwy. takes off to the right . . . follow this for about a quarter mile to the proposed camping area on the right.

WHERE TO PARK: Very pleasant, large camping area off the Old Kingsbury Hwy. gives even a large group plenty of room to maneuver their trailers . . . You park on firm, sandy ground, and a small stream runs through the area . . . You are located in Heavenly Valley's permanent open space area . . .
Alternate parking area: Near the summit of Kingsbury Grade turn north on North Benjamin at the brick-walled entrance to Kingsbury Village . . . travel on this wide, paved residential street until it becomes Andria Rd. Park at the end of the road and pick up road 14N32 which is a continuation of the paved road. This entrance to the trail system avoids the hazardous Kingsbury Grade crossing

and shortens your ride to Spooner by a mile and a half.

ACCOMMODATIONS: Use the above areas for day rides only until overnight areas are officially designated.

TRAIL FEATURES: It is necessary to cross Kingsbury Grade Hwy. in order to enter the trail system across the road . . . **Use extreme caution in crossing.** There are surges of heavy traffic on the road and there is heavy use by large trucks . . . Cross the road headed for a wooded area on the opposite side . . . parallel the highway west for a few hundred feet until you see an obvious fireroad . . . bear to the right, then left, climbing steadily and passing the jeep road which drops down to the right . . . None of this area is marked but the jeep roads make it an easy route to follow . . . Numerous fireroads come in from the right and left but continue on a northerly course until the jeep road ends against a bank . . . Eventually a new trail will follow the ridge east of the present route, but in the interim turn immediately left (at jeep road terminus) and drop down following a dry stream course for a few hundred feet till you reach the 14N32 jeep road . . . Head north all the way to Spooner Summit . . . **This is a**

very satisfactory route for beginners or any horsemen who want a spectacularly beautiful but easy ride . . . The trail is very gentle except for a three-quarter-mile steep pitch out of Daggett. Good short day rides can be enjoyed from either end of this route . . . Loop rides are possible by exploring existing fireroads.

 CAUTION: Lack of water on the trail . . . Bring your own drinking water . . . Water for horses in creeks and roadside springs along trail about two miles before you reach Spooner . . . Possibility of meeting with motorcycles or 4-wheel-drive vehicles, but not a serious problem here because of trail width.

CARDINET'S DIARY

August 25, day four. Immediately to the north and east of the Kingsbury site we took a logging road which rises rapidly. It apparently is mainly covered by the Minden Quadrangle map which is not available to us as it is outside the Lake Tahoe Basin. This is truly the "Rim" and within a mile emerges on perhaps the most magnificent overlook of the Basin. You look about 500 feet below for a view of the top of Castle Rock which stands 7904 feet tall! The road continues on an undulating course to a terminal point in the vicinity of Genoa Peak. From this terminal point a trail drops down to the west until it meets 14 N 32 upon which we continued to Duane Bliss Peak and beyond. In retrospect it appears a trail could follow on a contour from the terminal point and meet 14 N 32 farther on to the north. At a point of land probably centered in the lower half of Section 7 T 14 N, R 19 E a magnificent view of the Carson, Eagle, and Washoe Valleys is the high point of the day. It is a leisurely type of trail with nothing very steep except for a short stretch on the north. It is also dry and devoid of water until the last mile and a half. The riding time from Kingsbury to Spooner was five fours.

Watch for trucks as you cross Kingsbury Grade . . . easy fireroad riding awaits you on the other side.

This aspen-lined segment of the trail is a piece of cake after the hard riding of the first three days.

Cardinet

These road signs are your only clue to the existence of a staging area among the trees on the right.

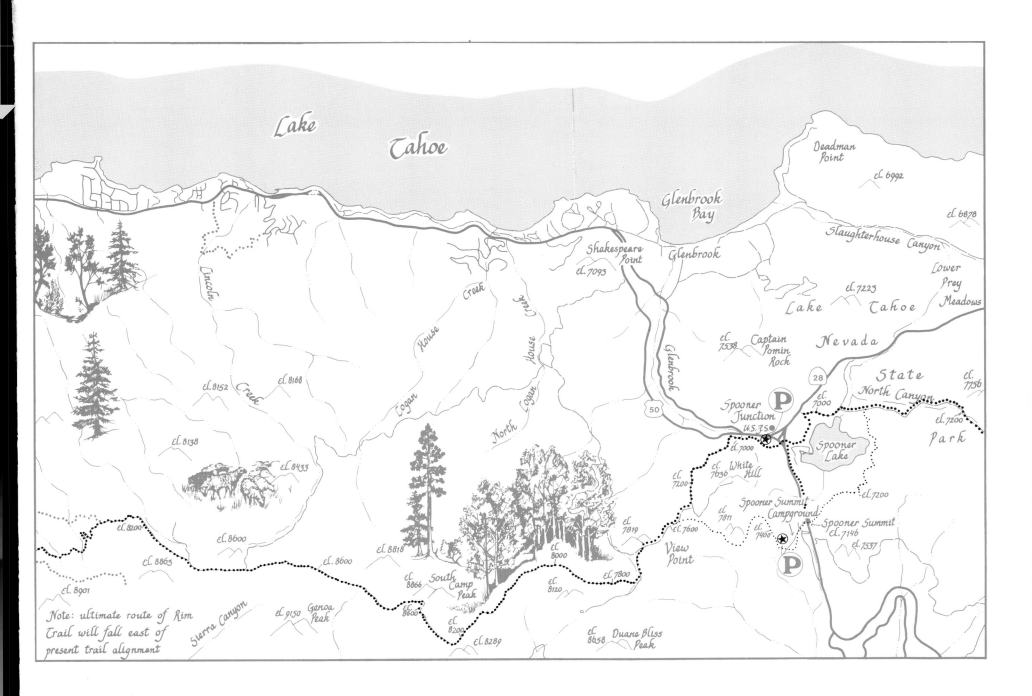

Lake

Tahoe

Deadman
Point

el. 6992

Glenbrook
Bay

el. 6878

Slaughterhouse Canyon

Shakespeare
Point
el. 7093

Glenbrook

Lower
Prey
Meadows

el. 7223

Lincoln

Creek

Creek

House

Logan

House Creek

North Logan

Creek

el. 8152

el. 8168

el. 8138

el. 8433

el. 8200

el. 8600

el. 8863

el. 8901

Note: ultimate route of Rim
Trail will fall east of
present trail alignment

Sierra Canyon

el. 9150

el. 8600

el. 8818

el. 8866

el. 8600

el. 8289

Genoa
Peak

South
Camp
Peak

el. 8000

el. 8120

el. 8200

el. 8658

Duane Bliss
Peak

el. 7819

el. 7600

el. 7800

View
Point

Captain
Pomin
Rock

el. 7538

Lake

Tahoe

Nevada

State

North Canyon

Park

el. 7756

el. 7200

el. 7200

el. 7200

Glenbrook

50

28

Spooner
Junction
U.S.F.S.

el. 7000

P

el. 7000

el. 7000

White
Hill

el. 7636

el. 7200

el. 7811

Spooner Summit
Campground

el. 7400

Spooner
Lake

Spooner Summit
el. 7146

el. 7537

P

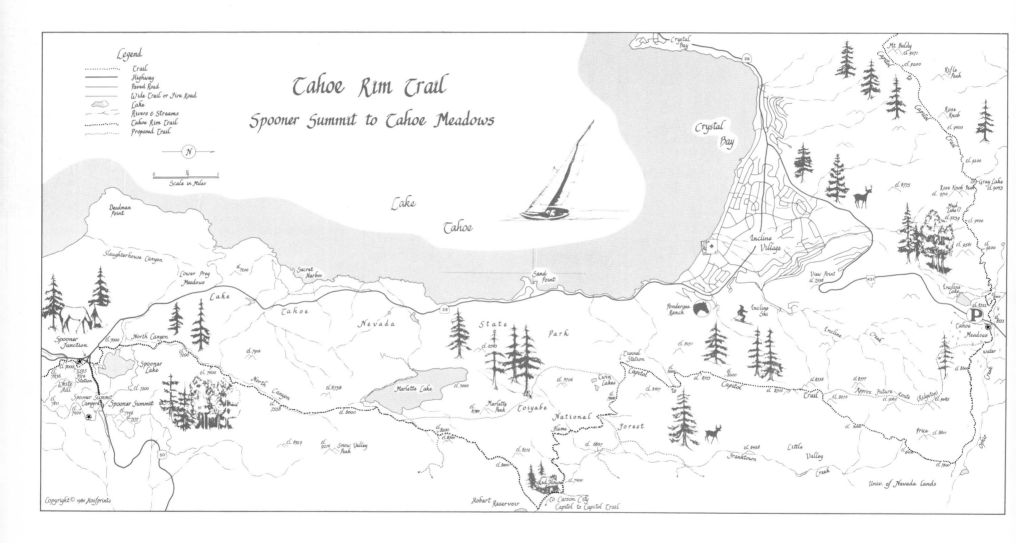

Tahoe Rim Trail

Spooner Summit to Tahoe Meadows

Legend

····· Trail
───── Highway
═════ Paved Road
▭▭▭▭ Wide Trail or Fire Road
     Lake
     Rivers & Streams
····· Tahoe Rim Trail
····· Proposed Trail

N

0 ½ 1
Scale in Miles

Lake Tahoe

Crystal Bay

Crystal Bay

Incline Village

Deadman Point

Slaughterhouse Canyon

Lower Prey Meadows

el. 7200

Secret Harbor

Sand Point

View Point el. 7590

Lake Tahoe

Nevada   State   Park

Spooner Junction

North Canyon   el. 7000

el. 7200

el. 7916

Spooner Lake

el. 7400

North Canyon

el. 8738

Marlette Lake

el. 7000

el. 8585

Ponderosa Ranch

Incline Ski

el. 8151

el. 8000

Incline Creek

Tahoe Meadows

el. 8322

el. 8513

water

White Hill
el. 7656
USFS Fire Station
el. 7000

el. 7000

el. 7811

Spooner Summit Campgrd.
el. 7146

Spooner Summit
el. 7531

el. 7400

el. 7558

el. 8000

el. 8780

Marlette Peak

Coiyabe

Twin Lakes

el. 8706

Tunnel Station

el. 8407

Capitol   to   Capitol

el. 8705

el. 8000

el. 8538

el. 8777

el. 8510

el. 8070

el. 8065

el. 8800

Approx. Future Route (Ridgetop)

el. 90.85

50

el. 8929

el. 9214

Snow Valley Peak

el. 8500

el. 8500

National   Forest

Flume

el. 8212

el. 8000

el. 8807

el. 6468

Franktown

Little Valley Creek

Capitol   Trail

el. 8050

el. 8400

Price   el. 8801

el. 7900

Red House

el. 7400

Hobart Reservoir

To Carson City
Capitol to Capitol Trail

Univ. of Nevada lands

Mt. Baldy el. 9271

Capitol

Capitol to Capitol Trail

el. 9200

Rifle Peak

Rose Knob
el. 9400

el. 9200

el. 8775

Rose Knob Peak
el. 9710

Gray Lake
el. 9083

Mud Lake l.
el. 9239

el. 9400

el. 9561

el. 9200

Incline Lake

28

431

28

Copyright © 1984 Hoofprints

SPOONER SUMMIT TO TAHOE MEADOWS

Diverse in scenery with commanding views of Lake Tahoe and the Carson Valley . . . timber country rich in Comstock and Virginia City history . . . this trail segment generally suitable for novice riders . . .

— George Cardinet

Tahoe Rim riders Elizabeth Fairlea and Dale Brooks.

LOCATION: Near Lake Tahoe Nevada State Park in Washoe County Nevada . . . Good paved highway services either end of this trail segment, Hwy. 50 at Spooner Summit and Mt. Rose Hwy. (431) at Tahoe Meadows.

WHERE TO PARK: You have several choices depending on your plans: for **Day Use** there is a very small staging area at Spooner Summit (on Hwy. 50 just east of the Summit) which is satisfactory if you are heading south on the Rim Trail toward Daggett Pass. Opposite the Spooner Summit Rest Area is a larger parking area with an equestrian entrance to Lake Tahoe Nevada State Park . . . At present it's a wide shoulder but it's the probable site of a large, improved staging area. For overnight in this area we recommend staging at the U.S. Fire Station at Spooner Summit . . . To park your trailer here you must have permission from the Forest Service . . . sounds ominous but they have a record of being very accommodating . . . Phone: (916) 544-6420. To enter the trail system from Spooner Summit Fire station (headed toward Tahoe Meadows) it is necessary to ride on the north side of Hwy. 50 on the wide shoulder of the road for 0.8 mile to the large roadside pullout area opposite the Spooner Summit sign . . . the fireroad entrance to the Park takes you around Spooner Lake where you pick up the trail at the northwest side of the lake. The Cardinet ride chose to cross Hwy. 50 opposite the Fire Station by crossing in the center of the Y formed by the junction of Hwy. 50 and Hwy. 28. They followed the fence line to a break in the wire, made a quick left, and rode around Spooner to the trail on the northwest side . . . The trails through Lake Tahoe Nevada State Park are well marked and lead through whispering pines.

ACCOMMODATIONS: The Spooner Fire Station has ample room for parking with water and toilets for your convenience . . . The small staging area at Spooner Summit also has water and clean rest rooms.

TRAIL FEATURES: Nineteen and a half miles or a seven hour ride from Spooner to Tahoe Meadows . . . From Tahoe Meadows to Tunnel Station the trail shares a common route with the Capitol to Capitol Trail, a good route for novice horsemen . . . Fireroads and single file trails are roughly brushed out and flagged . . . the terrain is moderate with a few steep areas. A good one day ride from the State Park is to ride as far as Tunnel Station and return. A recommended novice ride through the State Park is to take the fire trail to Marlette Lake or to follow the signs from Marlette Lake to Hobart Reservoir . . . Another good day's ride is to follow the fire road all the way to historic Red House . . . from Spooner to Marlette Lake is an especially beautiful ride through aspens . . . from Tunnel Station to Tahoe Meadows is ridge riding with continuing views of Lake Tahoe and Washoe Lake . . . Tunnel Station is the mouth of a tunnel which transported the water gathered at Marlette and Tahoe Meadows by flume through the mountain to a pipeline which was joined by other water from Hobart Reservoir at the Red House. From here it went by pipeline to tanks where it entered a siphon at the "Tanks" under the Carson Valley and ended up in Virginia City.

 CAUTION: Use extreme caution in crossing Hwy. 50 and in riding along its shoulder for 0.8 mile. Confirm access points with Forest Service. Reconnoitering is advised. The trail to Tunnel Station via Twin Lakes is rough cut and difficult to find . . . watch carefully for the trail taking off toward the north as you leave Marlette Lake basin . . . never fear, improvements are on the way.

The smile on Sid Hubbard's face tells you how pleasant it is to find a marked segment of the trail after so many miles of exploring!

Opposite this sign is a large widened area on the north side of Hwy. 50 with plenty of room for trailers and easy access to the Nevada State Park segment of the Tahoe Rim Trail.

Overnight parking is OK in the graveled parking area adjacent to the U.S.F.S. Fire Station.

From Fire Station the safest crossing of Hwy. 50 is in the center of the "Y" formed by the junction of Hwy. 50 and Hwy. 28. Follow the fence line to a break in the wire as noted in text. Highway is dangerous but fence is well set back.

CARDINET'S DIARY

August 26, day five. The need for a staging area at Nevada Tahoe State Park is vital to the continuity of the Rim Trail in its state of gracious and inspiring charm. All the requisite components are already present: toilets, water, shade. The crossing of the highway at the junction is by far the safest because of the view and the center island. Trail crossing warning signs should be installed.

The route to Marlette Lake and beyond is particularly charming and was especially so on the morning we rode through. An interpretative guide to the trail would be a project well worth pursuing, especially from Spooner on to Tahoe Meadows with its early day water system background still in evidence by the traces of the old flumes.

Leaving Nevada State Park at Tunnel Station a trail climbs and traverses the ridge between Tahoe and Little Valley with extensive views to both the Nevada and California sides. This trail was developed by Pat Fitzgerald of Reno, and he has made considerable improvements during the past year. At a point presumably near the mid-point of Section 7 T 16 N, R 19 E the visible remnant of an old road is followed which eventually joins the Ophir Creek Trail above the remnants of Price Lakes. The alluvial fan of last winter's slide is quite visible. Four-wheel-drive vehicles are creating a bog and disfigurement on Ophir Creek. The last mile and a half into Tahoe Meadows is a road of sorts. Riding time today: 7 hours.

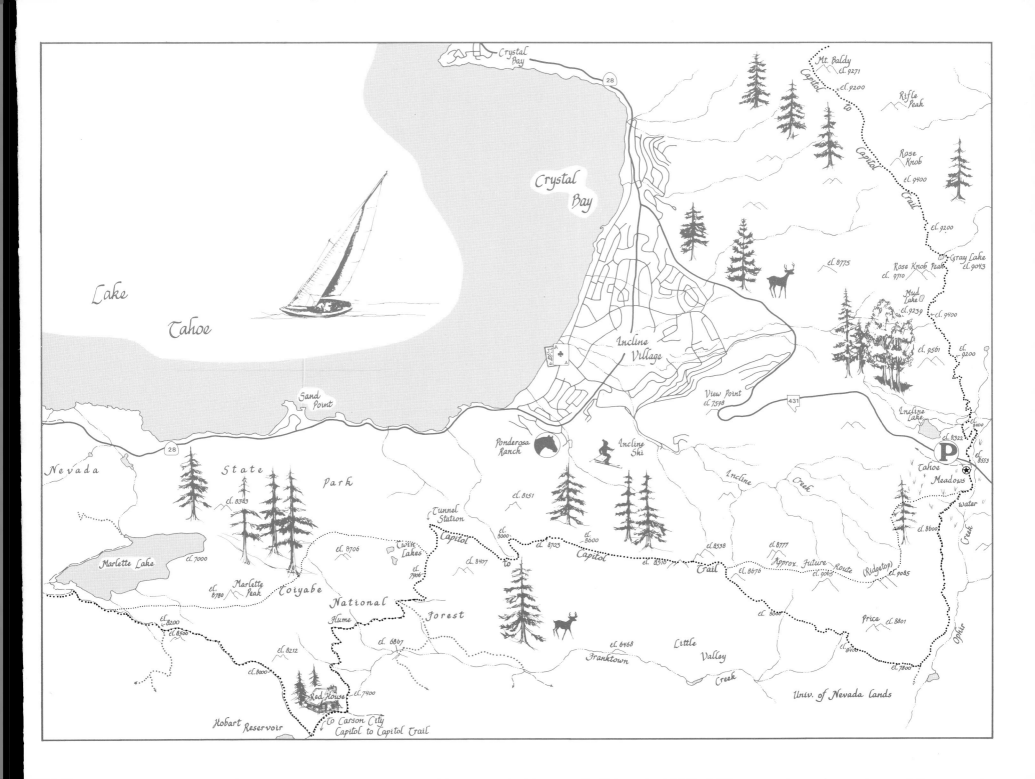

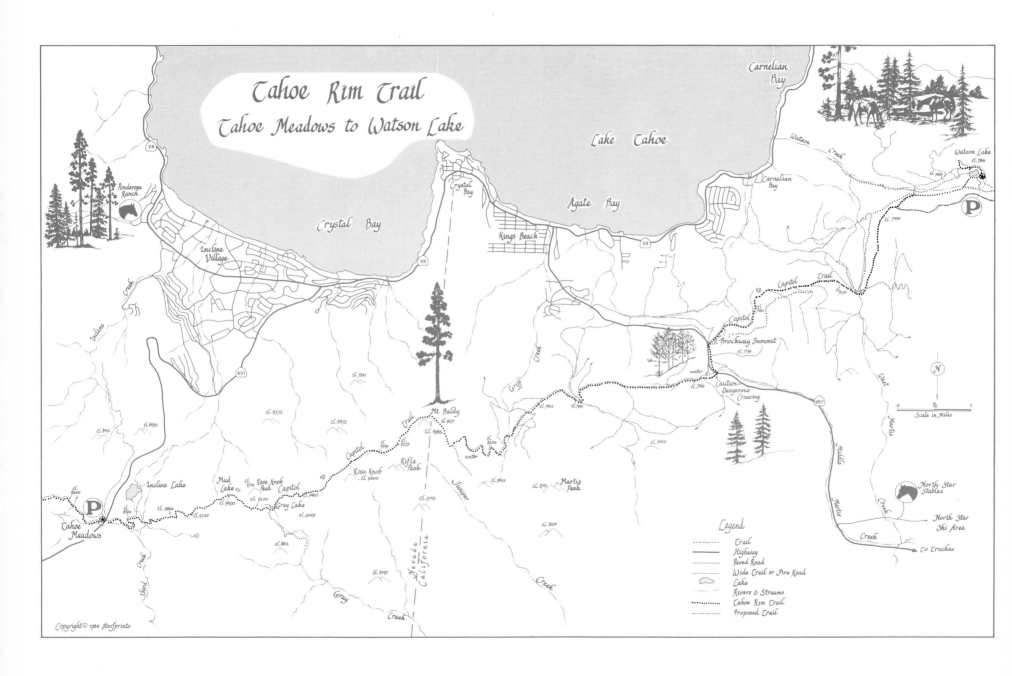

Tahoe Rim Trail
Tahoe Meadows to Watson Lake

Carnelian Bay

Lake Tahoe

Watson Creek

Watson Lake
El. 7800

Crystal Bay

Agate Bay

Carnelian Bay

Kings Beach

Crystal Bay

Ponderosa Ranch

Incline Village

Incline Creek

El. 7861

Mt. Baldy
El. 9271

Capitol Trail

Griff Creek

Brockway Summit
El. 7199

Capitol Trail

El. 7600
El. 7400
El. 7200
El. 7100

Caution Dangerous Crossing

El. 7400
water
water

El. 7600
El. 7800

El. 8575

El. 8872

Capitol Rd

El. 9499
El. 9275
El. 8965
El. 8100

West

Martis Creek

North Star Stables

Rifle Peak
El. 9141

Rose Knob
El. 9600

Rose Knob Peak
El. 9770

Capitol

Mud Lake

Incline Lake

El. 8422
El. 8450

El. 8800

El. 9200

El. 9400
El. 9100

El. 9400

Gray Lake
El. 9043

Juniper

El. 9603

El. 8771
Martis Peak

El. 7420

El. 8104

North Star Ski Area

To Truckee

El. 8000

Tahoe Meadows

El. 8400

El. 8812

El. 8497

Third Creek

Gray Creek

Nevada California

Creek

Legend

....	Trail
———	Highway
———	Paved Road
———	Wide Trail or Fire Road
⬭	Lake
~~	Rivers & Streams
••••	Tahoe Rim Trail
....	Proposed Trail

Scale in Miles

N

TAHOE MEADOWS TO WATSON LAKE

On this stretch of trail you have a magnificent panorama of the entire Lake, plus Donner Lake and the Summit . . .

— George Cardinet

LOCATION: On the rim of the North Shore of Lake Tahoe in Washoe County, Nevada, and Placer County, California. Nearby communities are Kings Beach and Incline Village which offer every commercial service you might need.

WHERE TO PARK: Approximately eight miles from Incline Village just off Mt. Rose Hwy. (431) . . . From Hwy. 28 turn north on Hwy. 431 heading toward Tahoe Meadows. Drive toward Mt. Rose ski area and turn east off highway right at crest of grade. If you pass a split log fence on the right you've gone too far . . . Take dirt road to the right leading into the camp area . . . Take it slowly as the dirt road is easy to miss and is very rough at the entrance . . . Park and camp in areas between road and creek to avoid encroaching on private property.

ACCOMMODATIONS: Available for day use and overnight . . . Campfires are allowed but permit is required. Contact the U.S. Forest Service, phone (916) 544-6420 or write: Lake Tahoe Basin Management Unit, P.O. Box 8465, So. Lake Tahoe, CA 95731 . . . Water for horses in Ophir Creek but bring in your own drinking water . . . A beautiful camp setting but no facilities.

TRAIL FEATURES: Eighteen miles, or six and a half hours of riding time between Tahoe Meadows and Watson Lake . . . The entire ride corresponds with the historic Capitol to Capitol Trail (which was officially reopened in 1982 with a 200-mile ride from Sacramento to Carson City — led by George

Turn in to camping area before you reach this log fence. Park and camp in area between dirt road and creek.

Cardinet, of course!) . . . From Tahoe Meadows head west where the Rim Trail traverses an adjoining piece of private property owned by Mr. and Mrs. Gordon McClean . . . Until a quarter mile past Stateline the trail is single-file horse trail changing to fireroads and logging roads as you pass through timber country . . . After leaving the relatively high, bare ridges east of Stateline Tree the trail drops down to level and moderate grades very satisfactory for novice riders . . . Midway in the ride it is necessary to cross Hwy. 237 at Brockway Summit which is **very hazardous** . . . It's worth your effort to get across because your reward after riding for four miles over dirt and gravel logging roads is the beautiful gem of Watson Lake . . . There's limited space at Watson Lake with room for only two to three rigs but according to George it was everyone's favorite spot and they all wanted to stay another day.

 CAUTION: Crossing Hwy. 237 at Brockway Summit is very dangerous . . . use extreme care.

Car is used here to illustrate appropriate dirt road. The beguiling little road on the left quickly becomes unmanageable for trailers.

CARDINET'S DIARY

August 27, day six. From Tahoe Meadows Trail 18 E 23 is followed through the Incline properties past Mud and Gray Lakes, Rose Knob Peak, Rose Knob, Rifle Peak, and Mt. Baldy and to a high point near Martis Peak on the California-Nevada Line. A magnificent panorama unfolds revealing the entire Lake, Donner Lake and the Summit, and the entire country north and east of Truckee. Here the party had a group picture taken at the State Line Tree, a tree which up to a year ago was so identi-

fied with a large old black and white sign and also exhibited the old green and white Forest Service directional signs. Another landmark we passed was Mr. Coyote, an old dead tree presenting a profile of a stylized coyote that has stood guard on the trail for years. It occupies a prominent position on the ridge just a bit south of the midpoint of section 33, T17 N, R18 E. It would seem appropriate to talk to Mr. and Mrs. McClean at Incline Lake to see about the advisability of rerouting the trail away from their

road entrance, skirting the meadow to the east of said entrance and picking up the present trail at the large pine which contains the Old Forest Service green and white sign indicating the trail to Mt. Rose. After climbing up past Mr. Coyote the trail follows the rim, affording a continuing panorama of the Lake and the north Shore. Leaving the State Line tree the trail rapidly descends on 16N 23 and 18N 02 to the vicinity of Brockway Summit. Here a very hazardous crossing of Highway 237 is necessary.

Road 16 N 73 is followed to a point in the SW quarter of Section 17 T 16 N, R 17 E where a dirt road is taken a short distance to Watson Creek which is then followed to Watson Lake. Road 16 N 73 is a miserable, high-traffic gravel road. A trail could easily be constructed off of but parallel to it through the second growth trees, all of which is apparently on Forest Service Land. A four-wheel-drive trail is indicated on the map just a bit north of 16 N 73 which we did not locate, but upon investigation it could prove useful. However, on the map it appears to traverse more private land.

Watson Lake is a delightful camp spot and as noted suits fine for a counterclockwise ride or hike on the Rim. Total riding time from Tahoe Meadows is 6½ hours.

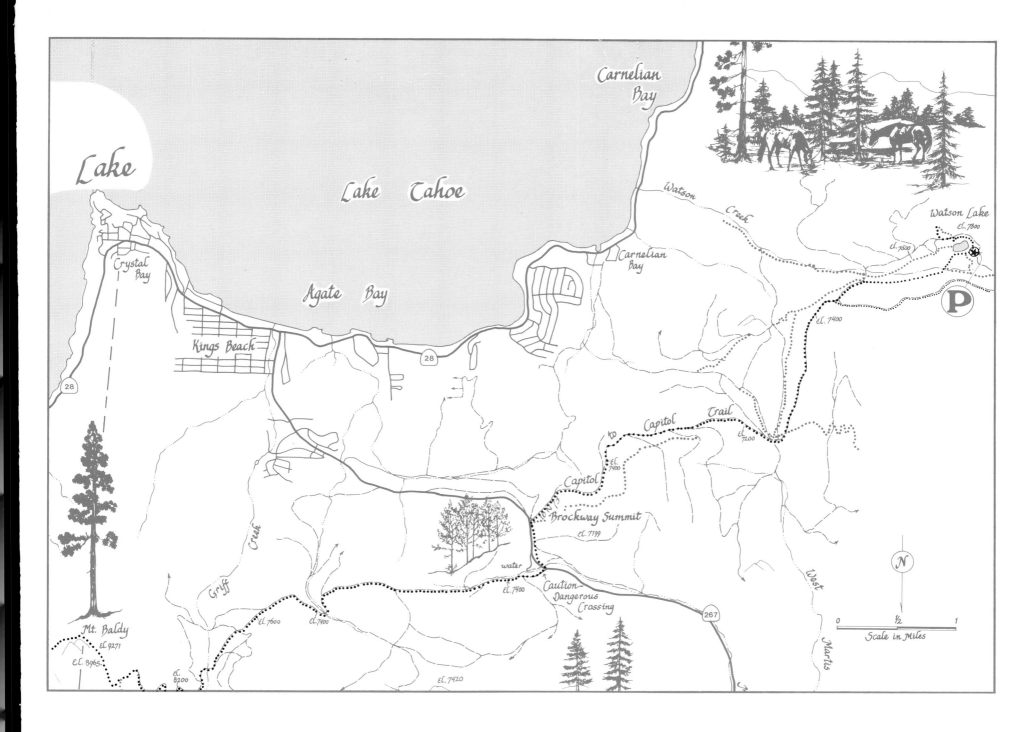

Carnelian
Bay

Lake

Lake Tahoe

Watson
Creek

Watson Lake
El. 7800

El. 7500

Crystal Bay

Carnelian
Bay

Agate Bay

P

El. 7400

Kings Beach

28

28

Capitol   Trail

*El.
7100*

Capitol

*El.
7400*

Capitol

Brockway Summit
El. 7199

Griff   Creek

water

El. 7400

Caution—
Dangerous
Crossing

267

West

El. 7600   *El. 7400*

N

Mt. Baldy
El. 9271

El. 8965

*El.
8200*

El. 7420

Martis

0   ½   1
Scale in Miles

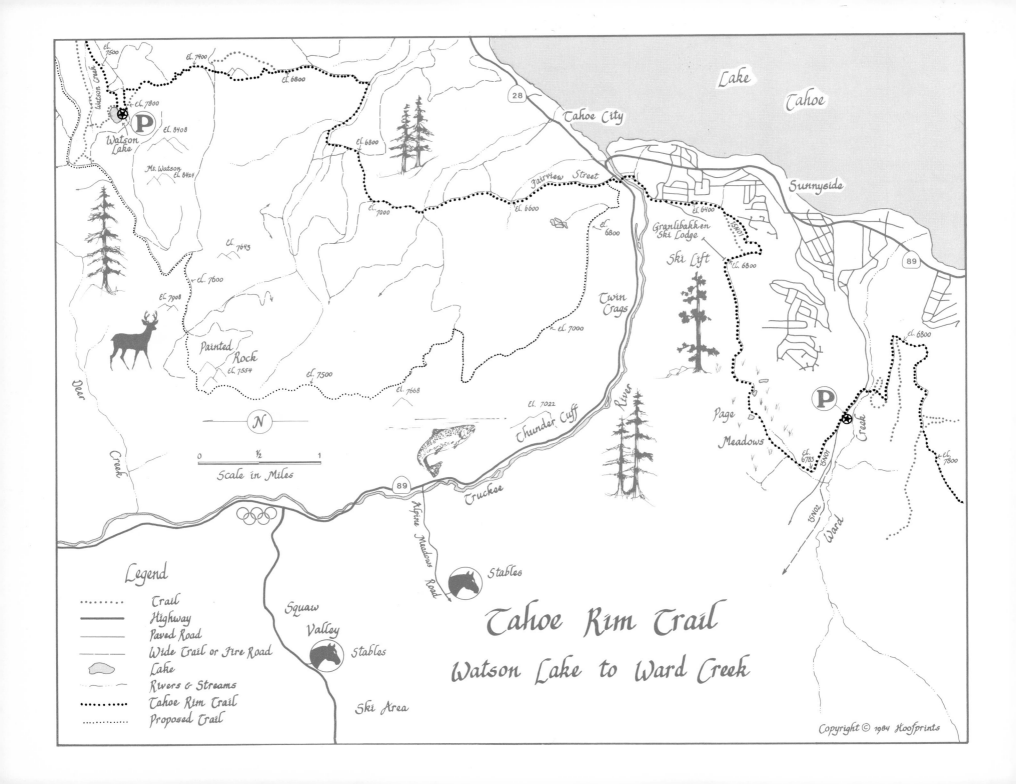

Lake Tahoe

Tahoe City

Sunnyside

Watson Lake
el. 7500
el. 7400
el. 6800
el. 7800
el. 8408
Mt. Watson el. 8424
el. 7643
el. 7600
el. 7908
Painted Rock
el. 7554
el. 7500
el. 7668
el. 7000
el. 6600
el. 6800
el. 7022
el. 6400
el. 6800
el. 6800
el. 6800
el. 7800
el. 6783

Fairview Street

Granlibakken Ski Lodge
Ski Lift
Twin Crags
Page Meadows
Thunder Cliff
River
Truckee

Deer Creek
Watson Creek
Squaw Creek

Ward Creek

15N01
15N01
15N02

28
89
89
89

Alpine Meadows Road

Squaw Valley
Ski Area

Stables
Stables

Legend

··········	Trail
———	Highway
——	Paved Road
—·—·	Wide Trail or Fire Road
⬭	Lake
⋮⋮⋮	Rivers & Streams
●●●●	Tahoe Rim Trail
·········	Proposed Trail

Tahoe Rim Trail
Watson Lake to Ward Creek

WATSON LAKE TO WARD CREEK

A little gem of a lake . . . everybody's favorite spot on the ride . .

— George Cardinet

LOCATION: Approximately 17 miles from Truckee . . . From Brockway Summit on Hwy. 267 take road 16N73 (a main haul road for timber) to Watson Lake . . . it's about four miles of gravel road.

WHERE TO PARK: This beautiful little spot is not easy to find . . . the best advice I can give is watch your mileage . . . Turn off Hwy. 267 onto road 16N73 and travel four miles on well compacted, well marked gravel road . . . stick to the gravel road because it is easy to get lost in a maze of fireroads crisscrossing the Tahoe National Forest and the LTBMU lands . . . Your landmark is a large rock painted "Bruce and Joe." I have no idea who they are but I shall be eternally grateful to them for providing us with a point of reference (if this rock has rolled away I really don't know how to help you!) . . . The fireroad immediately opposite Bruce and Joe rock leads downhill seven tenths of a mile on a rough, rutted road to Watson Lake . . . Until this road is improved I strongly advise that you park along 16N73 which has many wide areas, saddle your horses and pack your gear to Watson Lake.

ACCOMMODATIONS: Peaceful, spectacularly beautiful camping area and popular fishing spot . . . fire rings, tree sheltered camping area, shallow lake and nearby meadows . . . Watson Lake is a special treat on the Rim Trail route . . . a beautiful gem with trees down to the water line. A campfire permit is required here.

TRAIL FEATURES: Requires too much effort for a one-day ride but if you're looking for peace, beauty and adventure in an overnight camping experience, this is the spot . . . Use Watson Lake as a base camp and explore the numerous trails surrounding it . . . On fireroad 16N73 it's a seven mile ride to Tahoe City from Watson Lake . . . Camping at Watson Lake and riding back toward Tahoe Meadows is recommended at this time, although this is

the reverse of Cardinet's actual Rim Trail ride . . . **the rim trail route from Watson Lake to Ward Creek is not recommended at this time** because it requires too many complicated and hazardous road crossings in and around Tahoe City . . . As a segment of the 10-day Rim Trail Ride the route utilizes foot trails and fireroads through timber country as well as road travel through Tahoe City . . . Leaving from Watson Lake the trail drops down cross-country then onto Burton Creek State Park trails leading to Tahoe City roads . . . It is necessary to cross Hwy. 89 at Tahoe City from Fairway Drive at the west end of town . . . **This route is not recommended** until Rim Trail proposals are implemented. At that time the trail will divert to the north of Mt. Watson and arrive at the same point via Painted Rock.

 CAUTION: Again, until the Rim Trail improvements are made along this segment do not attempt to follow the actual Rim Trail Ride as led by Cardinet . . . instead enjoy the beauty of Watson Lake as a base camp for exploring the timber country . . . This is a very difficult segment of the Rim Trail unless you ride the route in reverse, heading toward Tahoe Meadows . . . Just don't wait too long to enjoy the beauty of Watson Lake!

CARDINET'S DIARY

August 28, day seven. We left Watson Lake on the adjacent road to the east taking another unnumbered road south which then turned west and dead-ended in less than a mile. At this point we took off cross-country southerly through an open corridor in the woods.
After a half hour we made contact with a motor-

cycle trail, in good repair, which led into a dirt road bearing generally west and southwest into Tahoe State Park. At the junction of an unnumbered road apparently in the northeast quarter of Section 31 T 16 N, R 17 E we followed in a northwesterly direction until crossing Burton Creek at a dam located on the common line of Sections 30T 16 N, R 17 E and 25 T 16 N, R 16 E near the intersection of Sections 36 and 31. Within a short distance we took a road bearing west and then south entering Tahoe City on Fairway Street on its western extremity. It is but a few feet down Hwy. 89 where it is crossed, and the trailer park bridge is used to cross the Truckee River. A block or two through the Park brings us to a gate and trail bearing south (pointed out to us by USFS Dan Fitzgerald), then on three blocks of pavement to enter upon Road 15 N 01 signed Ward Creek Trail. This was followed through Page Meadows and out to its juncture with Road 15 N 02 on Ward Creek. This was to be our camp for the night. As the route from State Line Tree to Ward Creek is largely woods and lacking in Rim scenics we recommend our route. If so decided it should immediately be set forth on City and County General Plans so that future development encroaches no further. It also seems possible that rerouting around the development south of the Truckee River would be possible. However, the present intrusion is minor. On our pre-ride we followed Road 15 N 02 to its apparent terminus just under Twin Peaks in a broad meadow. There being no discernible trail we retraced our steps. A bridge cave-in seems to have precluded traffic from the upper reaches of Ward Creek. It is an excellent trail, however. In Section 2 T 15 N, R16 E we found evidences of an old trail with a broken rustic USFS sign saying "Ridge Trail." It was impassable, however, as it was blocked by so many downed trees. The rehabilitation of this trail may be the most desirable route to Twin Peaks as opposed to Road 16 E 07 which we took on the ride. Riding time from Watson Lake to Ward Creek camp: 5 hours.

"Bruce & Joe" rock on your right is your landmark. Fireroad immediately opposite rock leads to Watson Lake. It's extremely rough and rutted, so unloading on 16N73 is recommended.

116

View of lake from camping area.

Polished rock burnished by Ice Age glaciers along the shore of Echo Lake . . . another of the many lakes viewed along the Tahoe Rim Trail.

Frances Coleberd

117

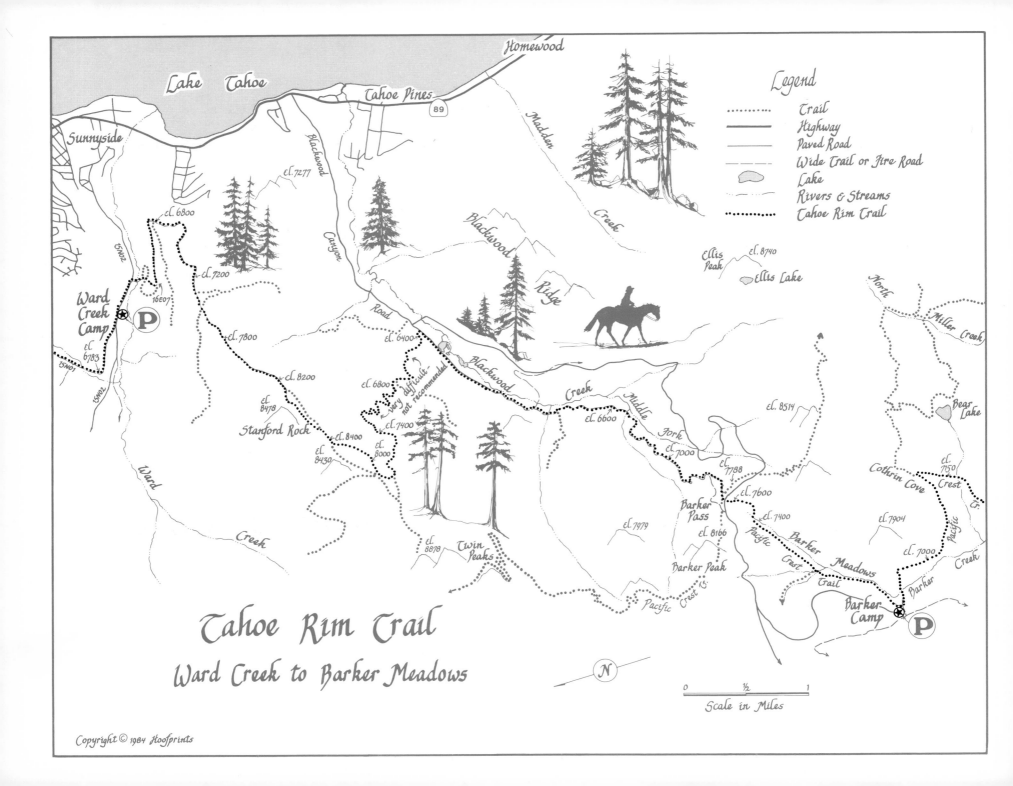

Tahoe Rim Trail
Ward Creek to Barker Meadows

Legend

··········	Trail
————	Highway
———	Paved Road
=======	Wide Trail or Fire Road
	Lake
	Rivers & Streams
••••••••••	Tahoe Rim Trail

Lake Tahoe

Homewood

Tahoe Pines

89

Sunnyside

Madden Creek

Blackwood Canyon

Blackwood Ridge

Ellis Peak   el. 8740

Ellis Lake

el. 7277

el. 6800

15N02

el. 7200

16E07

Ward Creek Camp

P

el. 6783

15N01

15N02

el. 7800

Road

el. 6400

Blackwood Creek

North

Miller Creek

el. 8514

Bear Lake

el. 8200

el. 6800

very difficult - not recommended

el. 7400

Middle Fork

el. 6600

el. 7000

el. 7788

Cothrin Cove

el. 7150

Crest

el. 8478

Stanford Rock

el. 8400

el. 8000

el. 8430

el. 7600

el. 7904

Barker Pass

el. 7400

el. 7000

Ward Creek

el. 8878

Twin Peaks

el. 7979

el. 8166

Barker Peak

Pacific Crest Tr.

Pacific Crest Trail

Barker Meadows Trail

Barker Creek

Barker Camp

P

Pacific Crest Tr.

N

0   ½   1

Scale in Miles

WARD CREEK TO BARKER MEADOW

A challenging ride through timber country with magnificent views of the Pacific Crest . . .

— George Cardinet

LOCATION: Approximately seven miles south and east of Tahoe City. Turn west on Ward Avenue which becomes Ward Creek Blvd. as you travel through a residential area on a narrow paved road.

WHERE TO PARK: Ward Creek Camp is a mile and a half from Hwy. 89 on the left hand side of Ward Creek Blvd. and on the north side of Ward Creek between the junction of Road 15N02 and Road 16E07. Just before you reach the camp area you will see a large gravelled parking area marked at the nearby creek with the sign "15N47 4 miles to Stanford Rock." George says correct designation of this trail is 16E07. For day use this area provides easy access to the trail. Continue to Ward Creek Camp for overnight stays.

ACCOMMODATIONS: Ward Creek Camp is a scenic, unimproved camping area with room for only a couple of rigs . . . Overnight stays are welcome here but because of the limited camping area and lack of facilities George recommends that you stage at Squaw Valley Equestrian Center (916) 583-7433.

TRAIL FEATURES: Moderate to steep ride through timber, meadow and brush with a spectacular view of Twin Peaks . . . from Stanford Rock views of Alpine Lakes and Squaw Valley beyond . . . You're traveling on fireroad trail and cross country but portions of this ride are **difficult and uncertain** because of the likelihood of snow at any time of year . . . also the ultimate Rim Trail will probably not use this route so it is important to verify this segment of your ride with the Forest Service . . . A good, reliable day ride from this area is Ward Creek to Twin Peaks and return.

CAUTION: If the Pacific Crest Trail is blocked with snow it will be necessary for you to pick your way from the Stanford Rock ridge down to Blackwood Creek on a steep switchback overgrown with stirrup high brush . . . very hazardous here because the brush is underlined with rocks.

CARDINET'S DIARY

August 29, day eight. We left Ward Creek on Road 16 E 07. After a rather steep first half mile a long, gradual climb was experienced past Stanford Rock which we climbed to a point approximately on the common line of the SE and SW quarters of Section 28 T 15 N, R 16 E where according to the map trail Road 16 E 07 bears north and our trail continues on Road 16 E 08. The former is apparently day seven's "Ridge Trail."

On our preride we had followed Road 16 E 08 up onto Twin Peaks. The trail is well blazed and is no problem in spite of extensive snow drifts. However, the trail petered out on reaching the summit. There was a blaze or two on the far slope, but otherwise there was no more evidence of the trail. It would have been possible to push through to the Pacific Crest Trail but inadvisable without trail work which we had no time for. Also we had been advised that at a point midway between Twin Peaks and Barker Pass the PCT was impassable because of snow. Consequently, on the actual ride we dropped off from the juncture of Roads 16 E 07 and 16 E 08 in

Well marked trail heads can be misleading. There's some rough riding ahead!

Section 28 on an old overgrown logging road which bore east for a half mile and then descended into Blackwood Creek on a series of switchbacks. We then proceeded up Road 15 N 40 and its extension 16 E 09 to Barker Pass and then on the PCT south and west. Our selected camp spot and recommended staging area was occupied by a logging crew so we used another less desirable site about a mile on down the road beyond where the PCT crosses said logging road. The crossing is not marked so it gave us a bit of a problem the next morning. Riding time from Ward Creek to Barker Camp: six hours. (Note: If Twin Peaks had been negotiable and PCT obtainable we would have made the ride in nine instead of ten days. I strongly recommended the rehabilitation of "Ridge Trail."

George Cardinet

Steep, difficult riding through timber country means there will be long stretches when you're well advised to take the load off the horses.

For day use an easy entrance to the trail is from a wide parking area marked "15N47 — 4 miles to Stanford Rock."

ELDORADO NATIONAL FOREST

Tahoe Basin Management Unit

Wilderness Regulations

Because Desolation is an extremely popular wilderness area and receives very heavy use during the summer months, it has become necessary to impose the following **restrictions** to assure solitude and protection of the wilderness resource:

1. A free wilderness Visitor Permit **is required** and **must be obtained** before you enter the Wilderness.
2. Permits will be limited to 700 overnight users per day to camp in the Desolation Wilderness from June 15 - Labor Day. Permits are also required for day use but are not subject to this quota. During the remainder of the year **NO** quotas will be in effect; however **wilderness permits are required.**
3. 50% of the permits may be reserved by mail or in person up to 90 days in advance; the rest will be issued on a first-come, first-served basis.
4. The maximum party size will not exceed 25 people.
5. Maximum length of stay may not exceed 14 days per visit.

Desolation Wilderness Visitor Permits can be obtained at the following offices:

(For west side entry)
U.S. Forest Service
Eldorado National Forest
100 Forni Road, Placerville, CA 95667
(916) 622-5061

Pacific Ranger Station
Pollock Pines, CA 95726
(916) 644-2348

(For east side entry)
Lake Tahoe Basin Management Unit
P.O. Box 8465
870 Emerald Bay Road
South Lake Tahoe, CA 95371
(916) 544-6420

NO TRACE CAMPING

No trace camping is an attitude that can lead to enjoyment of the wilderness without changing or damaging it.

Fire

Fuel stoves are recommended. There is a shortage of down wood in parts of the wilderness. Wood fires leave scars and sterilize the soil. If you must have a fire, build a small fire in an existing fire circle.

Firewood

Gather only fallen wood. Snags and silvery logs are part of the wilderness beauty and provide homes for animals. Leave them for all to enjoy.

Drown it!

Drown your campfire, stir it with a stick or trowel and **feel** the ashes to make sure the fire is out . . . **COLD!** Escaped campfires have destroyed many popular camps.

Noise

You can help preserve wilderness solitude by using techniques that blend with the surroundings, avoiding boisterous conduct, and by leaving firearms and radios at home.

Soaps and Detergents

Washing or bathing in lakes and streams will pollute them, even when using biodegradable soap. Keep wash water, fish entrails, and garbage away from bodies of water.

Sanitation

Use good toilet habits. Carry a small garden trowel for burying human waste at least 100 feet from water, trails, and campsites. Dig a hole 6-8 inches deep and cover it with loose soil or sod after use.

Construction

Construction of large rock fire pits, rock walls, and other "improvements" detract from the landscape and are now prohibited by regulation.

Trail Switchbacks

Switchbacks are expensive to construct and maintain. Cutting across switchbacks hastens destructive trail erosion and could injure yourself and others.

Pets

If at all possible leave your pet at home. If you must bring your pet, put it on a leash to minimize its impact on wildlife and other visitors.

Campsites

Where terrain permits, select campsites at least 100 feet from lake shores, streams, meadows, and trails. This helps to prevent permanent damage to fragile vegetation, and minimizes water pollution.

Pack it Out!

Pack it out, you carried it in. Aluminum foil does not burn, carry it out with your other litter. Animals and weather will bring buried refuse to the surface again.

Wilderness Regulations for which you may be cited & fined:

Fire — leaving a fire without completely extinguishing it.

Washing in, discarding wash water or fish entrails in, or otherwise polluting any lake, stream, or other water.

Permits are required. Wilderness permits are issued for one trip, for a specific length of time.

Cutting or otherwise damaging any timber, tree or other forest product; except as authorized by permit.

Firearm — Discharge of firearm or other implement capable of taking human life, causing injury, or damaging property in or around campsites, trails, across lakes, or near occupied areas.

Motorized Vehicles — use of motors or motorized vehicles.

Building structures such as rock walls, tables, stream dams, large fireplaces, storage caches.

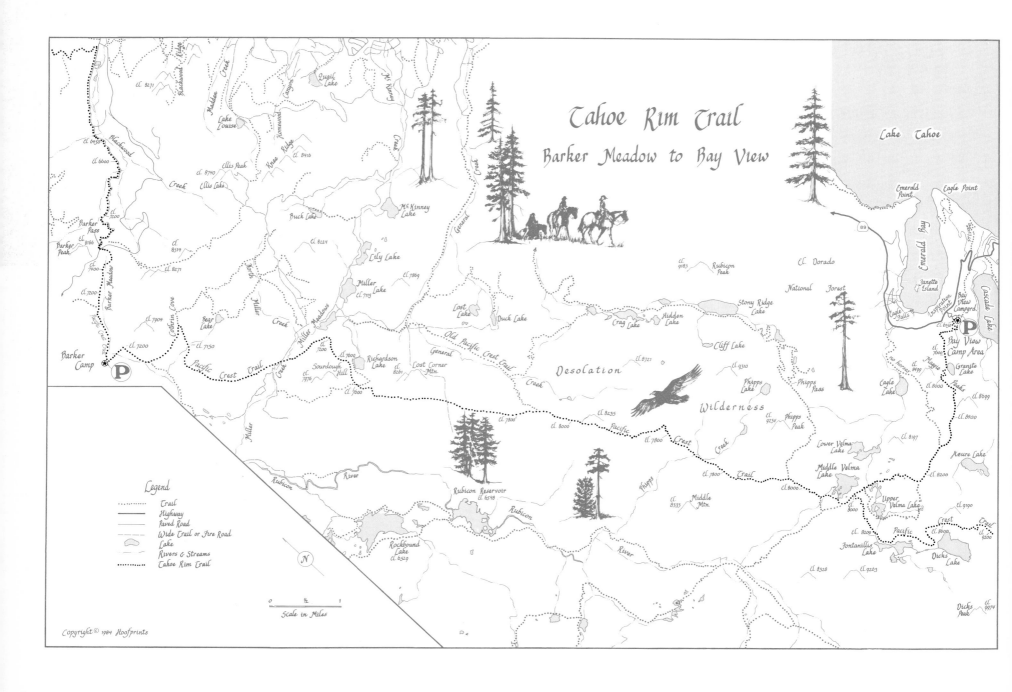

Tahoe Rim Trail
Barker Meadow to Bay View

Lake Tahoe

Legend

··········	Trail
——	Highway
===	Paved Road
- - -	Wide Trail or Fire Road
⬭	Lake
~~	Rivers & Streams
••••••	Tahoe Rim Trail

Scale in Miles
0   ½   1

N

Desolation Wilderness

El Dorado National Forest

Emerald Bay

Cascade Lake

Barker Pass
Barker Peak   El. 8166
El. 7400
El. 7200

Barker Camp P

Blackwood Ridge El. 8271
Blackwood El. 6450
El. 6600

Madden Creek

Lake Louise

Ellis Peak El. 8740
Ellis Lake
Grass Ridge El. 8416

Creek

McKinney Creek
Quail Lake

Buck Lake
McKinney Lake

El. 8224

Lily Lake

Miller Lake El. 7115
El. 7869

El. 8514
El. 8271

North Fork

Miller Creek

Miller Meadows

Cobrin Cove
Bear Lake El. 7904
El. 7150
El. 7200

Pacific Crest Trail

Sourdough Hill El. 7776
Richardson Lake
El. 7200
El. 7000
Lost Corner Mtn. El. 8261
General

El. 7000

Old Pacific Crest Trail

Lost Lake
Duck Lake

Crag Lake
Hidden Lake

Cliff Lake

El. 8721

Stony Ridge Lake

Rubicon Peak El. 9183

Phipps Lake
Phipps Pass
Phipps Peak El. 9234

El. 9310

Pacific Crest Trail

El. 8235
El. 7800
El. 8000

Rubicon Reservoir El. 6548

Rubicon River

Rockbound Lake El. 6529

Middle Mtn. El. 8333

Middle Velma Lake El. 8000

Lower Velma Lake

Upper Velma Lake El. 8000

Fontanillis Lake El. 8100

El. 8328 El. 9263

Dicks Lake

Dicks Peak El. 9974

Pacific Crest Trail El. 8600 El. 9200

El. 9190

Azure Lake El. 8197 El. 8200

Eagle Lake El. 8000

Maggie Peaks El. 8499 El. 8600 El. 8400 El. 8699

Granite Lake

Bay View Camp Area P
Bay View Campgrd. El. 7000

Cascade Lake

Inspiration Point
Cascade Falls
Eagle Falls

Emerald Point
Eagle Point

Jantte Island

89

BARKER MEADOW TO BAYVIEW

Ridge riding on the Pacific Crest Trail as you enter the Desolation Valley Wilderness . . .

— George Cardinet

Sandy Darby

LOCATION: Access to Barker Meadow staging area is from Hwy. 89 between the communities of Tahoe City and Homewood. From Hwy. 89 turn onto Blackwood Canyon Road at the Kaspian Recreation Area.

WHERE TO PARK: From the turn-off on Hwy. 89 to the top of Barker Pass you travel seven miles on a relatively easy grade haul road. At the Pass you will see a large mapboard on your right and a PCT trail sign. From this point you will drive one and three tenths miles to the point where you turn left down to Barker Meadow. You will be on good gravel road but use low gear to avoid trouble. The road is wide with wide pull outs. Logging roads come in from all directions. You can't miss the large staging area on the right with ample room for parking and turning trailers.

ACCOMMODATIONS: Nothing formal, but a beautiful meadow and nearby Barker Creek make this an inviting place.

TRAIL FEATURES: Approximately a seven-hour ride (21 miles) from Barker Meadow to Bayview on spectacularly scenic but, for stretches, hard to follow trail . . . From Barker to the Rockbound Lake overlook is a new section of Pacific Crest Trail in good condition (as of 1984.) The grade is gentle and invites a leisurely pace. It is banked, drained and sloped to minimize maintenance . . . the trail from that point on to the vicinity of Velma Lakes is barely maintained and poorly marked . . . In the vicinity of Velma Lakes you leave PCT and head east to Bayview on well marked granite trail. This segment of the Rim Trail in its entirety should probably be regarded as too rough for novice trail horses and horsemen . . . A less demanding day ride would be to stage at Barker Meadow and ride the new stretch of PCT trail as far as Rockbound Lake overlook and return to camp . . . For qualified adventurers to travel the full 21 miles the reward for mastering the precipitous granite trails is the scenic grandeur unique to Desolation Valley Wilderness.

 CAUTION: At the end of August portions of this trail were blocked to the Cardinet ride by snow . . . the same could happen to you. **Be prepared for Sierra weather** . . Carry warm clothing and rain gear . . . blankets are recommended at night for horses . . . Granite trails are in good condition after a rain but great care must be exercised at creek crossings where flash floods are a possibility.

CARDINET'S DIARY

August 30, day nine. The trail from Barker Pass south to a point opposite Rockbound Lake is relatively new construction. However, there is no evidence of maintenance this year. There is an excellent, delightful trail apparently re-routed to pass on the west bank of Richardson Lake. Some downed trees and evidence of motorcycle intrusion. There was only one wilderness sign to designate entry. Only one Pacific Crest Trail sign between Barker and Velma Lakes where we diverted to Bayview Camp. From the end of the aforesaid "new construction" to the vicinity of Velma Lakes the PCT has obviously been neglected for some years. Downed trees and erosion present a generally miserable situation and in many places create difficulty in following the trail. This section brought forth innumerable, unsolicited comments of varying degrees of concern and derogation. Blasting on Road 17 E 03 frightened the horses somewhat but fortunately we had posted guards before entering the critical area. The power drills were also a bit disconcerting. It is suggested that people be forewarned of drilling and blasting by placing warning signs some distance before the entrance to the area. This was not a stressful situation but this suggestion is made in the interest of better public relations. Riding time to Bayview: seven hours. (Note: It was necessary to descend to Bayview Camp and eliminate the next few miles to Echo Lake because of impassable snow in Dick's Pass.)

123

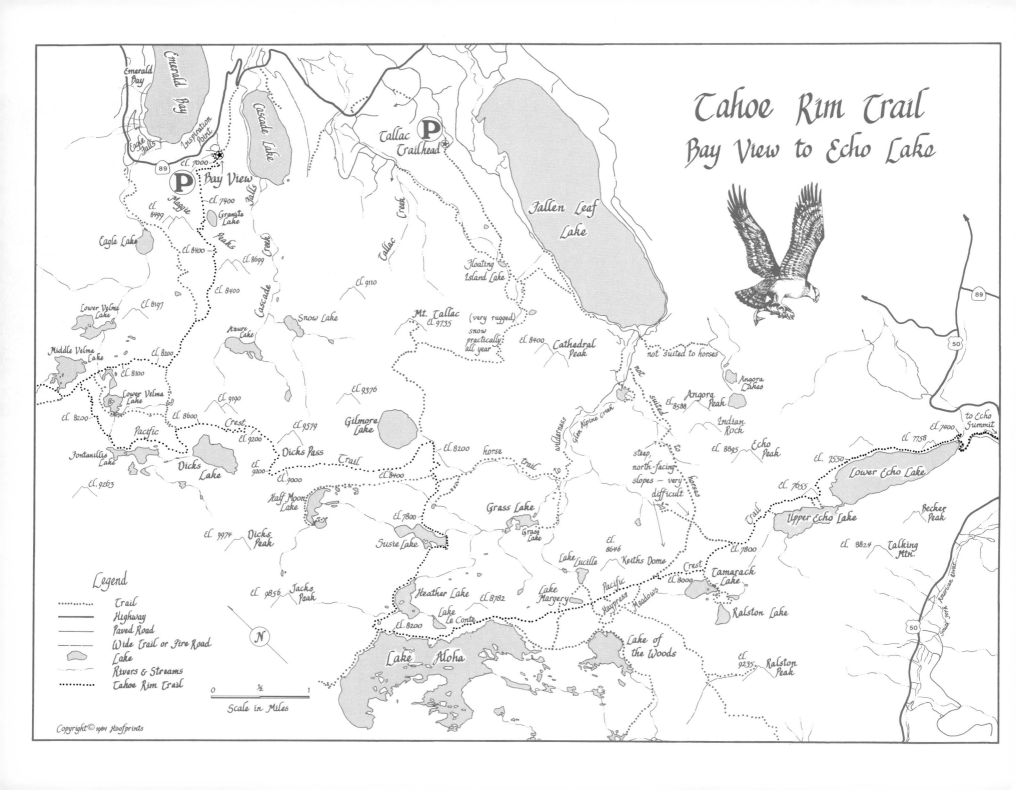

Tahoe Rim Trail
Bay View to Echo Lake

Emerald Bay

Emerald Bay

Cascade Lake

Inspiration Point
El. 7000

89

P Bay View

Tallac Trailhead P

Fallen Leaf Lake

El. 7400

Maggie
El. 8499

Granite Lake

Peaks
El. 8400

Cascade Falls

Tallac Creek

Eagle Lake

El. 8699

Cascade Creek

El. 8400

El. 9110

Floating Island Lake

89

50

Lower Velma Lake

El. 8197

Azure Lake

Snow Lake

Mt. Tallac
El. 9735

(very rugged) snow practically all year

El. 8400

Cathedral Peak

not suited to horses

Middle Velma Lake

El. 8200

El. 8100

Lower Velma Lake

El. 9190

El. 9376

Gilmore Lake

Angora Lakes

Angora Peak
El. 8588

Indian Rock

to Echo Summit

El. 8200

El. 8600

Crest

El. 9579

wilderness

Glen Alpine Creek

El. 8895

Echo Peak

El. 7400

El. 7758

Pacific

El. 9200

Dicks Pass

El. 8200

horse

trail

not suited

to horses

El. 7550

Fontanillis Lake

Trail

Dicks Lake

El. 9200

El. 9000

El. 8400

to

Lower Echo Lake

El. 9263

Half Moon Lake

El. 7800

Grass Lake

steep, north-facing slopes ~ very difficult

El. 7655

Upper Echo Lake

Becker Peak

El. 9974

Dicks Peak

Susie Lake

Grass Lake

El. 8646

Keiths Dome

El. 7800

El. 8824

Talking Mtn.

Legend

- ·········· Trail
- ———— Highway
- ———— Paved Road
- ———— Wide Trail or Fire Road
- Lake
- Rivers & Streams
- ·········· Tahoe Rim Trail

El. 9856

Jacks Peak

Heather Lake

El. 8782

Lake Le Conte

El. 8200

Lake Lucille

Lake Margery

Pacific

Crest

El. 8000

Tamarack Lake

Ralston Lake

N

Haypress Meadows

Lake of the Woods

El. 9235

Ralston Peak

Lake Aloha

South Fork American River

50

0   ½   1

Scale in Miles

Copyright © 1984 Hoofprints

BAYVIEW CAMP TO ECHO SUMMIT

The magnificence of the Desolation Valley Wilderness with access from a beautifully designed horse camp . . .

— George Cardinet

LOCATION: On Hwy. 89 between Emerald Bay and Cascade Lake, twelve and one half miles from intersection of Hwy. 50 and Hwy. 89 in South Lake Tahoe.

WHERE TO PARK: Heading north on Hwy. 89 the highway becomes narrow and winding and then a steady, uphill climb for the last three miles as you approach Bayview Campground . . . Easy access to the Campground opposite Emerald Bay's Inspiration Point. The road loops around a regular camping area with a second loop designated for horse trailer parking. There is room here for about five or six trailers . . . trailhead takes off from the parking area.

ACCOMMODATIONS: Overnight and day use of this area requires permission from the Forest Service, Lake Tahoe Basin Management Unit . . . Phone or write to Frank "Mac" Magary (LTBU, P.O. 8465, So. Lake Tahoe, CA 95731, (916) 544-6420). Well designed stock trail head complete with two large corrals, water supply, elevated ramp for unloading stock . . . Area has been remodeled to accommodate large stock trailers as well. Trails in this area can also be reached from nearby Camp Richardson Stables and Cascade Stables. Both stables invite overnight boarding for your horses . . . Guides are available, and from the Hubbard family's experience with both stables, guides seem to enrich your knowledge of the area without reducing the adventure . . .

TRAIL FEATURES: Great variety here for all levels of trail experience . . . well established horse trails popular with vacationers as well as granite footing to

Tree-shaded pipe corrals are only one of the many equestrian features at Bayview Camp.

challenge even the boldest riders . . . The trail winds through a glacier-scarred granite landscape with sparse vegetation surrounded by majestic snow-covered peaks into gentle meadows lush with wildflowers and the brilliant blue of a myriad of lakes and ponds . . . More breathtaking beauty can hardly be imagined but your sightseeing should be moderated by careful attention to the granite footing of the trails . . . trails are well marked and you're likely to share them with numerous hiking groups . . . Except for the austere landscape the popular use of this area makes the name Desolation Wilderness seem somewhat inappropriate . . . For riders the route to Echo Summit is to ride toward Velma Lakes, pick up the trail south of Lower Velma returning to PCT. Head toward Dick's Pass on PCT passing Lake

Aloha and Echo Lakes and on to Echo Summit.

A special feature of this area is that you can realize your dreams of a combined riding-fishing trip! Nearby stables can offer you a guide to the best fishing spots.

CAUTION: Day rides from Bayview up to the Velma Lakes area offer all the beauty and variety you could hope for in a trail ride . . . If you wish to follow the Rim Trail route in its entirety (past Echo Lake to the start of the ride at Echo Summit) you must plan carefully with the Forest Service because of general trail conditions, possible snow, and changing policies within the Wilderness area.

CARDINET'S DIARY

August 31, day ten. To travel the length of the Desolation Wilderness by horse on the Rim Trail without pack stock it is necessary to come out to Bay View Camp via Maggie's Peaks as we did. (One may then the next retrace their steps to Velma Lakes and then proceed south on the Pacific Crest Trail and leave the Desolation Wilderness at Echo Lake.) As Dick's Pass was closed by 40 feet of snow we proceeded south through the Cascade Lake properties after obtaining permission from their owner, Shrimp Ebright. As you descend the trail to Cascade Lake the prominence of Maggie's Peaks is readily descernible above you. Maggie's Peaks were so named not because of any possessory interest she had in them but because of certain anatomical features. Our trail took us around the west end of the Lake and virtually under Cascade Falls from which the lake is named. The trail takes you over the south rim of Cascade Lake across the valley of Tallac Creek back into the Desolation Widerness at Floating Island Lake. Here the trail traverses the ridge dividing Cascade and Fallen Leaf Lakes. After passing around the east end of Fallen Leaf Lake the trail crosses several meadows and our ride concluded at Camp Richardson at South Lake Tahoe. A light rain fell upon us during the day and increased in intensity during the evening and night.

Showers and a welcome clean up at Camp Richardson preceded a cocktail party and steak Bar-B-Q under an acre of awning hosted by Rob Ross of Camp Richardson stables who housed our horses for the night.

126

Cardinet

Reaching Fallen Leaf Lake after ten full days of riding, a Sierra rainstorm ushers the Rim Trail riders home.

BE A PART OF THE TAHOE RIM TRAIL'S FUTURE —

YOU CAN GIVE money, tools, material, or lend equipment, or more important give a part of you. Contribute to the planning, construction, and maintenance of one of the most spectacular trails in the United States. And it's all tax deductible.

THE TAHOE RIM TRAIL

The Tahoe Rim Trail provides an ideal means by which civic-minded organizations and corporations can channel their contributions toward a national and local cause of immense importance. Gifts will be used for acquisition, planning, and construction of the Tahoe Rim Trail, feeder trails, trail heads, educational/interpretive centers, rest areas, overlooks, picnic sites, and campsites.

Without the support of corporations as well as individuals and organizations, the Tahoe Rim Trail Program would be unable to keep pace with the ever-growing need for the construction and maintenance of the Trail and associated facilities.

The Tahoe Rim Trail offers individuals and corporations a tax-deductible and a speedy, flexible, and efficient means through which gifts can be allocated to urgently needed projects associated with the Rim Trail. The program consists of a not-for-profit corporation guided by an all-volunteer Board made up of industrial and civic leaders from both California and Nevada.

VOLUNTEERS ARE THE KEY

The low administrative and fund-raising costs are due not only to efficient staff operations, but also to the extensive use of volunteers. The Board and the Tahoe Rim Trail Executive Committee are composed entirely of volunteers.

Projects are carried forward by local fund-raising committees made up of volunteers who serve because of their concern for the Tahoe Rim Trail Project. Volunteers will be needed to assist with Trail planning, construction and maintenance, legal and administrative practices, publicity, fund-raising, and membership drives.

CONTRIBUTORS

Lifetime	$1,000.00
Trail Boss	500.00
Trail Planner	100.00
Trail Scout	50.00
Trail Blazer	25.00
Trail Guide	10.00
Tenderfoot	5.00
Planning	Time
Construction	Time
Interpretation	Time
Maintenance	Time

THE ADOPTION PROGRAM

ADOPT A TRAIL PLANNING SEGMENT: volunteer you or your organization or corporation to assist in analysis and planning a mile or more of a specific stretch of trail. The contribution might consist of historical, archeological, natural features, and wildlife research, engineering and design work, and any plan preparation necessary.

ADOPT A TRAIL CONSTRUCTION SEGMENT: volunteer you or your organization or corporation to assist in the construction of a mile or more of a specific stretch of trail. The contribution might consist of shovel and pick work, construction of a small bridge or rock wall, operation of trail building machinery, donation of materials and/or equipment.

ADOPT A FACILITY: volunteer you or your organization or corporation to construct a complete trail head, a comfort station, a picnic site, a campsite, a trail marker, an interpretive sign or display case, or an interpretive overlook.

ADOPT AN INTERPRETIVE PROGRAM: volunteer you or your organization or corporation to research and plan an interpretation program for a trail portion. Contributions might consist of all research and planning for brochures, books, maps, or wayside marker display. Research would include but not be limited to the history, archeology, geology, flora, fauna, soils, water, and hazards of the area. Or volunteer to prepare and present an interpretive program.

ADOPT A MAINTENANCE PROGRAM: volunteer you or your organization or corporation to maintain a trail mile, a comfort station, a campsite, picnic site, or interpretive device. Contributions may consist of rebuilding a section of trail, replacing trail markers and interpretive devices, paint, stain, or refurbishing comfort station, tables, and grill.

Will you join us in helping to secure the Rim Trail's future? The Tahoe Rim Trail, P.O. Box 10156, South Lake Tahoe, CA 95721.

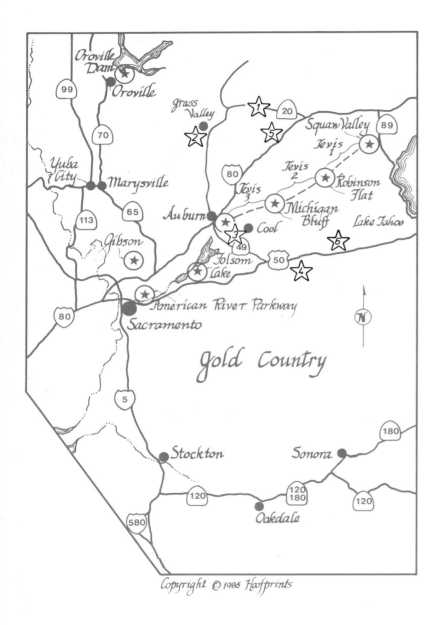

VI. Gold Country Trails

featuring

☆ Pioneer Trail
☆ Empire Mine State Historic Park
☆ Middle Fork Trails
☆ Black Oak Equestrian Campground
☆ Lowell Hill Road
(Area of Donner Emigrant Trail)
☆ Wright's Lake

⊛ Neighboring trail areas

A beautiful trail around Jenkinson Lake is one of the pleasures of staying at Black Oak Equestrian Campground.

GOLD COUNTRY horsemen galloped to the rescue as I stared overwhelmed at the mass of maps and mountains I would have to conquer in order to portray the trail systems of California's celebrated gold rush lands. My original plan of selecting one research-rider to blaze the way was promptly buried under the enthusiasm of many Sierra horsemen eager to share the good news of gold country trails. Their hills are alive again, not only with the controversy of modern day miners in search of a fortune, but also with modern day trail lovers dedicated to maintaining and improving their access to the land. How could I focus on only one rider with stories like this to choose from?

— the energy and unselfishness of the Jordan family who built a horse camp for public use,
— the perseverance of Ray Sherman and the Gold Country Trails Council in constructing an all-volunteer built trail,
— the determination of Jon and Carol Saunders who completely changed their lives in order to live near the trails,
— the horse savvy of Bab Verdugo who has been training horses since the 1930s,
— the depth of horse camping experience shared by the Twin Lakes Riding Club,
— the dedication of Maxine Stahl whose devotion to saving a trail was undiminished by her simultaneous activities of running a lumber business, writing a book, and competing on endurance rides,
— the generosity of Carol Jones who with a day's notice dropped everything to guide me along a trail.

The problem of choosing one rider in order to comply with the established format of this book was finally solved when I admitted to myself that I was indebted to all of the above for the Gold Country section and would frankly acknowledge it! If you're headed for the Sierra foothills these are good people to know, so let me introduce you!

I was a complete stranger to Carol Jones until I phoned her on a summer day in 1984 and asked for information on horse trails in the Placerville area. With the mention of trails and our mutual friendship with Heritage Trails Fund founder Nancy Dupont, Carol generously offered to give up a heavily scheduled day to join me in exploring the trails around Sly Park. As I got acquainted with the trails I got to know Carol. The first thing I learned is that

although her knowledge and love of horses and Gold Country trails would lead you to believe she'd been around both all her life, the fact is she's a convert from horseless city life.

"I'm a born and bred city girl," she confided. "I just happened to marry an old farm boy whose dream was to return to country living. We were married ten years before his dream came true with our move to the foothills of Mount Diablo. I knew nothing about horses but the property we purchased just happened to come furnished with a very willful little Shetland pony. It wasn't long before the pony and I were engaged in a battle of wills which I was determined to win."

To get on the winning side Carol decided she'd better learn something about horses. "I enrolled in a horse husbandry class to find out the basic things like which end of the pony to feed," she said.

From that humble beginning her knowledge of horses grew and so did her love. She readily admits that during the 15 years that followed her "first pony" experience her love of horses grew into an obsession. She owned many different horses during this time and also got her children involved in trail riding and horse shows.

"It was a wholesome, worthwhile activity for all of us to share. We were kept busy with classes in Western Pleasure, English Pleasure, jumping, and dressage. After years of competing in the show ring we turned wholeheartedly to trail riding," Carol recalls.

Carol's interest in trails led her to membership in the Concord-Mount Diablo Trail Ride Association which in turn led to involvement in the Association's summer riding camp. She was an instructor for two years and camp director for two years, "two very exciting experiences stemming from my involvement with horses."

As often happens with trail loving horse owners the time came when suburban trails didn't satsify the urge for country living and the move was made to Placerville. Since her family's move to the mountains, Carol has kept horses strictly for her own pleasure. Helping others is one of her pleasures, so she's involved with friends in a Quarter Horse breeding program. Her contribution is the training of young colts. Working with young horses is a long way to come from not knowing which end of the pony to feed!

Trail riding is still Carol's favorite horse activity and since her move to the Gold Country she's satisfied to ride the trails close to home. "I know there are gorgeous trails all over this state, but once I got up here in God's country I just didn't want to go anywhere else, she explains. "Once you find heaven, you hate to leave it."

Rides around Sly Park had made Carol familiar with the trail system, but she was as surprised as I was at the sudden appearance of a full-fledged equestrian campground. Welcoming us to the forested area featuring pipe corrals, tie rails, saddle racks, water, electricity, restrooms, and generous turnaround areas for trailers was retired contractor Leonard Jordan. He didn't look very retired as he wiped the sweat and dust from his face and brought the large caterpillar tractor to a halt. He had put in a full week of trail work and campground improvements, but in spite of his obvious weariness he was more than happy to answer our questions. It's just that we could hardly believe his answers:

"Yes, this is a brand new campground open to horses . . . No, I don't work for any park or government agency. I'm doing this on my own, with my daughter Marianne, my granddaughter Cherie, and my great-grandkids . . . No, we don't belong to any horse clubs or trail groups . . . No, nobody's paying us to do this. The Eldorado Irrigation District gave us the land to work with and w'ere putting in the labor on a volunteer basis . . . Yes, I'm using the Cat at my own expense . . . No, honestly, no organization is behind us. We just love horses and camping and decided to do something about it . . . If you want to know more than that you'll have to ask my daughter. She's in charge of this outfit!"

The "outfit" arrived in a few minutes later to confirm the words of grandfather Jordan. As incredible as it seemed to a Bay Area rider accustomed to countless committee meetings, fund raisers, and miles of red tape as requisites for every mile of trail built (not to mention horse campgrounds!) the entire Black Oak Equestrian Campground was being built by the unsolicited, volunteer labor of the Jordan family — with the blessing and cooperation of the water district and Sly Park rangers. While Carol and I stood in awe of the magnitude of labor and responsibility taken on by a single family — their work crew spanned four generations! — Marianne Jordan brushed off our hurrahs with an offer of cold lemonade and a simple explanation.

"Horses have played a major role in our family's history," explained Marianne. "My great, great grandfather was a wagon master. His home base was in Illinois but his westward excursions led to the establishment of the family in California as ranchers and loggers. In the San Joaquin Valley, Jordan Hot Springs, Jordan Peak, and Jordan Lookout Tower still bear the family name.

"Camping with our horses has always been an important activity for our family, and so has music. We're a family of fiddlers. In fact,

Marianne Jordan with her daughter, Cherie Minatre, her grandchildren, Jarrod and Amber Rose, and Sly Park Ranger Robert Chapin — the Black Oak Equestrian Campground trail crew!

my cousin placed first one year in a fiddling contest at Oregon State. Not too long after we moved to Placerville we found out he was coming for a visit so my daughter Cherie and I got the idea of combining everything we love to do in one big hoe-down — horses, fiddles, and camping! So the search began for a place to hold the event. Sly Park seemed like the perfect place and park officials agreed to the idea. There was only one problem — no place for people to camp with their horses."

It's safe to say that most people faced with organizing a major event wouldn't have simultaneously tackled a project as awesome as building a campground. But with sturdy pioneer blood pumping in their veins, Marianne, her father, daughter, and grandchildren got out the shovels, chainsaws, and tractor and set to work. Their enthusiasm was spurred by the help of friends and park officials. The Jordans worked for an entire month until the end result was a campground for the public's benefit. But first it had to be christened by the family's "Summer Ride and Mountain Hoedown!" From as far away as Oregon and Utah riders and fiddlers joined local music-loving horsemen for a three-day event of riding all day and fiddling

131

at night. Reenergized riders danced while tired horses munched their oats to the tune of a fiddle which has been in the Jordan family since 1905. The success of the first hoedown hints at its becoming a "yearly event". Regardless of the future of the Hoedown, Gold Country horsemen are one beautiful campground richer because of the ideas and energy of the Jordan family.

Grass Valley horse trainer Bab Verdugo.

Placerville trails had brought me the adventure of new friends. Now as I headed north to Grass Valley trails I looked forward to the guidance of an old friend as I explored Empire Mine State Park. To be honest, as I drove along that day on scenic, winding Hwy. 49 anticipating my rendezvous with Bab Verdugo, I was thinking less of trails and more of Bab's humor and his wife's hospitality. As sure as the sun would set that evening I knew I could count on some funny stories from Bab and a batch of June's fresh cookies with iced tea waiting for me at the Verdugos. I weakly vowed not to forsake my "tight schedule" and the research I must do for the alluring comfort of big chairs in the Verdugos' shady yard where old dogs lie against your feet while one yarn begets another and another till the shade turns crisp and you suddenly realize that a whole afternoon has passed into evening. In spite of deadlines it is hard to resist such days where anecdotes and refreshments are interwoven with the privilege of following a renowned horseman on his daily round of horse training. Reflecting on more leisurely times spent with the Verdugos I realized that Bab has treated me — his guest — much the same as he treats his horses. He's been generous with his time, patience, and wisdom. He has answered my questions with respect, intent on meeting my need rather than displaying his knowledge. The steady stream of stories as horses were groomed and hitched, stalls cleaned, visitors introduced, were entertaining, but there was more to it than that. Like a horse under Bab's tactful training, I've spent those gentle afternoons *being taught* without realizing there was a lesson going on at all.

Bab claims there's no secret to his skill. It's just that he has been training horses all his life. He credits his dad with everything he's learned from rodeo to pleasure-driving horses.

"I tried to copy everything I saw my Dad do with a horse. Besides regular training he was good with trick horses. We had horses that could kneel and bow and come to you on command. The real trick, though, was that Dad had to get work out of his horses . . . He worked them with plows and the Fresno scraper. Then if the boss wanted to go some place he had to be able to saddle them up or hitch them to a nice buggy. Dad worked on a number of different ranches, training horses and driving teams. The first big place he worked at was the Garvey Ranch in Southern California, and later there was the Harry Carey Ranch in Saugus. That's where I was given my first job, herding sheep and goats with saddle horses."

Following in his father's footsteps, Bab developed the skills of a true horseman on ranches throughout California. He also broke

Bab Verdugo with two-year-old Paint mare Summer. "Too many trainers are in a big hurry with young horses. They end up with nervous animals. I spend a lot of time just letting them stand quietly in harness."

some ground on his own, such as doing stunt work in two movies about the Civil War.

"One movie was called the *Swamp Fox*," he recalls with a grin. "The horses had to be versatile and so did I. I'd be a Confederate in the morning and a Union soldier in the afternoon. No problem, just a change of uniform! The other movie was *Come Spring* with Walter Brennan, Ann Sheridan, and Edgar Buchanan. In both movies I was riding and driving. I had two black mares, Molly and Belva. In a scene where I was a Northerner, I was supposed to be driving the bullion wagon. I was to get shot and fall out of the wagon. Well, I was willing to get shot, but I still held onto the wagon, so of course that scene was out!

"Molly and Belva never let me down. I had to make a buck so they had to do whatever I asked. I'd drive them in one scene, then I'd unhitch the horses and use them for riding scenes. I could pack them, ride them, drive them both single and double. Those were tough times in the '30s, after the Depression . . . those horses saw me through."

Bab has vivid memories of the tough times, but he is best remembered in the Bay Area for the good times he gave young riders. For 17 years he operated a training stable in Danville which produced some of the top Morgan horses in the 'sixties and 'seventies. Besides training riders in English and Western riding, Bab started an all-pony drill team. The good horsemanship and camaraderie resulting from that experience have ensured the Verdugos a wealth of friends. In spite of a move to Grass Valley six years ago ("Danville started looking more like a city instead of a ranch. Besides, I'd spent a lot of years in Plymouth before I moved to the Bay Area and I'd always liked the Gold Country") Bab has many loyal customers from the Bay Area who won't think of letting anyone else start their young horses. From my own experience I'd say it's Bab and June's hospitality as well as horse knowledge that keeps California horsemen knocking on their door.

I put a little more weight on the accelerator anticipating the "fringe benefits" of a job which requires an afternoon on beautiful Empire Mine Park trails in the company of a first-rate California horseman. I wonder if June is baking raisin cookies or chocolate chip?

Horsemen groups have played such a major role in the California trails movement it would be easy to conclude membership in those groups means nothing but work. What's become of just plain fun and simple enjoyment of your horse and the outdoors? If an overdose of political hassles and work parties is beginning to dampen your enthusiasm as a horse owner, I suggest you head for Wright's Lake the first week in August and make the acquaintance of the Twin Lakes Riding Club. These people know how to have fun!

It was late afternoon when I pulled into the Wright's Lake horse-camping area. I wasn't prepared for the beauty and the size of the area or the ambience of "good old days" when the partnership of man and horse seemed as natural as clouds and rain. Instead of being relegated to some out-of-the-way, "token" area designed to discourage horse use, horses and humans were enjoying their campsites around a choice meadow generous in size and welcoming. Small children tanned themselves on the fat, sun-warmed backs of their ponies who were content to stand chest high in sweet meadow grass. Teenaged riders were coming into camp from the trail, a few campers of various ages were headed out toward the swimming hole, and here and there among the trees I spotted occupied

Twin Lakes Riding Club horsemen come at a gallop across the campsite-fringed meadow reserved for trail riders at Wright's Lake.

hammocks and picket lines. It was truly a sight to gladden the heart of any horseman looking for new adventures.

What I had happened upon was the annual August camping trip of the Twin Lakes Riding Club. Active member Ed Whisman and his wife Meredith, president of the club, were eager to share camping tips pertinent to the area as well as information on the Orangevale-based club.

According to the Whismans the Club was started in the early 1960s by ten families, who liked to get together and ride. The Club is still oriented to families, so riders of all ages are welcome. The Whismans discovered the club in 1965 after their move from San Francisco to Orangevale. Their two children have been active in the wide variety of club-sponsored horse events, and for the entire family the Club is a big part of their lives. Both father and daughter are gymkhana winners!

"Our activities vary from year to year," explained Meredith, "and we always include some gatherings without horses as well as with them so we have something to offer nonriders. The main thing about this Club is that we're family oriented as well as horse oriented. We all learn and have fun together with events such as breakfast rides, English and Western gymkhana, and horse shows at the Club's arena. We have an annual Family Fun Day, trail rides, and poker rides . . . then we give the horse a break and go bowling or roller skating. But best of all is the Wright's Lake trip which is always planned for the first week in August.

"Wright's Lake is the place to go for total relaxation away from the hustle and bustle of city life. The air is clean and healthy . . . You can do things as a family here. You can swim, jog, ride, sail, picnic . . We do what we want when we want, so it's very relaxing." Ed Whisman concurs wholeheartedly about their good fortune in being intimate friends of Wright's Lake. Unlike his wife who grew up on a ranch in Indiana, Ed was a San Francisco boy who had little acquaintance with horses until they purchased their first one in 1963. His enthusiasm for horses and the family focus of the Twin Lakes Riding Club has been fueled by his appreciation for the scenic beauty of Wright's Lake and the friendly cooperation of the U.S. Forest Service rangers.

"We really feel welcome here. It feels like homecoming every August when we pull in and set up camp," says Ed. "Plan to spend a week when you come. It's unbearable to leave any sooner than that."

The Twin Lakes Riding Club welcomes new members. It meets on the first Wednesday of each month. Meeting places vary but are always announced to the public in the *Orangevale News*. Information on shows and trail rides is available at local feed stores and training stables. Prospective members must attend three meetings and be voted on for Club membership. All members receive the Club's monthly *Roundup* magazine. Additional information may be obtained by writing to Roundup, P.O. Box 361, Orangevale, CA 95662.

History comes to life on Gold Country trails, but a slice of history is being made today by Ray Sherman and members of the Gold Country Trails Council. Ray founded the Trails Council in 1977 after he and other Nevada County horsemen were inspired by Sharon Saare's slide show presentation, "Trails for Today and Tomorrow." Dedicated to the development of trails in the Sierra foothills, the Council spent two years working closely with the U.S. Forest Service, getting proper permits and authorizations, plus three additional years of physically working to build the trail.

"The Gold Country Trails Council literally built Pioneer Trail," says Grass Valley horseman Ray Sherman, "and we aren't through yet. This is the most beautiful country that I know of, and there ought to be many more trails than there are. Few people are fortunate enough to live in an area as pretty as this. It should be shared with as many people as possible."

In addition to the newly built 14 miles of trail which parallel the scenic corridor of Hwy. 20, seven more miles of trail are being developed with "infinite possibilities" for connecting trails throughout the Forest Service lands. Ray seems rightfully proud of this significant accomplishment by an all-volunteer crew. The support his group received from trail councils throughout the region encouraged him to reciprocate by serving on the board of the American Trails Foundation.

"The Foundation coordinates the activities of trail councils and organizations nationwide, works for beneficial trail-related legislation, and collects and disburses money for trail projects," says Ray in explaining why his "retirement" has been anything but quiet!

"I worked in Los Angeles County as a fireman for many years," says Ray. "When I retired I moved my family to Nevada County with dreams of country living. The first thing I did was buy a horse! I had wanted a horse ever since I was a 14-year-old working in the

Ray Sherman riding Rushcreek Alta in competition on the American River Ride in 1979.

To explore the trails in the Donner-Emigrant Trail area, I turned to Jon and Carol Saunders, two horsemen whose entire lives testify to their love of riding. Jon's devotion to horses and trails is best summarized in one statement of fact: He works at the Alameda Naval Air Base and commutes two and a half hours each way to his home in Newcastle. "It's the price I'm willing to pay for getting to do what I want." And what Jon wants enough that he'll tackle a five-hour commute is to live in the Sierra hills and ride the trails with his wife Carol.

Jon and Carol have both loved to ride for as long as they can remember. Carol's own experience with commuting on behalf of horses goes back to her school days when she would ride a bus three hours each way to reach a stable! Jon's childhood involvement with horses was limited to summer visits with his grandfather in Texas. Both Jon and Carol feel that their strong desire as children for more horse activity than they were able to have has stamped their lives as adults.

Friendly competitors and lifetime partners, Jon and Carol Saunders finishing up the Castle Rock Challenge Endurance Ride. Carol is on an Appaloosa mare and Jon is riding a 3/4 Arabian gelding.

horse arena at the Los Angeles stock yards. Also as a teenager in the 1940s I cowboyed on some ranches in Nevada and Northern California. Today I own three horses, but this dream didn't come true until after my wife, Laura, and I had raised six children and could claim 15 grandchildren! Out of the whole bunch I'm the only one interested in riding. They all share my feelings about the beauty of the Gold Country, however."

Since his move to Nevada County 15 years ago Ray has tried roping, cutting, trail riding, and driving. He enjoys helping local ranchers with their fall roundups, but his main love as a horseman is endurance riding competition. Carrying him along Gold Country trails are his three endurance horses, pure-bred Arab mare Rushcreek Alta, an Anglo-Arab mare named Raindrop, and an Arab-pinto mare named Liberty Bell. Ray Sherman's retirement is proof of what can happen when an individual doesn't give up his dreams. Pioneer Trail is proof of what can happen when a trails council turns dreams into labor.

"Before we met we had both bought horses and were both involved in endurance riding. What brought us together in the first plce is that our horses were boarded at the same barn. We started riding together and like it, so now it's a permanent arrangement," explains Jon.

The success of the arrangement is reflected in racing miles logged in endurance competition, 2,725 for Jon and 1,800 for Carol. Both are starting young horses for the 1985 racing season, a half Paso mare named Bonnie and a half Arab mare by Danshab named Coco. The newest member of the family is an eight month old Arab stallion who Jon plans to train for endurance racing. The Saunder's commitment to endurance riding is seen not only in his strenuous commute schedule but in Carol's work as membership secretary for theAmerican Endurance Ride Conference at the headquarters in Auburn. Jon was recently elected director of the AERC organization.

If the horses they own have even half the stamina you see in Jon and Carol they'll be tough to beat out on the trail!

The instant bond I felt with Maxine Stahl was inevitable. More than anyone else I had worked with on trails she understood my glazed eyes, my mixture of hyper-enthusiasm and bone-cracking weariness, my sleepless nights filled with ideas, my daily tasks filled with sleep. Maxine understood. She is also writing a book. *Practical Horsemanship for Distance Riding, A Beginner's Manual* is scheduled for publication in summer of 1985. According to Maxine its a "one of a kind book geared specifically toward those who want to get into long distance riding and don't know where to start." It's not surprising that I would turn to an expert for information on the Middle Fork off-shoots of the Tevis Trail. What is surprising is that someone as busy with her own projects as Maxine would stop in the middle of everything to help me with mine.

"In the middle of everything" aptly describes Maxine's activities as a Gold Country trail rider. Her book is the outgrowth of the four years she spent teaching horsemanship to overflowing classes in the Adult Education Program first in San Diego, then Placer and El Dorado counties. She gives private riding lessons, as well, and for her own pleasure is a vigorous competitor in endurance races. She helped organize the Mother Lode Trails Council in 1979 which has worked strenuously and with success to preserve local trails. Still, her perspective on all these achievements is that they are only sidelights to her most meaningful activities as wife, mother, and grandmother.

Hughes

A bright smile from a fast-moving, energetic lady, Carol Saunders on Arabian gelding Wizzard.

"My husband doesn't ride but it's his very supportive attitude, the moral support I get from Paul as my best friend that makes all this possible. I wouldn't have been able to do any of this without him behind me," relates Maxine emphatically.

Cooperation in the Stahl family seems to appear on many different levels. The day I interviewed Maxine in the small town of Cool she was answering my questions with one breath and handling the management responsibilities of the family-owned lumber and feed store with the next. Her office walls were covered with photographs and memorabilia of an active family enjoying each other's company. One photo that caught my eye was of Maxine giving riding lessons to her grandchildren. The lesson horse was her 19 year old mare Seaquest, a Mother's Day gift from her husand in 1969.

"I had ridden all my life, having worked on many cattle ranches in California. My grandfather was in the meatpacking business. There were no feed lots at that time so he went directly to the ranches to get the cattle. Ranches were enormous in those days, thousands of acres, not the five, ten-acre parcels we call ranches today. Granddad needed my help in bringing in the cattle. He'd put

137

me on a cutting horse and tell me which cattle he wanted cut out of the herd. Whenever I fell off he got furious, so I learned fast to stick on a horse! It was fun and exciting, especially since we always got the red carpet treatment at the ranches because we were their customers.

"I had two horses of my own till I was 18 then I did without horses for the next 18 years till Paul surprised me on Mother's Day," recalls Maxine. "He gave me a three-year-old mare who was my partner in learning dressage. From there we went on to competitive and endurance riding."

Maxine still takes every dressage lesson she can. Her advocacy of the discipline is based on her experience that "dressage is a definite aid in distance riding because you learn to communicate with your horse and 'gymnasticize' his athletic movements. I'll never quit dressage because there's always more to learn, but my big love is distance riding. You get to see places you'd never see otherwise and you meet lots of wonderful, interesting people!"

Meeting lots of wonderful, interesting people summarizes my personal experience in exploring trails with Gold Country riders. You'll understand immediately their love of the land once you take to the trails they've recommended. Not all people who love beautiful country want to share it. The welcome mat these horsemen have rolled out for you is a special gift of their time and the land they love. Why aren't they clutching it to themselves as others might? I think I have the answer. So much beauty and joy is experienced riding the Gold Country landscape it can't be contained, so you share it! In that spirit we've ridden and researched these trails. Welcome!

Distance rider and author Maxine Stahl on her grade mare Seaquest compete on the 1980 American River Endurance Ride.

GET READY, GET SET . . . *BEFORE* YOU GO

Horse camping tips from the Twin Lakes Riding Club

A combination of horse sense, common sense and the hard knocks of many years of horse camping experience with the Twin Lakes Riding Club resulted in this checklist provided by Meredith and Ed Whisman. These neighborly, Sacramento horsemen offer it to you with their best wishes! "Sure, it looks like work! But the rewards of good planning are more than worth the effort," says Ed.

Author's note: The Whismans have a cozy motor home so their list doesn't include tents, cooking equipment, etc. But if your facilities are like mine (an air mattress and a ground cover) I highly recommend that you read *Horse Camping* by George Hatley, published in 1981 by the Dial Press, 1 Dag Hammarskjold Plaza, New York, New York 10017.

An excellent *free* publication entitled *Techniques and Equipment for Wilderness Horse Travel* is available from the U.S. Department of Agriculture, U.S. Forest Service Information Office, 630 Sansome St., San Francisco, CA 94111, (415) 536-0122.

TO DO

Get feed
 Calf Manna
 Grain
 Cubes

Make feed boxes

Clean blankets

Check running lines

Get water buckets

Safety check truck
 and trailer

Gas and air for truck
 and trailer

Plan Meals

New canteen

Check raft and paddles and pump (Author's note: Not necessary for landlubbers of course but this crew was headed for Wright's Lake!)

HORSE STUFF TO TAKE

Saddles and pads

Bridles

Halters

Lead ropes

Running lines

Come along

Blankets

Spurs

Fly Spray

Silicone

Medicine, tranquilizers, oil (check with your own vet)

Food-cubes and Calf Manna, Barley, Oats, Corn Molasses

Lariats, water buckets

Brushes and comb

Nails, tools, rake

CLOTHING, ETC.

Jeans and shirts

Underclothes

Handkerchiefs

Light jacket and heavy jacket

Boots and shoes (mocs and tennis)

Swim suits, shorts

Camera

Compass

Maps

Watch

Axe and shovel

Knife

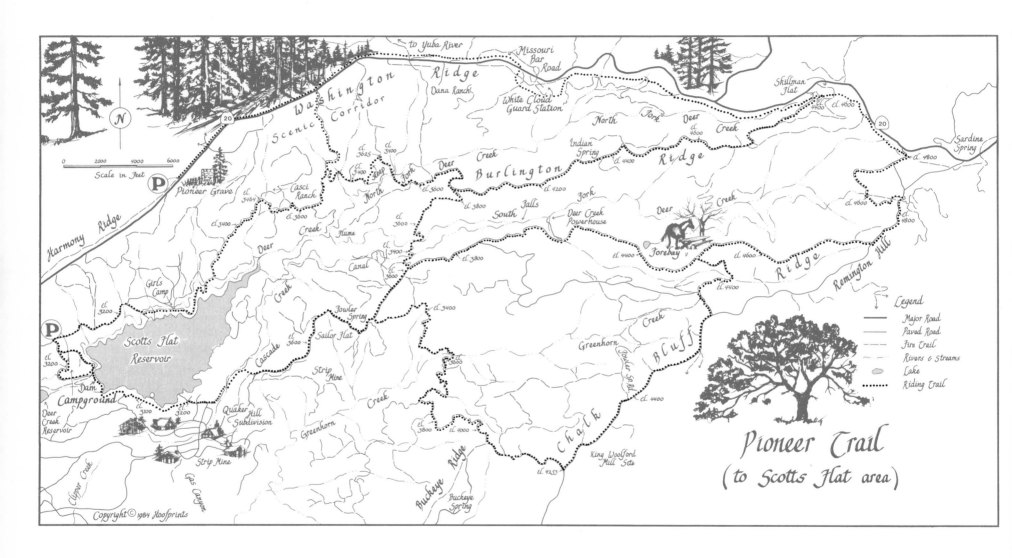

Pioneer Trail
(to Scotts Flat area)

Legend
— Major Road
— Paved Road
— Fire Trail
— Rivers & Streams
Lake
···· Riding Trail

Scale in Feet
0   2000   4000   6000

Copyright© 1984 Hoofprints

PIONEER TRAIL

"The most beautiful country I know . . . It ought to be shared with as many people as possible."

— Ray Sherman

REASONS TO GO: Easy riding through Tahoe National Forest lands along the route known as the Highway 20 scenic corridor . . . 14 miles of riding on well defined trails in a park-like setting framed by cedar and pine forests . . . A great connecting trail . . . it opens up countless hours of riding on U.S. Forest Service dirt roads . . . Look east from Chalk Bluff Ridge for a breathtaking unobstructed view of snow-capped mountains.

SPECIAL FEATURES: Entire length of trail built by volunteers — the dedicated, hard-working members of the Gold Country Trails Council! Pioneer Trail is named because of its proximity to historic Pioneer Grave . . . Nearby picnic and camping areas with an abundance of streams and springs for refreshing rest stops . . . or allow some time after a ride to enjoy one of the many excellent restaurants in the Gold Country communities of Grass Valley and Nevada City . . . you'll bask in the aura of the California Gold Rush!

LOCATION: Nevada County eight miles east of Nevada City on Hwy. 20.

WHERE TO PARK: Take Hwy. 80 to Auburn, then go north on Hwy. 49 to Nevada City. Pick up Hwy. 20 which is a good, paved road for trailer pulling and go approximately eight miles to the large parking area opposite the Pioneer Grave site on the south side of Hwy. 20 . . . There's good visibility when you turn into the parking area and plenty of room for up to 30 rigs . . . No parking problems, even on weekends . . . No amenities in the parking area . . . Nearby White Cloud and Skillman Flat campgrounds are for people only, but you can tie your horses outside the area and use the facilities.

Gold Country horsemen have every reason to be proud of their all-volunteer built trail.

View of Pioneer Trail leading out from staging area just off Hwy. 20.

TRAIL FEATURES: Easy side-by-side riding on five-foot-wide Pioneer Trail which is well marked and cushioned by pine needles . . . An addition of seven miles to this trail is planned for the near future . . . A combination of trail and fireroads yields about 40 miles of riding around the perimeter of the area and many more miles within . . . Pioneer Trail is the only marked route.

ACCOMMODATIONS: Day use at the Pioneer Grave parking area . . . Overnight parking for horsemen in new horse camping are at Scotts Flat Campground. It has six campsites with firepits and tables . . . area is large enough to accommodate 20 trailers. . . . Easy trail access from camp area . . . Campers must not leave horses unattended . . . For reservations phone Scotts Flat headquarters (916) 265-5302. Horseless members of the family can enjoy swimming, waterskiing, and fishing at Scotts Flat Reservoir . . . Concession stand at the main campground. Nearby Five Mile House restaurant serves sandwiches and dinners.

FEES: No charge for use of trails . . . Camping fees at Scotts Flat campground.

PARK SERVICES: A patrolman and fire crew work out of White Cloud Guard Station during the summer . . . Rangers patrol the area in trucks.

PARK RULES: No smoking while riding on the trail or roads . . . Dogs and fishing are OK . . . Grazing is permitted but there is very little feed in the area.

WEATHER: Ray's favorite months to ride here are May and June . . . trail is usable from spring to late fall . . . Snow in the winter blankets the trail system and gives it a rest.

 CAUTION: Wildlife here includes mosquitoes and yellow jackets . . . watch out for poison oak . . . Be aware of the sharp drop-off on the trail as it connects with the Forebay picnic area . . . Occasional public timber cutting may cause more traffic than usual along some stretches . . . In consideration of the many private property owners in the area, stick to the trail and the fireroads.

141

*It's day use only at Empire Mine State Park's grassy staging area, but for **group** overnight stays the Nevada County Horsemen are happy to share their very inviting club and camping facilities Phone: (916) 273-1507.*

EMPIRE MINE
STATE HISTORIC PARK

You're in the heart of the Gold Country with lots to see from the saddle and on foot . . . You don't have to like history to ride these forested backcountry trails, but it's an added plus if you do . . .

— Bab Verdugo

Grass Valley horseman Bab Verdugo introduces Audrey Hubbard to one of the historic features of Empire Mine State Park.

REASONS TO GO: Almost 800 acres of yellow-pine forest highlighted by the site of the largest, richest hardrock gold mine in California . . . Since the 1850 discovery of gold in a quartz outcropping, until the mine's closure in 1956, an estimated 5,800,000 ounces of gold were extracted utilizing 367 miles of underground passages . . . Before you hit the trail relive history on foot as you visit the historic mine yards and the magnificent formal gardens . . . Pay homage here to the memory of hardworking mules vital to the Mine's operation . . . Ride a mule on Empire Mine trails and you'll be right at home . . .

SPECIAL FEATURES: Historic structures and charming museum will put you in the appropriate mood to discover the beauty of Park trails . . . Little Wolf Creek, the first location of the miners in 1848 . . . Hardrock Trail and Osborn Hill Loop Trail, well marked with historical signs, add interest to your ride.

LOCATION: In the beautiful rural community of Grass Valley, California, where Gold Rush history is alive and well in the downtown area as well as the Park . . . From San Francisco Bay Area take Hwy. 80 to the Hwy. 49 Grass Valley exit. Go about 23 miles to the Empire St. exit, turn right onto E. Empire St. Proceed for 1.3 miles, crossing S. Auburn St., to the well marked entrance of the Park on the right.

WHERE TO PARK: On your way to the Park entrance you will pass a large, locked parking area on the right which is reserved for equestrian parking. Do not park here without first going to the main entrance and requesting the gate combination from the Park ranger. You will also be given a trail map and a report on trail conditions before you start out. Reservations are not necessary but the rangers request that you phone ahead if more than one rig is involved . . . The parking area is very generous in size . . . there are no special amenities here so tie to your trailer and bring your own water . . . Horses will find water along the trail in Wolf Creek.

TRAIL FEATURES: Mostly level riding on very well marked fireroads . . . almost impossible to get lost although much of the riding is through dense forest areas . . . Enter Hardrock Trail from the parking area and ride toward the Osborn Hill Loop Trail . . . staying on the periphery of the restricted area (no horses in the mining areas and the adjacent buffer zone) you can extend the limited mileage in the west side of the Park by crossing Hwy. 174 and picking up the trail straight across the road . . . go down an embankment, turn to the right and follow the trail to a fireroad called Pipeline Rd.

ACCOMMODATIONS: Day use only. For information call or write: Empire Mine State Historic Park, 10791 E. Empire St., Grass Valley, CA 95945 (916) 273-8522.

PARK FEES: No fees for trail use.

PARK SERVICES: A delightful Visitor's Center featuring special group tours and Mother Lode country memorabilia such as cards, photos, books and maps . . . Free maps for trail use . . . From April through November a movie and slide shows add to your knowledge of mining activity in the Gold Rush days.

PARK RULES: Stay on the trails and ride only in areas designated for horses . . . Park is open 9 a.m. to 6 p.m. from April 1 - Oct. 31. It closes at 5 p.m. between Nov. 1 and March 31.

WEATHER: Park is open year-round but spring and fall are the most popular months for trail riding . . . Bring plenty of drinking water if you're riding in the summer.

 CAUTION: It is critically important to stay on the trails . . . Open mine shafts and plugged mine shafts are dangerous (sometimes the plug rots out) . . . Keeping to the trails is also a good way to avoid contact with poison oak.

143

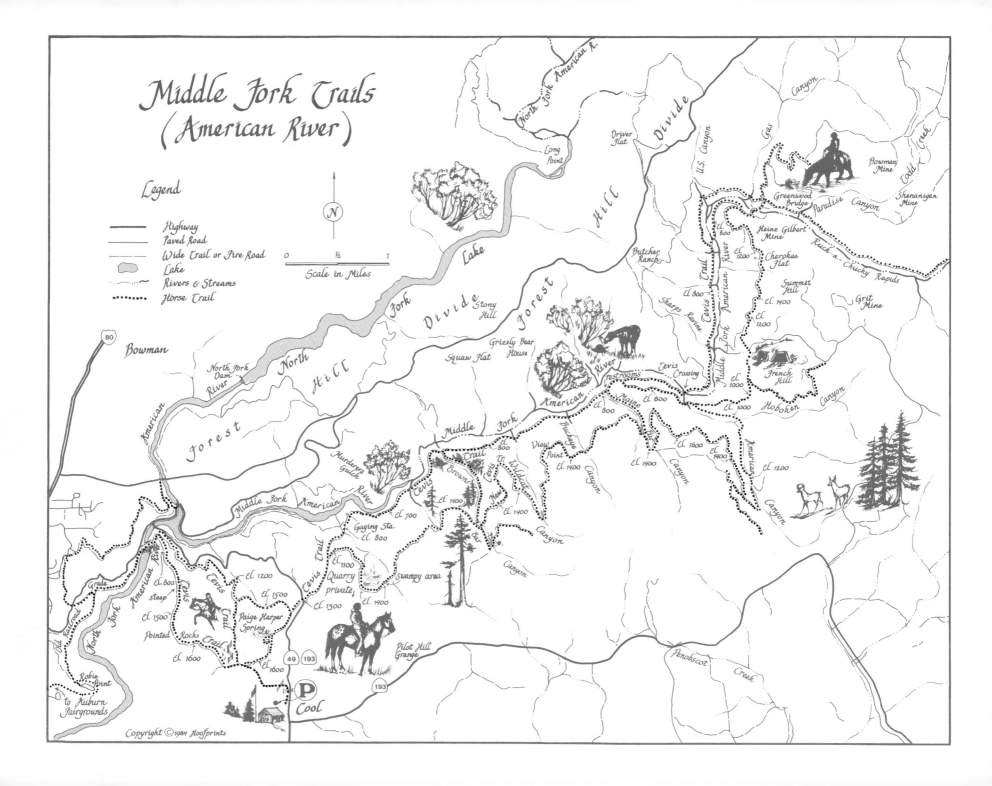

MIDDLE FORK TRAILS

"The essence of the Mother Lode country . . . Challenging trails along rivers and creeks where the gold mining took place . . . Beautiful, rugged, and full of wildlife."

— Maxine Stahl

Large parking area behind Northside Fire Station.

REASON TO GO: Views along the trails of the Middle Fork of the American River . . . Gorgeous views of the American River Canyon as you climb away from the river . . . Varied terrain with fig, oak and pine trees, grapevines and ferns . . . Historical remnants from the Gold Mining days — Murderer's Gulch, Cherokee Flat, Grizzly Bear House, Grit Mine and Ruck-a-Chucky Rapids add interest to your ride! Bear and cougar tracks to keep you sharp . . . Real adventure riding!

SPECIAL FEATURES: Fishing and swimming in the calmer sections of the river . . . Trail crosses many small creeks, a refreshing feature on hot summer rides . . . Many nice picnic areas.

LOCATION: In the town of Cool between Auburn and Placerville. Going either way the road is narrow and winding for about three miles . . . Drive carefully as you'll be tempted to look at the beautiful scenery instead of the road! From Placerville take Hwy. 49 north to Cool approximately 17 miles. From Auburn take Hwy. 49 south to Cool approximately 6 miles.

WHERE TO PARK: Staging area for horses is at a large, gravel lot behind the Northside Fire District station. It's right off the highway on the west side of Hwy. 49. Parking area holds six to eight rigs, fewer in winter as ground is less firm. Weekend parking is not usually a problem . . . Enter the trail system directly across side street opposite the driveway . . . Head north toward Pointed Rocks on the Tevis Trail . . . Pass through two gates (close the gates, cattle are being leased). Plans are under way for a

horse watering area at the parking lot. For now use a bucket to get water from the Fire Station.

ACCOMMODATIONS: Day use only. For overnight parking use the Fairgrounds in Auburn phone: (916) 885-6281. NATRC has also developed a bed and breakfast directory for horsemen on the road! Write to: NATRC, P.O. Box 20315, El Cajon, CA 92021.

TRAIL FEATURES: A very popular area with endurance riders . . . great trails for conditioning your horse for competitive rides . . . Trail varies from flat to steep; rocky in some areas but generally excellent footing . . . It's a 10-mile ride from the staging area to the trail paralleling Sliger Mine . . . several loop trails are possible within this mileage, including Brown's Bar Loop and Main Bar Loop . . . These well maintained trails are a combination of wide fireroads and single file trails . . . Brown's Bar Loop is the recommended route for less experienced trail riders . . . Main Bar is extremely steep for two miles and not good for beginners.

FEES: None.

PARK SERVICES: California State Department of Parks and Recreation rangers patrol fireroads . . . They are assisted by a segment of Auburn unit of the Folsom Volunteer Horse Patrol . . . For further information phone California State Department of Parks and Recreation at Folsom (916) 988-0205, at Cool (916) 885-4527.

PARK RULES: Dogs are allowed . . . grazing along the trail is permitted . . . Fishing is OK with a Fish and Game permit . . . No smoking or overnight camping and no firearms.

WEATHER: Park is open all year. The trail from Cool to Main Bar is good year-round but it's best to avoid other sections after a rain as they can be quite slippery.

CAUTION: Stay on the trail to avoid encroaching on private property . . . All river crossings are potentially hazardous, especially when river is up before July. The crossing used by the Tevis riders is designated as Tevis Crossing on the map . . . It is considered the least dangerous of the three crossings, but still beware of rocky footing.

A wilderness setting? No. The riders are just across the road getting cold drinks in the little town of Cool.

BLACK OAK EQUESTRIAN CAMPGROUND

All the necessities for a great camping experience with your horse, plus the added bonus of being isolated from the general campground area . . . an excellent area for families and large groups . . .

— Marianne Jordan

If crisp, clean mountain air turns you on you'll love this High Sierra feeling at just 3,500 feet! . . . Miles of trail riding around the lake and pleasant summer temperatures make this an inviting place . . .

— Carol Jones

Gold country horsemen Carol Jones and Leonard Jordan proudly display improvements to equestrian area.

REASONS TO GO: Deep forest riding around beautiful Jenkinson Lake with a water surface area of 640 acres! . . . Wide variety of terrain ranging from flowery meadows to heavy timber . . . Many scenic lake views, plus the reward of a dip in the lake after a long trail ride.

SPECIAL FEATURES: Jenkinson Lake is the principal source of water for the El Dorado Irrigation District which operates and manages the Sly Park Recreation Area . . . Bordering the southeast end of the lake is the Mormon Emigrant Trail . . . Fishing, swimming, and all types of boating to fill the time of any horseless members of your family while you enjoy the trails! . . . This is truly a has-something-for-everyone recreation area.

LOCATION: Sly Park Recreation Area is in El Dorado County, 42 miles east of Sacramento via Hwy. 50. Take the Sly Park Rd. exit at Pollock Pines, turn right on Sly Park Rd. and travel a little over five miles on good, but winding, road to the Park entrance. Ask the ranger at the gate for the key to the locked equestrian parking area which is one-eighth mile further up the road.

WHERE TO PARK: Turn in at the Black Oak Equestrian Campground entrance at the corner of Sly Park Rd. and Mormon Emigrant Trail. Mormon Emigrant Trail is closed in winter and not always clearly defined on maps, yet it offers access from Hwy. 88 approximately five miles below Silver Lake, over Iron Mountain, and ends at the lake and equestrian camp . . . Twenty-one individual sites

(both drive-through and back-in) provide ample parking for horse trailers, camper trucks, and R.V.s . . . there's a large assembly area for overflow parking.

TRAIL FEATURES: Approximately 12 miles of horse trail in Sly Park with many more miles possible on adjacent logging roads . . . Trails are newly constructed by the California Conservation Corps crews and various horse groups (including the family crew headed by Marianne Jordan!) . . . "New" trail means narrow trails in many areas and minimal marking, but the enthusiasm and dedication of both Park officials and trail users is responsible for continual improvement of the trail system . . . There are enough steep areas to make this a good conditioning trail, but not enough

146

mileage within the Park for a competitive ride . . .

To enter the trail system around the lake: Ride out the entrance of the Black Oak Equestrian Campground and cross Mormon Emigrant Trail at its intersection with Sly Park Rd. Four white posts mark the entrance to the trail system (a sign may be there by now). Trail will be marked from this point . . . Ride toward the boat ramp following the blue ribbon markers on this single-file trail to Hazel Creek Meadow . . . plan your rest stop or picnic here as you'll find shade, a grassy area, rest rooms, and trees to tether your horse . . . cedar rail fencing designates the area, so you can't miss it . . . A unique feature of the ride around the Lake is that the equestrian trail is separate from the hiking trail . . .

ACCOMMODATIONS: The generous cooperation of the El Dorado Irrigation District and Sly Park officials, plus the spirited labor of the Jordan family and their friends, have produced a horse camping area that is unsurpassed for thoughtful design and convenience . . . The camp is designed primarily for group use and by reservation . . . The third week of each month is set aside for individual horsemen and their families . . . It's a very popular area and early reservations are encouraged. Phone (916) 622-4513 or write to El Dorado Irrigation District, P.O. Box 1608, Placerville, CA 95667. The camp is open to the general public on weekdays if not reserved. Facilities include tables, pipe corrals, barbecue pits, fire rings, saddle racks, vault type toilets, water for horses and humans, and some electricity . . . Each site has a hitching post.

FEES: An appropriate fee schedule is being worked out but will be in the following range: Group rate, $50 per night for first 50 people, $1 for each additional person . . . Nonreservation camping, $6 per night per each motor vehicle . . . Day use, $2.50 per day . . . Special rates for senior citizens.

Scenic lakeside riding but horsemen are strongly advised to stick to the trail and not to trust the footing of the water's edge.

PARK SERVICES: Rangers who really care about your enjoyment of the area! . . . The El Dorado Irrigation District will provide you with a map and a brochure (at main Park entrance) which is of general interest . . . a map designed for trail riders is in the works!

PARK RULES: Park is open year-round . . . leashed dogs are allowed in camping areas but not on the trails . . . Firearms and chainsaws are not allowed in the Park . . . Quiet hours are observed between 10 p.m. and 6 a.m.

WEATHER: Delightful summer temperatures are an added bonus, with an average of 75 to 80 degrees dropping into the 60s at night . . . The south side of the Lake offers cooler, shaded riding, so the Jordans suggest starting your ride on the north side in the cool morning hours and riding back on the south side in the afternoon . . . An average rainfall of 40 inches is received between November and April and considerable portions of the trail are muddy and slippery . . . phone rangers for trail conditions (916) 644-2545.

 CAUTION: These are new trails which are still quite rough in areas . . . horses should be well shod . . . Carry your own drinking water. There is some stream water on the trails for horses . . . The trails take you close to the Lake which offers a very scenic ride. However, **the water's edge is not safe footing for your horse** . . . you can't depend on the shoreline to support your horse's weight . . . Bring mosquito repellent and rejoice in the fact that there's no poison oak at this altitude!

147

Mule Spring sign reads: "Watering and resting point on Donner Trail. This was the furthest point to which pack animals could travel in bringing food to the stranded Donner Party in the winter of 1846-47. From here rescue parties carried 50-pound packs through deep snow to Donner Lake."

Photos by Jon Saunders

Woodsy staging area is a welcome feature for summer riding.

148

LOWELL HILL ROAD
(area of Donner Emigrant Trail)

Very easy riding through beautiful forest lands . . . an area of historical interest with the diggings of Dutch Flat and the route of the Donner party nearby . . .
— Jon and Carol Saunders

It's hard to get lost with landmarks like this — the penstock leading to Dutch Flat powerhouse.

REASONS TO GO: A great trail system for beginning trail riders or people wishing to train and condition a young horse . . . very easy terrain . . . generally level riding on logging roads.

SPECIAL FEATURES: Beautiful canyon views . . . Mule Springs is the site where wagons carrying supplies to the ill-fated Donner Party could go no further . . . Dutch Flat was on the route of thousands of immigrants who flooded into the Gold Country in the 1800s . . . Dutch Flat was the end-of-track for regular transportation service for the Central Pacific Railroad Line penetrating the Sierra, its creation due to tireless Chinese laborers and hundreds of mule and horse teams . . . Pack a history book in your saddle bag for the fullest enjoyment of this area!

LOCATION: In Placer County between Dutch Flat and Highway 20 . . . The Dutch Flat exit is 60 miles northeast of Sacramento and 70 miles west of Reno off Interstate 80 . . . Road conditions for trailer pulling are excellent.

WHERE TO PARK: Take Dutch Flat exit off Hwy. 80 25.63 miles east of Auburn, turning immediately left onto Ridge Rd. Continue 0.4 mile to Sacramento St.; turn left toward Dutch Flat. Follow this street for one mile, across a railroad track and into the town of Dutch Flat. Curve right onto Main St. and watch for the post office on the left (0.1 mile). Turn left at the post office and drive 1 block (100 yds.) to the

staging area . . . According to PG&E permits are not required for recreational use of this area in spite of posting . . . Very large parking area with plenty of room for turning large rigs . . . No amenities in the parking area but there are rest rooms at Hwy. 80 exit about 1.5 mile from staging area . . . Saddle up. Continue straight on the road (north) past a pond and downhill. Keep following the road to the river, across the dam, past a power generator, uphill, and past another pond. Swing to the right at the junction with Lowell Hill Rd. This sounds complicated, but just follow the road.

TRAIL FEATURES: Twenty miles of wide, well maintained logging roads excellent for "schooling" on the trail . . . not marked consistently but stick to the obvious road and you'll find it hard to get lost . . . Trail is mainly level with only one descent and climb . . . an abundance of fireroads crisscross the main trail . . . great for exploring! A tiny pond on the right lies next to the otherwise unmarked trail to Mule Spring . . . nice open grassy area perfect for a picnic or rest. Connect with the Pacific Crest Trail at Emigrant Gap . . . Shady trails with the added interest of going around Dutch Flat powerhouse and on to Dutch Flat north forebay . . .

Competitive trail rides and carriage drives possible here with special permits. Contact U.S. Department of Forestry, 13760 Lincoln Way, Auburn, CA 95603. Phone (916) 885-4517.

ACCOMMODATIONS: Day use only . . . convenient to restaurants, stores, and gas stations along I-80 . . . bring your own drinking water . . . water for horses in swimming hole along the trail.

FEES: None.

PARK SERVICES: Very friendly, knowledgeable rangers who patrol in trucks . . . maps available at the U.S. Forest Service office.

PARK RULES: Open year-round.

WEATHER: Hot summers here! . . . but trails are shaded in many areas and don't forget the swimming hole . . . Phone ahead to Forest Service office if you're planning a late fall ride . . . possible snow on the trails!

 CAUTION: "No problems with this area," say Gold Country riders Jon and Carol Saunders . . . "A great place to relax as you ride the trails."

149

WRIGHT'S LAKE
(access to Desolation Wilderness)

Everything for the family here . . . Beautiful riding trails entering the wilderness, but you can also swim, jog, sail and picnic. A place for total relaxation.

— Meredith Whisman

REASONS TO GO: Access to the spectacular scenery of the 63,475-acre Desolation Wilderness Area of the El Dorado National Forest . . . beauty and adventure guaranteed as you and your horse challenge rugged, rocky trails or bask in the splendor of flower-banked mountain meadows . . . The overwhelming phenomena of nature and geologic history form a magnificent backdrop for trails which invite endless exploring and a lifetime of return trips . . . the spectacle of the Sierra is all the reason you need to hitch up and go!

SPECIAL FEATURES: Camping areas scented with pine . . . rampant wildflowers in July and August . . . fishing in stocked creeks, with numerous lakes offering incredible scenic beauty . . . rugged granite terrain . . . glaciated canyons under the reign of majestic volcanic rock . . . plan to see snow as late as July!

LOCATION: South of Lake Tahoe in the El Dorado National Forest, bordering Desolation Wilderness . Eight miles off Hwy. 50 on Wright's Lake Rd. . . . nearby communities are Kyburz and Strawberry.

WHERE TO PARK: Wright's Lake Rd. exits off Hwy. 50 and is a paved, steady uphill climb for three and a half miles to Chimney Flat. For the last five miles the road levels out and changes to a packed rock surface leading into the camping areas. The Wright's Lake Horse Camp is at the south end of the parking lot . . . a generous-sized, scenic area with abundant room for large groups and large rigs . . . park under the trees bordering the meadow, and highline horses in campground area.

TRAIL FEATURES: A popular area with adventurous trailriders for over 20 years! . . . The trails are too challenging and the scenery too beautiful to recommend this as a day-use area . . . plan to spend a weekend at least, but a week would be better! **Trails are very rocky,** and well shod, sure-footed horses are a must if you are to enjoy all the trail possibilities here. Still, many riders enjoy this area on a less strenuous basis . . . they relax at the beautiful campsite and stick to the less challenging, but still inspiring, fireroad trails which are plentiful . . . riding toward Lake Sylvia, Beauty Lake, Lyons Creek, or toward the historic Wilson Ranch (a fourth generation family of cattlemen) is considered easier . . . If you're ready for more rugged riding and are prepared to tackle narrow trails, sometimes steep and slick with granite, ride toward Twin Lakes, a spectacular and difficult three miles . . . The Orangevale-based Twin Lakes Riding Club takes its name from many years of riding and camping in this area.

ACCOMMODATIONS: Beautiful campsite for horsemen! . . . a very special tree-rimmed meadow reserved for trail riders warrants a long visit. Phone El Dorado National Forest Information Center (916) 644-6048 for current weather and trail information and for group reservations.

FEES: None.

PARK SERVICES: Very friendly rangers who welcome your use of the horse camp and trails . . . A resident ranger (summer only) is located adjacent to the parking area. He can provide you with wilderness permits, or write ahead to El Dorado National Forest Information Center, 3070 Camino Heights Drive, Camino, CA 95609, (916) 644-6048 . . . An adequate trail map is available at the campsite or through the U.S. Forest Service offices.

PARK RULES: Wright's Lake Horse Camp is only a few miles from the Desolation Wilderness boundary, so wilderness regulations are in order. The regulations along with the information and advice compiled by the U.S. Forest Service will be helpful in planning your trip . . . a reprint is included in this text . . . Horses are not allowed in Wright's Lake.

WEATHER: Snow till July or August is not unusual here, so be sure to phone rangers for up-to-date report . . . "Hail the size of golf balls" reported members of the Twin Lakes Riding Club after a sudden summer storm . . . somehow their enthusiasm for the area was still intact! Bring a heavy blanket for your horse no matter how hot the daytime weather appears to be . . . and don't forget the mosquito repellent for your own comfort; they are particularly vicious in early summer.

CAUTION: Veteran Wright's Lake campers Meredith and Ed Whisman caution horsemen to pay close attention to their animals . . . colic can be induced by a change in the environment . . . so check with your veterinarian as you prepare for your wilderness trip . . . When organizing a group ride the Whismans come prepared with mineral oil and tranquilizers in the event of colic . . . Granite on the trails can be very slick . . . Placerville horsewoman Patty Logan recommends that you acclimate your horse at home to cows and cow bells before hitting wilderness trails . . . Another caution: don't let all the concerns deter the adventure . . . Wright's Lake is an experience too beautiful to be missed!

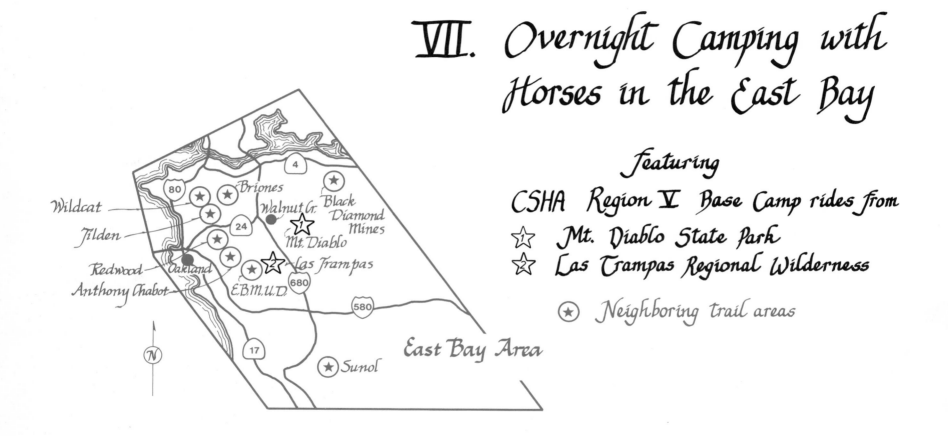

VII. Overnight Camping with Horses in the East Bay

featuring

CSHA Region V Base Camp rides from

☆¹ Mt. Diablo State Park

☆² Las Trampas Regional Wilderness

⊛ Neighboring trail areas

East Bay Area

Wildcat

Tilden

Redwood

Anthony Chabot

Briones

Walnut Cr.

Black Diamond Mines

Mt. Diablo

Las Trampas

Oakland

E.B.M.U.D.

Sunol

Camping with horses at Barbecue Terrace on Mt. Diablo dates back to the early 1940s. Thanks to the planning policies of the State Parks systems and the East Bay Regional Park District, with its 53,000 parkland acres in Alameda and Contra Costa Counties, this activity is still possible today.

OVERNIGHT CAMPING WITH HORSES IN THE EAST BAY

An Interview With Bob Cooper

BOB COOPER *is just the man to talk to about camping with horses in the East Bay—he rode on the first California State Horsemen's Association, Region V, Seven-Day Ride in 1975 and has been an organizer and participant in the ride every year since. In 1984 the Seven-Day Ride changed format and became the Region V Base Camp Ride featuring the camping areas and trails of Mt. Diablo State Park and Las Trampas Regional Park. Again, Bob was one of the organizers, trail workers and trail masters which made the ride possible. The immediate success of the ride — 70 riders of all ages and varying levels of trail experience — inspires an enthusiastic discussion of the history of the Region V Ride, what it has accomplished for trails in the East Bay and tips on organizing your own camping trip with horses. When he's not volunteering his time on a trail crew or leading a trail ride mounted on his appendix Quarter Horse gelding, Bob is a computer programmer at Lawrence Livermore National Laboratory. Originally a city boy from Chicago, Bob credits a summer on a dude ranch for getting him "hooked on horses." His love of riding has greatly benefited both East Bay trails and Bay Area horsemen.*

Q: How did the CSHA Region V Ride get started?

Cooper: As you know the East Bay Regional Park District has provided a fantastic Park system throughout the East Bay. Our goal, as horsemen, was to see these Parks linked together by connecting trails so we could introduce more people to trail riding, as well as to the Parks . . . We needed some distance instead of just a few miles in various unconnected Parks.

Q: It's generally known that you succeeded with your goal. But how receptive were the Park officials. Was it a fight or a cooperative venture?

Cooper: Definitely a cooperative venture! From the beginning the Park District has been very positive in working with horsemen groups . . . I can't even imagine putting on a ride of this magnitude without

the blessing and the help of the Park . . . We would plan a ride, see what was feasible and say to the District, "We need a connecting trail from here to here. Can we possibly get it?" The District was very responsive. It would become an action item for them and we gradually started making a loop, the "Golden Loop" as the founders, Bruce Lee and Heber Brown, called it.

Q: Considering all the Trail Councils and horse clubs I know who've had protracted struggles with various agencies to preserve trail access for horses, that just sounds too easy! What's behind all this cooperation?

Cooper: Nothing mysterious. Just some good planners working for the Park District and some dedicated horsemen willing to do their share and more to make it happen. It hasn't just been hard-working horsemen, either. All the members of the East Bay Trails Council, hikers, joggers and bikers have worked real hard for a successful trail system. We've been particularly fortunate in the leadership we've had from the EBRPD, Hulet Hornbeck, for instance. Over the years we've developed a great relationship, a real rapport with Park managers and staff in the various Parks and in the East Bay water property, too (EBMUD). It hasn't been just one person who's been a good connection. We've worked directly with different Park managers, and recently most of our dealings have been with Bob Doyle, Park District Trails Coordinator . . . Bob has been a strong lobbyist with the Park directors for the financing of the new trails. It's been pretty well established that if the Park will just give us the place the horsemen will come in and put up the tie stalls, purchase materials, and do the installation . . . The Park has put in the waterlines, done any grading required, and brought in portable toilets for camping areas.

The ranger at Las Trampas (Charles Johnson) was absolutely thrilled when we started preparing

an area for the Base Camp Ride. He saw us put in over 300 hours of volunteer help in this one Park alone . . . 200 hours on the trails and 100 hours on the campsite. He was delighted with people like Gene Anderson and his friends who like to get out on the trails and flex a muscle or two . . . Gene is a retired Battalion Chief of the San Francisco Fire Department who spends about three days a week working on Las Trampas trails as a volunteer. With the Park's blessing he has put in key linking trails that get riders off the fireroads.

Q. Las Trampas was one of your Base Camp areas, I know, and I'd like you to describe it as a camping area. But first, could you explain why the decision was made by the Region V Seven-Day Ride Committee to give up camping throughout the Park system, in favor of the Base Camp idea?

Cooper: Our initial goal had been accomplished. Connecting trails between East Bay parks are an established fact, plus we had introduced new riders to the trails as we had hoped. Depending on the weather, between 35 to 75 riders have participated each year since 1975. The next factor was cost. Moving our campsite everyday meant we were dependent on a caterer and a hay truck to feed people and horses. That was the major cost of the ride. With base camp rides where we stay put and ride out on different trails everyday we can do our own cooking and people bring in their own hay, cutting costs. Also, we were finding that more and more people coming on the rides were having a hard time taking off work for seven days and preferred the Base Camp Rides where they had more of a choice in length of stay. The rides are attracting a variety of people, and frankly, some people preferred less strenuous camping. You can put more comfort into a base camp as opposed to a camp that has to be moved every day.

Q. You say "variety of people"? How would you describe your riders?

Cooper: The ride is open to everyone with a horse. We have no other requirements as such. We get all ages and all levels of ability. There's an equal balance between men and women. There are some teenagers, but it's mostly an adult ride because it's held during the school year. We've had riders come from all over the state, but the San Ramon Valley Horsemen make up about a third of the ride.

We do tell people that almost any trail in the East Bay requires some athletic ability on the part of horse and rider. We encourage people to condition their horses well before a ride, but we try to accommodate horses in poorer condition and less experienced trail riders. We can do that by offering a variety of rides out of the Base Camp. It's unfortunate, but we have to suggest to some people that they not finish the ride because of a poorly conditioned horse. In that case we have a trailer standing by. A couple of days this past year we had temperatures over 100 degrees and we had some horses really feeling the heat. We like to think our ride inspires people to learn how to take better care of their horses, and to get themselves in condition too!

Q. Could you briefly describe how a ride works? How do you organize a ride and what kind of schedule do you follow on the trail?

Cooper: Along about September we plan the where and the when of the ride. We get our flyers put together in time for the California State Horsemen's Association statewide convention in the Fall. CSHA sponsors the ride and covers it with CSHA insurance. We also get a blanket policy which covers the Park District. About ten workers, plus spouses and various friends, form the basic committee that plans the ride and sets up camp. The main thing about planning a ride like this is that we try to remain as flexible as possible . . . We take into account the experience and physical condition of each horse and rider . . . We customize the ride with an easy route for our beginners and a tougher, longer ride for the "gung ho" riders who want more miles in a day.

In 1984 our first Base Camp Ride was camped at Las Trampas. The first day we made a loop of Las Trampas trails, riding from Bollinger Canyon to the east side of Las Trampas using a new connecting trail put in by Gene Anderson.

On the second day from Las Trampas we rode through EBMUD land over to Moraga. The heat really got to the horses on this ride. We were all pretty weary when we arrived at the grounds of the Moraga Horsemen's Association for lunch.

On the third day we were still trying to recover from the second day so we relaxed around camp and took a short ride around Bollinger Canyon. That isn't all bad! For a lot of people the highlight of the ride is the friends you make, the socializing that takes place before you settle down to a barbecue dinner. A nice tradition of these rides that's developed over the years is Bruce Lee's wife, Bobbie, bringing up caviar hors d'oeuvres the last day of the ride. Then there's Larry Read, a past president of CSHA, who brings up a cook trailer providing cooking facilities for up to 70 people!

Our second Base Camp Ride was staged at Mt. Diablo at the Mitchell Canyon staging area. We rode mostly on the north side of the mountain on trails put in by the Concord-Mt. Diablo Trail Ride Association. On the third day we rode the trail to Eagle Peak. That trail was originally put in to accommodate one of the first Seven-Day Rides. Our group was probably the first to use that particular trail.

Q. How would you summarize the results of all your hard work in putting this ride together?

Cooper: We've given a lot more people an outdoor, overnight camping experience than would have had it without this organization . . . It's a great ride for East Bay riders without horse trailers who have been able to join the ride at various points . . . A lot of neophytes have had a good introduction to camping with their horse . . . A lot of people have happy memories they'll never forget.

Trail boss Bob Cooper on his Quarter Horse gelding, winner of the Concord-Mt. Diablo Trail Trials in 1984.

155

GOOD OLD DAYS AND . . .

This 1944 photo first appeared in the Oakland Tribune. Do any of these trail riding chefs bring back memories for you? Left to right: Lloyd A. Martinelli of Ygnacio Valley; Kent M. Weaver, nationally known horse show and trail ride judge; Paul Brunelle, from Concord, chief cook; George W. Smith of Walnut Creek, trail master; Ray M. Walsh of Concord, ride chairman for Concord-Mt. Diablo Trail Ride Association.

What's a trail ride without a good cook? Quality control test being administered by Paul Brunelle on 1944 Mt. Diablo Trail Ride.

Concord-Mt. Diablo Trail riders leaving Barbecue Terrace for journey back to Concord (early 1940s).

GOOD NEW DAYS IN THE EAST BAY

It is a tribute to the planning and hard work of the many horsemen groups in the East Bay area, as well as the farsighted policies of the East Bay Regional Park District, that the trail rides of the 1940s are still going strong today. There have been some changes, though. As late as the 1960s you had miles and miles of riding across East Bay hills, uninterupted by subdivisions and highways, just to meet up with the group. Then the "ride" began. When the "ride" ended you didn't load your horse in a trailer, but still had miles and miles ahead of you on your way home! Instead of sticking to trails in Park lands you crossed open country as a guest of one of the area's many ranchers. Most of the ranchers were avid horsemen themselves, and were hospitable to responsible riders who didn't forget to close the gates!

The changing character of the modern-day trail ride has only intensified the need of horsemen to protect their access to trails so that future generations will have the pleasure of horses and open country available to them.

Riders in the 1980s keep up the tradition on a Mt. Diablo trail ride.

Sandy Darby

In the 1940s horsemen generally rode from their backyard paddocks over the hills to meet for a Mt. Diablo trail ride. In the 1980s the horse trailer plays a major role. Generally horses must be transported from a boarding stable along busy streets and highways to the beginning of the trail ride . . . Times change but the important thing is horses are still with us and the ride goes on!

Sandy Darby

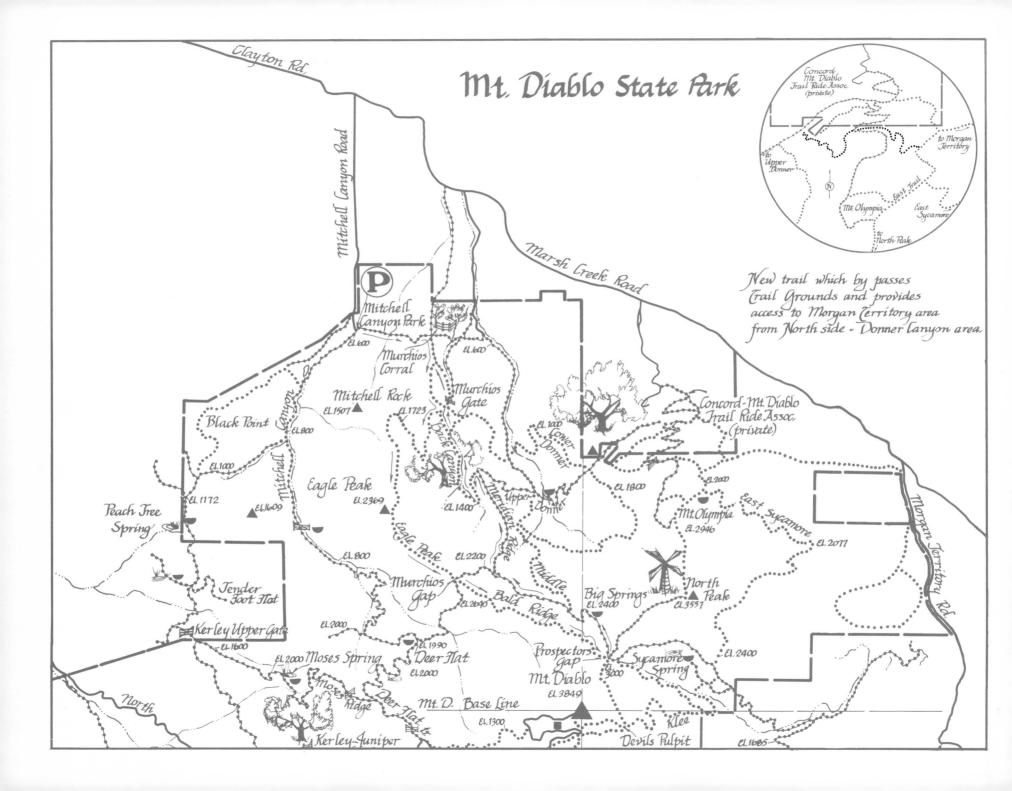

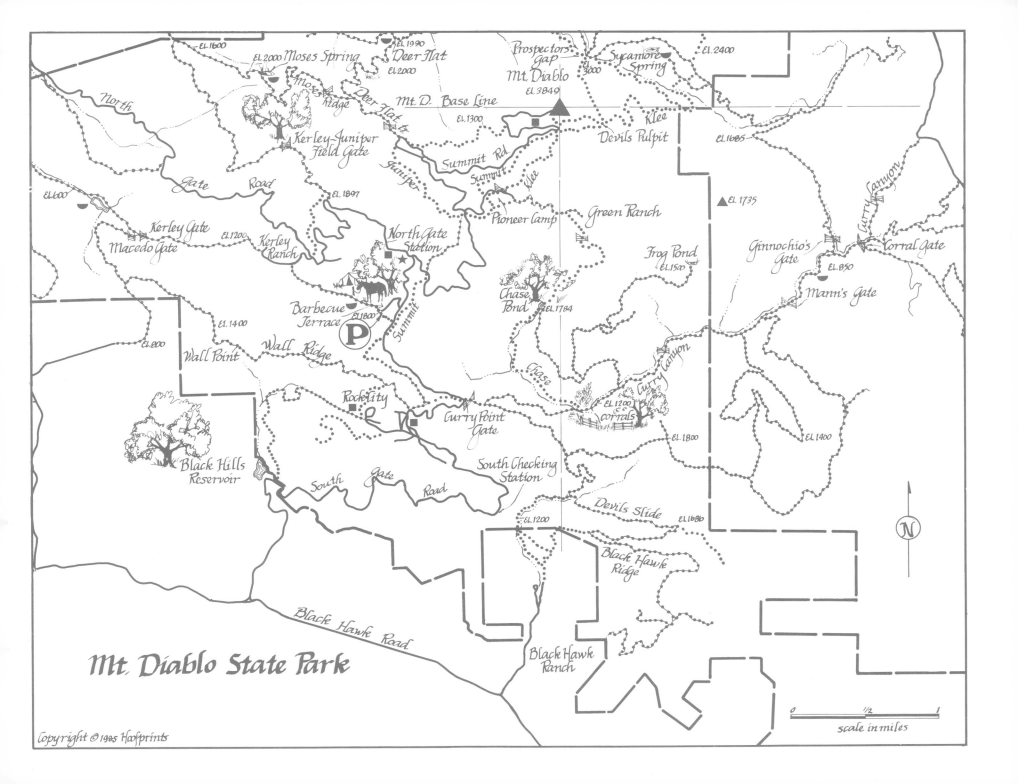

MT. DIABLO STATE PARK

This mountain offers a real challenge on a great variety of trails . . .

— Bruce Lee

REASONS TO GO: A vast park with an extensive system of trails. You can work just as hard as you choose to because you have so many choices: flat land, gentle grades, little hills, big hills and one huge mountain . . . The higher you go the more magnificent the views! On a clear day you can see the peaks of the Sierra Nevada to the east. Turn toward the west and you'll see Mt. Tamalpais and the Golden Gate. Easy to see on any day are the confluence of the San Joaquin and Sacramento Rivers . . . The rugged, untamed landscape is decorated with Digger pines, scrub oak, junipers, and giant live oaks, to name a few. Yellow aster, Mariposa lilies, and poppies soften the craggy hillsides.

SPECIAL FEATURES: Connecting trails give you access to seven East Bay parks . . . The southern loop trail enters the Skyline Trail system through EBMUD-San Leandro reservoir property and on through Las Trampas Regional Park. The northern connection picks up the Skyline Trail via Briones Regional Park and San Pablo-EBMUD lands. Connecting trails give you access to seven East Bay parks . . . The southern loop trail enters the Skyline Trail system through Las Trampas Regional Park, and the northern connection picks up the Skyline Trail at Briones Regional Park . . . Lots of deer, an occasional fox, bobcat and badger are sighted at Mt. Diablo . . . Great horseman facilities! This is the home of the Concord - Mt. Diablo Trail Ride Association . . . Museum at the Summit is open on weekends . . . The Summit on Mt. Diablo gives you the "second best view in the world," second only to Kilamanjaro!

TRAIL FEATURES: Access to at least 150 miles of trails with tremendous variety of terrain—flat and easy to the most difficult . . . This is the home of competitive trail riding and endurance racing . . .

There are good trails here for conditioning at speed, but riders should be sensitive to the fragile areas where erosion might take place . . . There is varying trail width all through the Park . . . Bald Ridge and Eagle's Peak are beautiful, challenging rides, but good judgment is needed on these trails as there are some steep, rocky areas.

LOCATION: A major entrance for horsemen is on the north side of the mountain. Take Ygnacio Valley Road to Clayton Road, from Clayton Rd. turn right on Mitchell Canyon Road and follow it to the entrance of the Park.

WHERE TO PARK: For day use or overnight park trailers inside the Park entrance on Mitchell Canyon Rd. Horse trailer parking is separate from auto parking . . . Area is very pleasant with many shade trees and a year-round creek . . . There is a restroom and parking for at least 25 trailers . . . A second day-use parking area is reached by taking Stone Valley Road to the far north end of Green Valley Road . . . this is the former site of the Friedan-Rossi ranch . . . A new access to the east side of the Park has been gained with the acquisition of the Morgan Territory . . . From Marsh Creek Rd. turn west onto Morgan Territory Rd. and go one half mile to the Park entrance on the right . . . No facilities here at present, but it is a time-saving entrance for people coming from the Valley. (Note insert on Diablo map.)

ACCOMMODATIONS: Group overnights are encouraged here with fantastic horseman facilities at Mitchell Canyon, Barbecue Terrace, and Pioneer Camp . . . Barbecue Terrace features 80 pipe tie-stalls, water, restrooms and 80 campsites. (Groups larger than 50 require a special permit.) Pioneer Camp can accommodate up to 30 people and has 10 tie-stalls, water and pit toilets . . . You can drive to all camping areas to bring in supplies . . . All camp areas require reservations which can be made by phoning the Park directly. (415) 837-2525, or write to MT. DIABLO STATE PARK, P.O. Box 250, Diablo, CA (94538) Early reservations are strongly advised. You

can reserve up to three months in advance for Barbecue Terrace and up to seven days in advance for Pioneer Camp. Plan ahead, because these are very popular camping areas, especially in the spring.

Murchio's Corral is also a nice resting place for riders, with shade trees and a corral for your horse if you wish to take a long lunch break . . . There isn't any water at the Corral but there are water troughs at Juniper Camp and year-round springs at Big Springs.

FEES: At the north entrance to the Park you'll be greeted by an "Iron Ranger" (Honor Box) to collect $2 per vehicle and $1 per horse . . . Overnight Fees: Barbecue Terrace, $50 per night for up to 50 people . . . $30 per night for up to 30 people at Pioneer Terrace. Families and small groups will be charged $6 per night, per person, plus $1 per horse. There is an additional $3.50 service charge for reservations. Fees are subject to change but since **advance reservations are required** for overnights there won't be any surprises.

PARK SERVICES: Ranger jeep patrol on the mountain and a mounted ranger patrol in the works! . . . You can always find a ranger at the North Gate entrance (go east on Ygnacio Valley Road to Walnut Ave., turn right on Walnut and go to Oak Grove, right on Oak Grove and a quick left takes you to the Park entrance.)

PARK RULES: Stay on trails . . . Don't short-cut . . . Don't ride on the edge of steep, narrow trails . . . Prevent erosion by crowding the uphill side . . . Park vehicles in authorized places. Don't block fireroads with trailers, as they must be kept open at all times for emergency access . . . Don't ride horses on pavement except when crossing the road . . . No dogs are allowed and absolutely no smoking on the trails . . . Plant life is protected here, and trails should not be cleared without authorization from the Park ranger.

 CAUTION: There are many areas with poison oak so stick to the trail and designated camping areas . . . Mt. Diablo trail veteran Bruce Lee says he hasn't seen a rattlesnake here in 20 years but that doesn't mean they aren't out there!

160

BRUCE LEE TRAIL
Mt. Diablo State Park

. . . Mr. Lee has been a tireless and enthusiastic volunteer. He has furthered the objectives of trail programs both in Mt. Diablo and throughout the East Bay. Through his efforts the interests of all California trail enthusiasts have been served. We all owe a debt of gratitude to Mr. Lee and hope he recognizes that the designation of this Trail is a small token of our appreciation for his efforts . . .

— William S. Briner,
Director California Department of
Parks and Recreation
in dedicating the Bruce Lee Trail
January 31, 1985

Bruce Lee.

The dedication of the Trail was a public event which took place two weeks before Bruce died in February 1985. When news of his passing reached the Board of Directors of the East Bay Regional Park District they adjourned their meeting, "not in memory of Bruce, but in honor of Bruce," said District Property Manager Hulet Hornbeck.

The reasons to go are special here — the Bruce Lee Trail is a scenic 10-mile link for riders, hikers, and bikers between Mt. Diablo State Park and Black Diamond Mines Regional Preserve, named in honor of one of the finest men I have ever known. Whether he was dealing with a horse or a human, Bruce brought out the best in that individual's ability to cooperate and perform. It is a fitting tribute to his memory that the Trail named for him represents the cooperation of four public agencies, the East Bay Regional Park District, the California State Department of Parks and Recreation, Contra Costa County, and the town of Clayton.

In recognition of Bruce Lee's extraordinary dedication to trails the board members of the East Bay Regional Park District broke precedent by naming a trail for a person.

Trail's end for the Bruce Lee Trail is at the Black Diamond Mines Regional Preserve south of Pittsburg and Antioch . . . 3,433-acre park with great historical interest . . . Black Diamond Mines was an active mining area for almost 100 years. In the 1850s Welsh and English coal miners developed more than a dozen major coal mines, making the Black Diamond area the largest coal mining development in California. The last coal mine was closed in 1902, and the East Bay Regional Park District has closed most of the openings into the mines. A few have been rehabilitated to accommodate tours open to the public . . . Today the trails over gentle rolling hills are quiet and peaceful, and riders are generally unaware of the 150 miles of mining tunnels beneath the pabk.

The Park District has recorded nearly 100 species of birds in the park, including the golden eagle . . . Animal tracks are more often seen than animals. The fireroads are imprinted with tracks of bobcats, coyote, grey fox, and mountain lion . . . Spring wildflowers enliven a landscape of rolling hills of valley grassland, oak, and chaparral.

Bruce Lee's long time friend, George Cardinet stands at the Center St. (Black Diamond Way) entrance to the trail leading to Black Diamond Mines Regional Preserve. The new entrance and the new trail were both dedicated in Bruce's honor.

EBRPD

The park is in Contra Costa County south of Pittsburg and Antioch. The main entrance is at the end of Somersville Road off Hwy. 4, but because the road is narrow and winding, horsemen should go to the northeast boundary and park at Contra Loma. Road conditions are good entering Contra Loma Park. Exit off Hwy. 4 at Lone Tree and continue south past the Antioch golf course to Empire Mine Rd. adjacent to the airport. About 100 yards from the intersection of Lone Tree and Empire Mine Rd. you reach Frederickson Lane which takes you into the park.

The Park offers approximately 10 miles of mainly fireroad trail with some minor trails traversing over 3,000 acres of gentle, rolling hills . . . There's no pavement in the park . . . The trails give the rider a safe and easy feeling.

Contra Loma Park borders Black Diamond Mines on its NE boundary. It is requested that horsemen park here and take the Contra Loma trail into Black Diamond Preserve.

Mitchell Canyon entrance to the Bruce Lee Trail.

Coming from Mt. Diablo, riders will descend to an urban trail segment of Bruce Lee Trail . . . View of the trail at the Marsh Creek Rd. crossing at Donner Creek.

Mitchell Canyon's inviting campsites are sheltered by trees and bordered by a year-round creek.

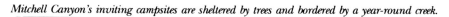

LAS TRAMPAS REGIONAL WILDERNESS

Beautiful facilities and extensive trails for a base camp ride . . . .

— Bob Cooper

Oak-clustered hills of Las Trampas Regional Park.

REASONS TO GO: About 4,000 undeveloped acres with expansive trail system . . . Las Trampas Ridge and Rocky Ridge provide spectacular views of the San Ramon Valley and Mt. Diablo, the Coast Range, and San Francisco Bay . . . Abundant animal life in the form of placid beef cattle and bounding deer . . . Great variety of vegetation. Black sage and buck brush, elderberry, gooseberry, and creek dogwood are only a few examples . . . It's easier to list the names of animals and plants than it is to describe the "on top of the world" feeling you have midst such vast open space.

SPECIAL FEATURES: A geological masterpiece created by two major faults of the Bay Area, Las Trampas and Bollinger . . . The same wind that will enliven your horse on Rocky Ridge has created wind caves in the large stone outcroppings . . . Grazing cattle meander on the hills and along the Valley Trail. Bird-watching horsemen may be distracted by a golden eagle . . . Easy to reach for horsemen pulling trailers . . . Rental stable nearby on Bollinger Canyon Rd. Phone (415) 837-7076 or 572-5553. Las Trampas Stables next door to Little Hills Ranch.

LOCATION: From Hwy. 580 take Crow Canyon Rd. north to Castro Valley, or from Hwy. 680 take Crow Canyon Rd. south at San Ramon to Bollinger Canyon Rd. Follow Bollinger Canyon Rd. to the parking lot, a distance of four and one half miles.

TRAIL FEATURES: Approximately 53 miles of generally well marked trail . . . If you have obtained an EBMUD trail permit you have a connecting link between Las Trampas and Redwood-Chabot Parks to the west . . . Much of the trail is wide enough for fast gallops, but there is enough climbing on narrow trails to give you a varied ride.

WHERE TO PARK: Parking lot at entrance to park is ample . . . Bring your own drinking water . . . There is spring water in the creek at Devil's Hole for your horse, but can't be relied on in the summer . . . There are toilets in the parking lot.

ACCOMMODATIONS: Park is open for day use without reservations . . . There are picnic areas near the parking lot with tables and barbecue units. These facilities are available on a first-come-first served basis . . . Information on overnight reservations can be made by phoning supervisor Charles Johnson (415) 837-3145. Camping area has tables, toilets, water, and corrals for 30 to 40 horses.

FEES: No fees for day use. Consult with ranger on overnight fees.

PARK SERVICES: The park has rangers on foot and in four-wheel-drive vehicles . . . Adequate maps are available at the park entrance in parking lot.

PARK RULES: Open year-round . . . Motor vehicles limited to Bollinger Canyon Rd. and to the parking lot . . . Firearms not permitted in the park.

WEATHER: Very hot in the summer, but always a breeze on Rocky Ridge. In very wet weather the trail riding is severely limited to only a few miles . . . Spring rides are a great time to see the abundant wildflowers — star lilies, Mariposa lilies, the fragrance of sage!

 CAUTION: Extensive, well marked trails give you a "no problem" ride. Be sure to close cattle gates.

EAST BAY AREA TRAILS SUMMARY

YOU CAN'T ride or camp in the East Bay without feeling a tremendous sense of gratitude for the East Bay Regional Park District and the area's active horsemen. They deserve the credit for an extensive array of opportunities to enjoy your horse. For the trail user, the East Bay is an inspiring model of cooperative effort and promises fulfilled. But to safeguard their sport from constant urban pressures, horsemen are wise to live by the old adage, "One isn't lazy about what one loves." In the East Bay area, as throughout California, policies and actual facilities for camping with horses are in various stages of review and development. Trail riders are urged to be "persistent and patient" in working with the Park District, the Trails Council, and horsemen groups. "Horse care" in the 1980s involves more than exercise, grooming, and feed — it means getting to know:

East Bay Regional Park District — 11500 Skyline Blvd. Oakland, CA 94619-2491 Phone: (415) 531-9300, Reservations: 531-9043. Trails Coordinator, Bob Doyle, 531-9300.

East Bay Trails Council — meets the third Wednesday of each month, 7:30 p.m. Park District Headquarters.

San Ramon Valley Horsemen — P.O. Box 403, Danville, CA 94526.

Concord-Mt. Diablo Trail Ride Association: — P.O. Box 419, Clayton, CA 94517.

Tilden-Wildcat Horsemen's Association — Es Anderson, 1020 Middlefield Rd., Berkeley, CA 94708. (415) 841-5335.

Moraga Horsemen — George Wagnon, 264 Lakefield Place, Moraga, CA 94556; (415) 376-5247. Same for Moraga Junior Horsemen's Assn.

Heritage Trails Fund - 1350 Castle Rock Rd., Walnut Creek, CA 94590. Phone: Nancy DuPont (415) 939-6357.

Park Summary (Spring 1985)

Day use and overnight with horses (**reservations required for camping.**) Other than Mt. Diablo State Park the only developed horse camping areas at present are **Chabot Regional Park,** 4,674 acres east of Oakland-San Leandro (415) 531-9043, and **Del Valle Regional Park,** 3,445 acres, 10 miles south of Livermore, (415) 443-4110, and **Las Trampas Regional Wilderness** (as described in text).

At the following Parks horse camping facilities are limited or nonexistent at present. If you don't mind "roughing it," overnight stays with horses are still possible on a **special permit** basis.

Black Diamond Mines (as described in text). Phone: (415) 757-2620.
Sunol Regional Wilderness, 3,479 acres south of Pleasanton-Livermore. Phone: (415) 862-2244.

Day Use Only:

Briones Regional park, 5,030 acres near Lafayette, Orinda, Pleasant Hill, and Martinez.

Contra Loma Regional Park, 771 acres south of Antioch.

Dry Creek Pioneer Regional Park, 1,200 acres in the hills east of Hayward and Union City.

Garin Regional Park, 1,014 acres in the Hayward hills.

Redwood Regional Park, 2,129 acres in Oakland and Contra Costa Cty.

Tassajara Creek Regional Park, 451 acres north of Pleasanton.

Tilden Regional Park, 2,065 acres in Berkeley.

Wildcat Canyon Regional Park, 2,378 acres in the hills east of Richmond and north of Tilden Regional Park.

Mission Peak Regional Preserve, 2,546 acres atop Mission Peak and adjoining Monument Peak east of Ohlone College in Fremont.

Morgan Territory Regional Preserve, 1,525 acres southeast of Clayton and north of Livermore. Access to Mt. Diablo State Park.

Sibley Volcanic Regional Preserve, 381 acres in Oakland and Contra Costa County.

Cull Canyon Regional Recreation Area, 360 acres in Castro Valley.

Don Castro Regional Recreation Area, 100 acres between Castro Valley and Hayward. Limited horseback riding.

Little Hills Ranch Regional Recreation Area, 100 acres in Bollinger Canyon west of Danville and San Ramon.

Shadow Cliffs Regional Recreation Area, 249 acres in Pleasanton.

Point Pinole Regional Shoreline, 2,147 acres of land and water on the Richmond shoreline of San Pablo Bay.

Ohlone Regional Wilderness, 5,516 acres in southeastern Alameda Cty. between Sunol Regional Wilderness and Del Valle Regional Park.

The verdict is in: There's great riding in the East Bay! Improvements to the trail system are constantly being made, such as the work being done in 1985 on the old State Riding and Hiking Trail between Martinez and Mt. Diablo. According to Trails Coordinator Bob Doyle, it's "the finest urban horse trail in the area." Trail planning and development is an ongoing process, so keep in touch!

APPENDIX

167

Jean Wilkinson expertly managing a team of Morgan horses on a drive through open country.

168

Carriage Driving on the Trails

Marsha Jo Hannah
Peninsula Carriage Driving Club

Background

There is a new sport gaining popularity in the equine world, or more accurately, an old mode of transportation being rediscovered — carriage driving is making a comeback! Participants hitch one or more horses, ponies, donkeys, or mules to a two-wheeled cart or four-wheeled carriage, then go for a drive with their "turnout".

There are as many kinds of carriage driving as there are drivers, with a great variety of shows and organized activities available. Common show events include Pleasure Driving classes (roughly the equivalent of Western or English pleasure riding classes), Costume classes, and Obstacle classes (similar to Western trail classes) — each with a host of variants based on the type of vehicle, number and type of animals, way they're hitched, etc. There are even Combined Driving Events, which are similar to three-day events in the hunter-jumper world. CDE's include Dressage, Obstacles, and a Marathon; these are analogous to ridden dressage, stadium jumping, and cross-country jumping. Of course, in driving, the objective is to go around each obstacle cleanly, not over it!

However, many drivers, like many riders, aren't into the competitive side of horsemanship; they just want to have fun with their animals. For them, there are pleasure drives, the equivalent of trail riding. At present, the choices for places to drive are limited to driving on city streets or on existing horse trails, neither of which is really suitable.

There are many problems with driving on the street, the most serious of which is the automobile. Automobile drivers tend to feel that the roads belong to cars — never mind that the law still permits carriages on the road, and even gives them the right of way. Modern drivers also do not have any inkling of the potential unpredictability of horses, so are unprepared for the animal shying or bolting, and sometimes even provoke it by honking as they pass. Collisions, when they happen, almost always result in serious injury to the horse and/or driver. Also, most roads are now paved with asphalt or concrete, which can easily cause a steel-shod horse to slip. Furthermore, prolonged driving on pavement is thought to cause serious leg problems for the horse, as the hard surface of the road has no "give" to it.

Lynn Quam

Marsha Jo Hannah and Shadow. This photo was taken by Marsha's husband, Lynn, at their ranch near La Honda. While Marsha's Ph.D. in computer science led to a research position at SRI International her desire to master a completely different kind of challenge led her to the world of donkeys and carriage driving.

Bab Verdugo schools a two year old filly while enjoying the shade and spaciousness of Nevada County Fairgrounds.

The major problem with existing horse trails is that most of them are designed for riding horses moving single file. Most trails are a narrow path, perhaps three feet wide. Access is controlled by gates four feet wide or step-over stiles, amounting to small jumps. In rough terrain, the trails wind around, sometimes making sharp turns.

Carriages, however, are the precursor to the automobile, are about car-sized, and have many of the same limitations. A cart or carriage suitable for a horse is approximately six feet wide; with one horse hitched, the turnout is easily 15–20 feet long. A sharp turn with a horse and cart might be made on a 20-foot circle; with a pair of horses and a four-wheel buggy, a 30–40-foot circle would be needed. Backing such a turnout is somewhere between difficult and impossible, depending on the training of the horses and the experience of the driver. Carriages have slightly more ground clearance than a car, but their wheels are more fragile; driving over large rocks or across a slope can result in broken spokes from the side pressures. Also, many carriages do not have brakes. Instead, they rely on the horses pushing forward into their collars on upgrades or backward into their breeching on downgrades to control the vehicle. An equipment (or training) failure on a steep grade can lead to an accident, so most carriage drivers prefer to stay on fairly level trails. One interesting difference is that a horse and carriage uses three ruts — two for the carriage wheels, plus one between them for the horse.

170

Finding suitable trails

Clearly, present alternatives for carriage driving are less than optimal. What is needed are trail networks designed with carriages in mind. In many cases, such trails will be highly suitable for other users, such as horse riders, hikers, trail bicyclists, and perhaps even people in wheel chairs. Such trails enhance the safety of a park for everyone, as they provide ready access for fire trucks and other emergency vehicles.

What follows is a description of components of an "ideal" trail system. Parenthetic comments indicate acceptable alternatives. Notes are also made of things to avoid.

Let's start at the beginning — a potential driver arrives at the trailhead to begin his drive. Like any horseman, he arrives with his truck and trailer. Unlike the rider, he also has a carriage to haul. This is handled in one of several ways.

Usually, the towing vehicle is a pickup or flatbed truck which also hauls the carriage. This means that, in order to unload the carriage, the trailer must be unhooked from the truck, which is then driven ahead 20–30 feet so the carriage can be rolled off down ramps. Clearly this requires a lot of space; it also requires that the parking area be flat enough to safely unhook a trailer, which may not have a parking brake, and to park a carriage once it is unloaded.

Henry Boyd, DVM on a China Camp State Park trail with his Morgan mare.

Another alternative is to use a four-horse trailer, hauling the carriage in the back of it. This requires room for a large truck and long trailer, plus 20–30 feet behind the trailer for room to unload the carriage.

Occasionally, a second vehicle will haul the carriage, either in a truck bed or on a separate trailer. This means that for each turnout there has to be space for two rigs to park, turn around, etc.

Sometimes a small cart will be hauled attached to the trailer. This may require extra space to the side of the rig in order to unload.

The bottom line is that the parking area needs to be a large one, and the flatter the better. Drivers, like riders, prefer to go out in company, so anywhere from two to twenty turnouts may show up. Adequate parking is a must. Onstreet parking is suitable only if the road has wide shoulders and is very lightly traveled; unloading horses along a busy highway is an invitation to a runaway. Also, carriages tend to invite a lot of interest from passers-by; hitching up in view of a busy road leads to rubbernecking and accidents.

OK, now we're ready to go driving, so we get onto the trail. Trouble is, most of the trail control mechanisms that will keep out unwanted four-wheel drivers will also keep out a carriage turnout. The best solution is probably a gate 8–12 feet wide, with a key given out by request, subscription, or some such means.

The trail itself should be a minimum of 8–12 feet wide; more is better since turnouts will occasionally meet on a trail. For safety, turns in the trail should be such that they can be made in one sweep on a circle with a diameter greater than 30 feet. The trail should be reasonably level across the roadbed (under 10% grade, to avoid breaking wheels), not too steep along the roadbed (maximum 15% grade locally, average grade under 5% — remember, braking is done by the horses), and free from large rocks, ruts, chuckholes, etc.

Every mile or so (particularly on hills), there should be what drivers call a "blow spot". This is a place to pull over and rest the horses. It is also a good place to let another turnout pass, or to turn around and head back if something has gone wrong. Such places should be fairly flat, so the horse doesn't have to strain into the traces to keep the carriage from rolling down a slope. It should also be large enough to turn a carriage around in one swing, or to rest several turnouts at once.

The surface of the road should be fairly firm dirt or fine, packed gravel. Loose dirt is slippery, dusty, and turns to mud at the slightest rain or fog. Coarse gravel is hard on the horses' hooves and on some bicycle-type tires; loose gravel is also slippery. Asphalt is hard on horses' legs as well as being slippery on slopes (but access to a level asphalt trail is better than driving on the street!). Dirt or gravel trails should be graded at least once a year in late spring to remove weeds, smooth out the winter ruts, and fix up slides or washouts.

The optimal length of the trail varies with the driver. Five miles is probably a reasonable minimum, and few drivers will want to go more than 25 miles round-trip. However, everyone's needs are probably best served by a network of trails, offering lots of variety.

At picnic areas (and in the parking area), the usual amenities are appreciated — a stout hitching rack to park the horses at, a restroom for the driver, and a source of water for the horses. Shade trees are nice to rest under, especially in the hotter summer months.

Where are suitable sites for driving trails? Most parks that used to be farms or ranches will have existing dirt roads that only need to be mapped and maintained. Lands along the Bay may have dikes that are already topped with small roads. Mountainous parks may have suitable logging or fire roads; some places will have flat, open ridge tops which are glorious for driving.

There are undoubtedly many places already suitable for carriage driving or which can be adapted with a few modifications. Carriage drivers just need to know where they are. We hope this book will lead you out of the arena toward a new trail adventure.

Peaceful canyon trail at the Rancho del Oso end of Big Basin State Park.

RATING THE DIFFICULTY OF CROSS-COUNTRY DRIVES

Marsha Jo Hannah

IN THE PAST, cross-country drives have been described in very general terms by their organizers. This has occasionally led to people traveling significant distances to attend drives, only to find that the event was beyond their capabilities; worse yet, people have risked themselves and others due to their not realizing the true difficulty of the drive.

To alleviate this problem, the Peninsula Carriage Driving Club has developed a system for rating its drives into classes, designated 1, 2, 3, and 4, in order of increasing difficulty. What follows is an informal description of these classes, along with some comments regarding the application of this system.

Class 1 drives are *novice-level.* Drives in this class should offer no problems for novice drivers, young or out-of-condition horses, or antique carriages. The terrain should be quite flat; hazards should be non-existent; the distance should be relatively short; and the pace of the drive should be slow. The drive should leave the impression of a nice, safe (perhaps even slightly boring) outing.

Class 2 drives are *intermediate-level.* These drives should be suitable for experienced drivers educating green-broke horses about the real world or for student drivers expanding their skills by driving experienced horses in new situations. Grades should not exceed 7%, and hazards should be few and either mild or avoidable. The impression of participants should be that it was a fun, but not taxing, drive.

Class 3 drives are *advanced-level.* These drives will require significant experience on the part of drivers and horses; also, horses and vehicles must be in very good condition. Grades should not exceed 15% and should average less than 5%, and hazards should be no worse than moderate. The impression left by the drive should be that it was some-

what challenging, but not requiring peak performance at every instant.

Class 4 drives are *expert-level.* These are intended only for the best of drivers, well-trained and extremely fit horses, and light but stout vehicles in perfect condition. Essentially anything goes here, although nothing should be included which is inherently unsafe. The impression left by such a drive should be a feeling of extreme accomplishment with perhaps a bit of relief that it is over.

Clearly, objectivity is required in rating any drive. A drive organizer must realize that he and his horse are likely to be too familiar with their favorite drive. It is, therefore, prudent to seek outside opinions as to whether any elements of the drive might hold terrors for the average turnout. A reasonable approach is for a small group of drivers to preview the route in their turnouts, then assign a rating. Ratings should never be assigned on the basis of memories of what the area looked like last year, nor from having gone over the route on foot, on horseback, or in a jeep — it looks different from behind a horse.

In announcing a drive, the organizer should publish some details as to why it was given its rating. Minimal information should include the length of the drive, the expected driving time, the average grade and worst grade along the route, the types of hazards to be encountered, the availability (or lack) of pull-outs, and an indication of what equipment is recommended (e.g. breeching).

The final assessment as to the rating of a drive rests with the individual driver. If in middrive you discover that it is beyond the capabilities of you or your animals, then by all means turn around and go back. On all drives, the safety of the participants must be the first goal.

SITES OF SUCCESSFUL ORGANIZED DRIVES

Peninsula Carriage Driving Club
P.O. Box 620448, Woodside, CA 94062

THE FOLLOWING PLACES have been used for organized carriage drives sponsored by PCDC.

CTETA Horse Park (Combined Training Equestrian Team Alliance). Located in Woodside, on Sand Hill Rd., between Interstate-280 and Whiskey Hill Rd. 272 acres, developed as a horse-trail, cross-country hunter-jumper facility. Open-to-lightly-wooded, rolling range land, containing a variety of jumps, connected by a network of nicely disked 8'-wide paths. Very pleasant driving, mostly classes 2-3, some class 4 available; breeching/brakes advised; plentiful parking; grounds often dusty; watch for squirrel holes. Two arenas large enough to accommodate driven dressage. Temporary stabling on premises for events. Facilities currently available only during the dry months, but plans exist for graveling some of the trails for year-round driving. Open free to the public for casual driving (use of the grounds for training or use of a dressage arena is $5/turnout/day), except during jumping shows; check with manager for schedule. Contact CTETA, P.O. Box 620010, Woodside, CA 94062; or call Bob Smith, (415) 851-7855 evenings.

San Francisco Watershed. Located north of Woodside, off Cañada Rd., between Edgewood Rd. and State Hwy. 92. Graveled service roads lead through the back of the old Filoli estate and behind Crystal Springs Reservoir, mostly through the woods, but with occasional glimpses of the estate and the reservoir. Rustic picnic area available. Special permit required to get keys to multiple gates. Theoretically drivable year-round; rated classes 1-3. Parking on-street along Cañada Rd., Edgewood Rd., or Runnymede. Contact San Francisco Water Department, 1000 El Camino Real, Millbrae, CA 94030.

Wunderlich County Park. Located at 4040 Woodside Rd., Woodside. Dirt logging roads through second growth redwoods, somewhat narrow and steep; rated class 3-4. Special permit required to get gate key. Parking for about 10 trailers. Contact ranger at Park (415) 851-7570.

Somers Field. Los Altos Hunt Pony Club facilities, located on Woodside Rd. approx. 1/4 mile west of Wunderlich Park. Large, grassy meadow rated class 1-2; limited parking, approach from parking area rated class 4. Special permit probably required.

Menlo Circus Club Polo Field. Located in Atherton, off of Valparaiso Ave., at Elena. Large, well-groomed lawn, rated class 1. Limited parking, expensive permit/negotiation required. Contact Menlo Circus Club, 190 Park Ln., Atherton, CA 94025, (415) 322-4616.

Cañada Road. Located north of Woodside. The portion of Cañada Rd. between Edgewood Rd. and State Hwy. 92 is closed to automobile traffic on the 1st and 3rd Sundays of each month, 10 am-4 pm, April through October. Wide, 2-lane, paved road open to public, shared with bicyclists and hikers. Gently rolling hills, with nice views of Crystal Springs Reservoir. Limited parking along Edgewood Rd. or Cañada Rd.

SITES FOR INDIVIDUAL DRIVING

The following sites are used by individual PCDC members for occasional driving.

Shadow Cliffs Regional Park. Located west of Livermore, (along road that parallels railroad tracks.) Ex-gravel pit on Del Valle Creek with graveled roads along the levee. Mostly flat, with steep climbs onto and off of the levee; rated classes 2-3. Suitable for two or three turnouts to use; levee road somewhat narrow for organized drive. Ample parking; day use fee; horses not permitted near lake. Used regularly by Joan Case, (415) 828-3281.

Sycamore Park. Small park located west of Livermore, just off of State Hwy. 84. Flat, grassy area with graveled roads through sparse trees, rated classes 1-2. Seasonal stream with an easy ford. Limited parking for trailers, otherwise has potential for an organized drive. Used regularly by Joan Case, (415) 828-2181.

Briones Park. Located near Lafayette and Pleasant Hill. Large park with many fire roads. Terrain may be steep for an organized drive. Used occasionally by Joan Case, (415) 828-3281.

Pt. Reyes National Seashore. Used occasionally by Joan Case, (415) 828-3281, and by Carole Mercer, (415) 851-4363. Bear Valley Rd. reputed to be very nice, but open to horses weekdays only.

Almaden-Quicksilver Park. Located near San Jose. Terrain may be a bit steep for an organized drive. Used occasionally by Virginia Hammerness, (408) 269-6068.

SITES POSSIBLY SUITABLE FOR DRIVING

The following sites have been suggested as potential places to drive.

Garin Park. Between Fremont and Hayward. Lots of fireroads.

Sunol Regional Park. Near Sunol.

Coyote Hills Park. In Newark, along the bay.

Sawyer Camp Rd. Parrallels Interstate 280 north of State Hwy. 92, through S.F. Watershed. Paved, 2-lane road, permanently closed to automobile traffic. Some recent trouble with speeding bicyclists not staying in their lane. John and Irene Buchner know more, (415) 871-7371 evenings.

Pescadero Creek Park. Located on Pescadero Rd. between Pescadero and La Honda. Old Haul Rd. a bit steep in spots and narrow for an organized drive; probably OK for 2 or 3 experienced drivers. Service roads along ridges near Jack Brooks Horse Camp may be suitable, although trailering in/out of there isn't for everyone.

MISCELLANEOUS CONTACTS:

The following people/organizations have expertise in driving and/or organizing drives in other areas.

Pat James. Has organized drives at Pebble Beach. (One of THE finest drivers in the US — get in touch!) 2561 Michigan Avenue, Modesto, CA 95351; (209) 526-1106

Golden Gate Carriages (Carolyn Bernardi). Has the carriage concession in Golden Gate Park in San Francisco. Leave message with answering service at (415) 761-8272.

Napa Valley Carriage Co. Does carriage tours of the Napa Valley wineries; (707) 253-2611.

John Jenkel. Has carriage concession at Pier 39 in San Francisco, does CCF carriage drives around Sebastapol, (707) 823-7083.

California Carriage Foundation. c/o Mrs. Florence Stradan, Sect'y-Treas., 10075 Sheldon Rd., Elk Grove, CA 95624.

The photos, drawings and articles on mules are presented courtesy of the American Mule Association, artist Tori Thompson and Robert M. Miller, DVM. Tori Thompson is a full-time artist who also makes time to edit the Mule Association Newsletter.

drawings by Tori Thompson

176

WHY I'M A MULE LOVER

— *R.M. Miller, DVM*

Dr. Miller is the highly respected Thousand Oaks veterinarian whose articles frequently appear in Western Horseman *and* Equus *magazines.*

ALTHOUGH I've worked professionally with horses most of my adult life I had little contact with mules until about a dozen years ago. I'd been a wrangler, a teamster, a packer, a cowhand, and eventually a veterinarian doing equine practice. But in all those years I had contact with perhaps a dozen mules, and I had never ridden a mule. Even as a packer, I only packed horses.

One day I asked a colleague, Dr. Bob Bradley, why he raised mules. "Why," he said, "once you ride a mule you'll prefer them to horses."

"That's ridiculous!" I replied.

Bob looked offended, then said, "Okay, I'll tell you what. I'll loan you a mule, and by next year you'll be converted!"

Bob loaned me Jerry, a 27-year-old gelding who had been a cowhorse, part of a stagecoach team, a roping mule, and a bit of everything else. Jerry converted me to mules in 30 days. But first I put him to the test. I rode him up a bluff no horse could have negotiated. He went up it like a goat. He taught me that if I wanted to ride down the side of a cliff or cross a swollen stream he would decide where to go down or where it was safe to cross the creek. I learned quickly that mules have judgment and make decisions, and I learned to respect their judgment.

After a month we went on a two-day trail ride. There were 65 riders. Three of us were on mules. In the cool of the morning the horses were excited. One man got bucked off and broke his hip. The mules were quiet and relaxed. The trail went straight uphill. The temperature at noon was 100 degrees. Sweat poured off the horses, streaming from their fetlocks in a steady flow. The three mules started at the back of the column in the drag. By noon they were up front and wet only behind the ears.

That night I decided to test the myth of mule wisdom. As soon as the ride ended I offered Jerry hay and water. He wouldn't touch his hay for one and a half hours. He refused water until he was cooled out, three hours after we quit riding. There was no question that of 65 riders I was the best mounted man there, and the two next best were mounted on three-year-old mules! Moreover, we were riding the only barefoot animals on the mountain. I began to see the practicality of the mule.

Tori Thompson

When I got home I called Bob. "Okay," I said. "You win! But I know that Jerry is an exceptional mule, and that's the only kind I want."

We spent a few years hunting for a mule of Jerry's caliber, but we had no luck. There weren't that many good mules around at the time. Meanwhile we became regular spectators at Bishop Mule Days where I began to notice other things about mules:

I looked at hundreds of mules but couldn't find wirecut scars.

At the Bishop Fairgrounds I noticed that there was never the squealing and fighting that occurs in a bunch of horses. As a veterinarian, I noticed the lack of lame animals I see at every horse show. I didn't see sick mules . . . I also noticed that most of the mules were cold-jawed and poorly trained, but I saw enough good performers to convince me that a mule with the proper conformation can be trained and perform like a horse.

I examined the mules at the finish line at the race track and in the winner's circle. I asked how long they had raced. Some of them were eight, nine, and ten years of age. Their legs were tight and smooth. I hardly saw a splint, a lump, or a swelling. I saw mules come off the track and soon after be used in a trail class. I saw mules working a dozen different events at a single show.

My wife, Debby, didn't share my enthusiasm at the time, but I just had to have some good mules. So I bred a couple of our own good Quarter Horse mares and raised two handsome mules. I knew that spoiled mules can be a real problem so I did all the early training myself to be sure they were gentle, well mannered, and had no vices.

Now I learned more about mules. I learned what highly social creatures they are, how affectionate, intelligent, and what a sense of justice they have. They are amiable. They rarely start fights but they know how to win one, as many a horse or dog has learned. They are not as flighty as horses but they are wary. They have a great sense of self-preservation. They're really a remarkable animal with many admirable attributes including strength, persistence, caution, and high intelligence.

I started riding my mules and one day persuaded my wife to get on one of them, Jordass Jean. She did so reluctantly, only commenting that her gaits were fantastically smooth. Later that day I told her that I was going to find a ranch to put the mules on for awhile so they'd learn to work cattle. She said, "You can do that with your mule, but I'm going to show my mule."

"What do you mean, 'your mule'?" I asked. "You've been telling me that the mules were my project and that you'll stick to horses. Where do you get this 'my mule' stuff?"

Debby had been converted, too, and now we both ride mules!

My daughter was next. She had a POA mare and a beautiful Quarter Horse mare, a half sister to Jordass Jean. Ray and LaVerne Ordway, from Fresno, were trying to find a home for a 17-year-old mule named Sally. Ray, an old-time California reinsman, had trained Sally and used her as a working cowhorse. LaVerne was secretary of the American Mule Association and Sally belonged to her. Sally is out of a Tennessee Walking mare. In her youth she posed for the old AMA logo. Anyway, Sally came to live with us and was immediately confiscated by my 13-year-old daughter, Laurel. She rides the push-button mule everywhere, usually bareback, and has used her to win a bunch of awards in parades, mule shows, even open horse shows.

With my whole family converted to mules, I decided to sell off my Quarter mares, just keeping one in case we decided to raise another mule. I even sold my old roping horse that I used for brandings and roundups. I have mules who can do that sort of thing now.

Even if I didn't like the animals themselves I'd enjoy being around mules because I like the people involved with them. I find that only a special kind of person has an affinity for mules. People who lose their temper, lack tolerance and empathy, and are domineering and aggressive will probably dislike mules. You need to have a sense of humor, a sense of justice, and a real love for animals to be a mule person. Not all horsemen like mules, but I've noticed that all mule lovers like horses.

The mule business is much freer of the intensity that plagues the show horse business. There's less money involved. There's no breeding potential in your mules so there's less pressure. You can't be in the mule business for status, prestige, social image, or ostentatiousness. None of these fits with mules. Most of the people involved with mules simply like the animals and are not motivated by pretentiousness.

One of my clients, a trainer who specializes in combined training at a rather elite stable, recently bought a couple of good mules and is having a ball with them. However, I've been told that some of his customers are disdainful of the mules. I happened to be at the stable one day examining an expensive horse owned by an elegantly dressed lady. The trainer rode by on one of the mules. The lady waited til the mule had gone by, then curled her lip and sneered, "Mules!"

"Right!" I said, smiling to myself. "MULES!"

178

Oroville Mercury photos by Tami Dingler

An honest to goodness mule train accompanied by riders on mules and horses tours the Northern California countryside, an organized event sponsored by the Elegant Ears Mule Club. Mule teams and mule riders came from Marysville, Oroville, Sacramento, and Sutter to participate in the nostalgic event. The mule train assembled in Bangor, 70 miles northeast of Sacramento and set out for a full day's enjoyment of driving and picnicking. Oroville Mercury reporter and horsewoman, Tami Dingler reports that the highly successful day has become an annual event! The train leaves Bangor Park in the morning traveling along Avocado Road. After a turn onto Dunstone they stop at Honcut Creek for lunch and return in the afternoon on Bangor Park Road. Some of the wagons are equipped with the comforts of home, hay bales to seat the passengers and tape recorders playing the song, "Mule Train!"

Case

Case

CANDID REFLECTIONS ON DONKEYS

— by Joan Case

Joe and Joan Case of Mt. Diablo Ranch are best known as the family belonging to champion standard jack, Texas. The gentle, brilliant colored Texas is "a good friend" on a mountain trail and a dazzling performer in the show ring. Texas has been a popular attraction in parades, on television, at the Cow Palace and in the 1984 Olympics. The Cases are great promoters of donkeys and Joe's articles have appeared in Western Horseman and California Horse Review magazines. Before their entrance into the equine world, Joe and Joan were first involved with donkeys as hikers who enjoyed the strength and companionship of the donkey as a pack animal.

Above: Joe and Joan with Vallee Hubbard line up to show that donkeys come in three sizes! Opposite page you get a taste of the variety of ways to enjoy a donkey . . . they're useable and huggable!

THE DONKEY personality is gregarious and affectionate. They possess a great sense of humor, sometimes to the point of mischievousness. These are intelligent and cautious animals that can't be rushed. Some people call this stubbornness and others call it good sense. Don't travel with a donkey if you plan to speed through the countryside, leaping chasms, fording swift rivers, and ignoring slick or mushy footing.

Before hitting the trail with a donkey, make sure he is well trained "at halter" and understands (and obeys) basic commands. Also, your donkey should be in good physical condition to carry a load. If the animal is responsive and quiet at halter, then packing, riding, or driving them is fairly easy to achieve. It is as though they were born to carry or pull a load, provided that load is of reasonable weight and is not binding, rubbing, or unbalanced. They will balk or sit down if overburdened. They are not stupid.

Donkeys make great companions packing on the trail. They are gentle, stable animals and their walk is a comfortable (though not fast) speed for their human hiker friends. They are usually willing to go along with you as you cross bridges and most other obstacles, provided the footing is stable and safe for their small hooves and provided you allow them time to look at and smell the proposed crossing. They are thinking animals and won't go where they feel it is unsafe. Their tough, elastic hooves do not need to be shod unless you are going cross-country for days on a lot of weathered granite like you might find in the Sierra mountain range.

Riding donkeys is fun and driving them even more fun. They are natural trotters and can be quite flashy in harness. Their tendency not to bolt and run is a character trait appreciated by all donkey owners.

Unlike the horse, the donkey has a tough, but small, upright and cupped hoof that is great for the desert rocks but sinks in mushy surfaces. They instinctively know that and avoid such areas. You must get them to trust you and spend some time and persuasion on the business of mud, water, or snow training. Reward them with kind words and quiet strokes. Patience in getting them to trust you and enlisting them as a team member in completing a journey will get you safely across many kinds of terrain. They cannot be beaten or hurried into submission. Abuse creates a most unpleasant animal. Conversely, spoiling a donkey through lack of discipline creates an equally unpleasant animal.

"SUMMER" ON THE TRAIL

by Doni Hubbard

THE FRIEND on my right grabbed my arm just as the friend on my left grabbed my purse. My daughters shrieked as two auctioneers rushed toward me and I felt the common glare of 500 pairs of eyes. I blinked back at the sea of faces focused on me as the specter of my husband's face hovered above the chaotic din of shouting and applause. *Could I possibly undo the damage I have done?* Too late . . . no turning back now. My fate had been sealed by my impetuous right hand which had ignored the restraint of a now incredulous friend. A fusion of excitement and resignation raced through me as I retrieved my checkbook from the other horrified friend who held my purse.

"Mom, Mom! Did you mean it? Did you do it?" was answered by my gesture of handing a check to the two men standing before me glistening with sweat and triumph. No, there was no turning back now.

If my account of how it felt to be the top bidder on a yearling filly at the 1981 Paint Horse Sale at Watsonville seems outrageously dramatic, you fall into one of three categories:

1) You have never bought a horse at an auction, or

2) You have bought so many horses at auctions you are calloused, or

3) You have no empathy for the guilt a normally responsible wife feels when she buys a horse while her innocent husband is off on a fishing trip.

The shocked, mildly hysterical friends who had tried to prevent my rashness by futile grabs at my purse and arm weren't easing the pain, either, with their threats to testify on my husband's side in the event of any possible divorce case. While they hooted my impetuosity my gleeful teenaged daughters heaped hugs and praise on my generosity. Both charges were false. I was neither generous nor impetuous, but only I knew the truth. Buying the slender, chestnut overo filly had been a cold, calculated move. True, the calculation had taken only a minute or two, but its roots could be traced back almost 30 years.

On my tenth birthday my father had presented me with a library card instead of the pony I'd been praying for since my seventh birthday. He could have bitten the bullet and said, "You're one of five children. You know we can't afford a horse." Instead he chose to put my dreams "on hold" in a constructive manner.

I had a blurred, watery view of the Wellwood Murray Memorial Library card as my Dad explained, "Someday you *will* own a horse. In the meantime read everything you can on horses, learn all you can from books, and when the time is right you'll be ready for a horse of your own."

Dad was right. Many books and many years later I owned not one, but several horses, and my daughters were living the kind of childhood I had dreamed of.

In no way do I feel I was shortchanged. My dependence on books for my horse experiences put me in the company of the greatest horsemen in the world. Will James, Alois Podhajsky, Margaret Cabell Self, James Fillis, Captain M. Horace Hayes, to name a few, were horsemen whose advice I devoured. All the while the dream grew that someday I'd be carried along the trails by a young horse who was living proof of the training techniques I'd studied. The purchase of the yearling filly, "APHA Sometime," called "Summer," was the perfect opportunity to transform my dream into reality.

By the time the filly came along I'd had enough experience with real live horses and enough knowledge of my own shortcomings to modify my dream. After observing the hard knocks of a few others who had plunged into training with a good book in one hand and a rope attached to a young horse in the other, I knew I wanted an extra character in my story — a knowledgeable, experienced horseman for on-the-spot correction. I knew this would cost some money, but so do vitamins, coat conditioners, saddles, fancy riding clothes, and even short stays in the hospital. I've never understood horse owners who will spend money like water on all of the above, while from the back of their badly mannered horse brag that they've never spent a dollar on a trainer. I guess I spent too many years in the library and as a school teacher not to place a high value on good instruction. Horses are no exception to the rule that you can't build something solid on a poor foundation.

To build a good foundation with my future trail horse I turned to Walter Wright from San Juan Bautista. His interview published in my first book, *Favorite Trails of Northern California Horsemen,* drew immediate favorable response from horsemen all over the state frustrated by 'problems.' Walter's emphasis is on giving all horses, regardless of their breeding or intended use, a thorough basic education including breaking to hobbles, "sacking out," and brief work on the long lines before any work under saddle. A young horse under Walter's supervision spends very little time in the arena before being taken out on the trail. According to Walter, too many people stay in the arena and school a horse to the point of souring him when trail work early on would have kept the horse interested and built his confidence in the rider. (It's a matter of experienced judgment here because you can get in real trouble by heading out on the trail with a horse that isn't ready, i.e., not responsive to your legs and hands).

In the case of Summer we were working with a yearling filly too young for any amount of riding. So after a few weeks of basic ground work as mentioned above she was turned out in pasture (she kept company with about 15 horses on 300 acres) to get a practical education from some no-nonsense broodmares. I agonized for days over Walter's advice to take this step. (I had a taste of what it will be like when our girls first go off on their own!)

"She'll be a better horse if you give her a chance to learn some things on her own. She'll have more to think about if she has to figure out where the good feed is, and the water, and she'll learn to handle herself around other horses. You want a good trail horse, so let her learn a few things on her own in the hills. If she can't handle it, then you don't want her anyway," Walter had advised. I gulped hard and agreed to his plan.

After three months in pasture Summer came back to us, thin, but without a scratch. She had survived kindergarten, and her attitude was more gentle and willing than when we had first worked with her.

"Give the old mares credit," said Walter. "Trainers don't like to admit this but sometimes a horse needs lessons he can only learn from another horse."

Summer was still too young for riding, but stabled in our large paddock at home we had daily opportunities to work with her on the ground. She learned about baths, clipping, and farriers, and responded eagerly to being ponied along the trails. In the meantime, I was back in the books growing more convinced that if this was to be my "perfect" trail horse I didn't want to rush any part of her training. We'd take our time and use her as an opportunity to learn all we could about horse handling.

A whole new adventure opened up to us when as a two-year-old Summer was trained to pull a cart. Again it was the classical horsemen of my library days who inspired this turn of events. From them I

Summer as a yearling looks eager for her next lesson.

learned that a time-honored method of preventing a training problem or curing one is to give a horse, even one not intended for carriage driving, some time "between the shafts." While a rider's weight on the back of a young horse can be damaging, most young horses by the age of two are physically able to pull a light cart at a moderate pace and distance. Harness work gives the opportunity to condition the young horse and develop obedience without placing the burden of weight on his back. Besides, I was working on a book of new trail adventures and the art of carriage driving in open country was making an exciting comeback!

No one is more respected in carriage driving circles, particularly in training young horses to drive, than Bab Verdugo of Grass Valley. "He's never in a hurry with a young horse," was a frequent comment I heard about his training. An unhurried approach suited us just fine. After four months at Verdugo Training Stable, Summer was entered in her first driving classes and won two seconds and a third! We were thrilled! The animation and beauty of driving classes is a worthy end in itself, but of particular satisfaction to me as a confirmed trail rider was that Summer was proving to be a calm, steady young horse, unruffled by new surroundings. So far, all my long-cherished theories on horse training were working to a T. We were right on target with Summer's training as a two-year-old so the tall, sleek filly came home for a well deserved vacation. Except for daily handling, being trailered to different sites, and ponied along the trails, she would receive no more schooling until she was a solid three-year-old. At least that was the plan. Where I made my mistake was in spending all my time with horse books when I should have been reading up on children!

Two months later I was watching with dismay as the long-legged, mud-caked filly cautiously picked her way around the oozy paddock. Constant rain for a month had made horse activities in the suburbs pretty miserable.

"If only this horse were old enough to ride," I said to my daughters as we watched the filly slipping and sliding across the paddock. "It sure would be nice if we could put her in training at some nice barn instead of keeping her in this mud."

My wishful thinking met with a curious response from both girls. Sheepish smiles, a giggle, stares at the floor and ceiling. With Christmas only a week away it didn't take much prodding on my part to get the whole story.

"Mom, Summer doesn't need to go to a trainer. We've been riding her. We're breaking her for you as your Christmas present," sixteen-year-old Vallee said in her softest voice. I probably would have been furious if my mind hadn't flashed back to the time I gave my mother two German Shepherd puppies for Mother's Day.

Any parent will immediately understand my feelings at that moment — anger, pride, curiosity, gratitude clashed within as my eyes fastened on my daughter's perfect white teeth, the result of my having made some orthodontist wealthy for life. All could have been lost so easily — the teeth, the child, the horse. By God's mercy everything seemed to be intact. Everything except my perfectly planned training schedule.

Every horse book worth reading has emphasized the need for flexibility on the part of the trainer. There are basic rules, but all animals are different. Be prepared for the fact that horses won't have read your training book and won't always behave as they should. Children are a lot like horses, I decided.

So much could have gone wrong, but the true story of my daughter's first experience of giving a horse its first ride was nontraumatic.

"I was sitting on the fence brushing her," explained Vallee, "when I just couldn't resist sliding onto her back. She was great, Mom, really! She just looked back at me kind of puzzled, then started walking around the paddock. She didn't seem scared, and since it was so slick in the

184

Walter Wright gives an approving smile as Vallee Hubbard completes her first "official" ride on Summer.

paddock I jumped off, put a bosal on her, and rode down the road."

Once the shock wore off I accepted my Christmas present with grace. Walter Wright supervised Vallee's riding for the first month while I proudly clicked away with the camera. Walter gave Vallee high marks for her handling of the horse, but also warned, "Don't think all training is this easy. Not one in twenty horses will be this steady this early." I like to think our good fortune is not a matter of odds but rather of the careful preparations the horse had received up to this point.

Now it was time to put the books aside and take to the trails in earnest. Under the guidance of expert horsewoman, trail competitor, and judge Nancy Smith Kasovich, and with continued instruction from Bab Verdugo, we still had a lot to learn.

EVALUATING THE YOUNG TRAIL HORSE PROSPECT

with Nancy Smith Kasovich

WHEN OUTSTANDING horsemen speak reverently of another horseman, my ears perk up. With so many varying opinions in the horse world, I was curious about the solid agreement on Nancy Smith Kasovich of Santa Rosa. The phrase "great horsewoman" popped up immediately whenever her name was mentioned during my two years of research for *Favorite Trails*. "She has more understanding of a horse and how to improve performance than anyone I've known," "a fantastic competitor . . . I don't know anyone who can get more out of a horse than Nancy," were typical of the comments which sparked my eagerness to meet her. My chance came in an interview five years ago which transformed me from enquiring writer to ardent fan. She is a thinking, sensitive person whose character and experience offer a wealth of advantages to any horse she trains.

Nancy's marriage to nationally known polo player Bob Smith ended with his death in 1977. As a young girl who had exercised polo ponies at Golden Gate Park she had known the trainer for 13 years prior to their marriage. Her own reputation as a young but highly reputable horsewoman was already established, so it was only natural that she would join the ranked seven-goals player in a career of buying, training, and selling polo ponies. When she wasn't occupied with taking horses unsuitable for polo and reschooling them for jumping and endurance competition, she was busy galloping Thoroughbreds around the track.

"I can't think of a nicer way to be described than as a good horsewoman," Nancy had said in our interview in 1980. "I credit the compliment to the fact that between my grandmother's influence (one of the first owners of Thoroughbred race horses in Australia) and Bob who tried to teach me everything he knew, I learned to do things right with a horse

simply because I never had a chance to see things done wrong."

"Learning to do things right with a horse" was what my experience with Summer was all about, so four years later I returned to Nancy's Santa Rosa home (which she shares with husband Tom Kasovich and son) for her highly prized evaluation of the Paint filly as a trail horse prospect. Nancy's full-time employment with Sonoma County means that horse activities are no longer the dominant theme, but have to be squeezed in to an already busy, productive life. I was ecstatic that Nancy had agreed to take a day out of her very full schedule to focus her years of experience as a trainer and NATRC judge on Summer's potential. Summer's attitude toward the event? While Nancy and I got set for the interview with notes, tape recorder, and camera, my partner calmly munched her oats in the trailer, secure in the knowledge that even if pronounced a complete dud by NATRC standards, the Hubbard family was already hopelessly attached to her.

185

Nancy demonstrates an alternative means for providing additional control in handling a young horse on the ground. A regular nylon lead is looped under the chin and over the noseband for added leverage.

"When I agree to look at a horse for a customer the first thing I do is to get an overall picture of the horse. After all, trail riders are out not only for the ride but also to see beautiful country. They want an animal that is both versatile and calm so that they can get across varied terrain and not be constantly worried about keeping the horse under control . . . a horse may have the greatest conformation and be very well bred, but if he doesn't have the right attitude he won't do the job. For performance horses I give first priority to what goes on in their heads. Start with the head. Look at the eyes. I want a horse that will look at me, watch me, and show some sense."

"With this horse I would like it better if the eye was bigger and deeper set . . . Her eyes are small, but kind and alert. On the other hand, she looks like a typical three-year-old who might use any excuse to act silly . . . When someone is trying to sell you a horse, ask the owner to get on first and give you a demonstration. It's important to see how the horse reacts to the owner and, conversely, to see how the owner reacts to the horse. If they seem reluctant to climb in the saddle, maybe you should be, too. Theoretically, the horse should go better for its owner, and in watching you can get a pretty good idea of how it will perform for you . . . But just because a horse doesn't go perfectly for its owner doesn't mean I'd give up on it. I'd ride the horse myself to reaffirm what I saw. For instance, maybe the horse appeared gate-sour, didn't want to enter the arena. Is the horse actually dead set against co-operating, or is it just that a weak rider has allowed this bad habit to develop? I won't know for sure 'til I'm in the saddle . . . But before anyone saddles up I want to see the horse in a large paddock moving freely. The natural action of the horse is very important . . ."

186

Summer's first free move in the arena was to sniff the earth and roll! Nancy liked that indication of a relaxed attitude. The horse obviously felt unperturbed by strange surroundings. Her degree of relaxation was almost embarrassing! It took a few pops of a longe whip to get her moving, but when she did move Nancy was impressed with her "very catty, very athletic" action. The other positive sign was that immediately upon the command of "whoa" the high speed antics came to a halt. Giving a horse some free time in an arena gives you a chance to evaluate attitude as well as action. For instance, how easy is the horse to catch? Summer passed this test with flying colors even though it meant being introduced to equipment she'd never seen before . . . a cow halter.

"As I continue to observe the horse unsaddled," said Nancy, "I'm interested in the owner's answer to my question, 'What has this horse done?' Now, if you had told me that this horse hadn't done much of anything, I would have to be suspicious of anything else you might tell me because the legs tell the story. At three years of age she has wind puffs which are a sign of being worked too soon. It's more normal to see these on a horse that's five or six years old. Horses this young can have some training, such as you've given her, but how much work depends on the tightness of her legs. This is a good-sized mare, but she isn't mature. I would have liked it better if this horse had been started at three and a half years instead of two. *(Refer to the first chapter of this saga for an explanation of what went wrong with our perfect schedule!)* She has good, dense bone, but it's round bone which has a tendency to wind puffs, instead of the flat bone you look for in a good endurance horse . . . She has nice length to her leg, good sloping pasterns, and a good cannon bone. Overall, the conformation is very pleasing, except that I would say she stands a little close behind, and I would have liked to see more angle to her shoulder. I would give her an "excellent" rating in the withers which shows her Thoroughbred breeding (Summer is a registered Paint with a heavy dose of Thoroughbred in the pedigree) . . . In looking at the

"You can't beat a cow halter for getting control of the front end of a horse. It's humane, but when you talk with this, they listen. NEVER TIE A HORSE WITH A COW HALTER, but it is excellent for teaching a young horse to stand quietly. You can't begin to train a horse until he pays attention. Respect and attention go hand in hand. Get his respect, he'll give you his attention and like you more besides. In fact, there's no other way to get him to like you. Try to win him over with apples all the time and you'll end up getting clobbered!"

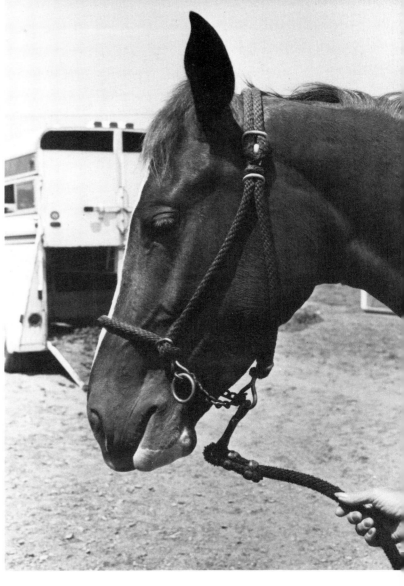

top line of the horse I see that she stands higher behind than in front which may make it harder for her to gather herself and means more pressure on the front legs . . . Her calm attitude, the length of her stride, her athletic action and generally good conformation indicate a horse with trail potential, but we can't be sure 'til we see her under saddle . . . One thing I would insist on with this horse is that she not be rushed in her training . . . lots of walking in the hills, but very little loping. Her attitude is relaxed and kind, but she's no deadhead . . . . definitely worth taking your time in training her."

187

Evaluation of the horse includes observing the horse's manners while being led and saddled. For her first ride on Summer Nancy's choice is a gag snaffle which gives a little more control through poll pressure . . . Summer reacts with a horse laugh to the new mouthpiece.

Before we take to the trails Nancy evaluates the horse in the arena to check how she bends and responds to leg pressure. Summer gets an A rating in that department thanks to her previous training.

"Don't be in a hurry with a young horse. Pick easy terrain and begin a gradual program of conditioning. To get this horse ready for NATRC competition as a four-year-old I would ride her every other day, either in the arena or on the trails. We'd do lots of walking. Something as long as a four-hour ride would be okay as long as we only walked. Assuming I started her in the summer I'd stick to walking 'til October. Then give her "time off" all through November and December. In January we would start up again with two weeks of "warm-up" riding in the arena . . . still nothing but walking. Then we'd spend the next few weeks walking in the hills, alternating with trotting in the arena. Then we'd build up to four weeks of trotting in the hills and cantering in the arena. At this rate I figure that by the middle of April she could do a good four-hour ride in the hills and be ready for the novice division NATRC spring ride on Mt. Diablo! You have to allow for some variations in all schedules, but this is a good basic one to build on. The main things to remember are lots of walking, and don't rush!"

*"Expose young horses to new sights and experiences . . .
    This filly has a willing attitude, so when she's
cautious give her plenty of time to look things over and
she'll reward you by being a confident horse. I always
try to ride alone when I'm training a horse because
then they don't develop the tendency to buddy up and
they're not always trying to rate the other horse. Also,
I'm freer to make corrections as I need to. But before
you start riding a young horse on your own it doesn't
hurt to ride out with a seasoned older horse for the
first time. Maybe it will take more than one time before
    you feel comfortable riding a young horse on your
    own. You have to do what you feel comfortable doing
    as a rider, based on your own experience and ability
    . . . Summer takes a good look at picnickers, sleeping
        bags, a picnic table, and garbage can
            clustered midst the trees.*

*"This filly has a calm attitude, but she wants to jump
everything in sight! A good trail horse has to step quietly over
obstacles . . . with patience and practice she'll learn!
Often the same lesson will have to be repeated until
good habits are established, but keep a positive attitude
and the horse will respond."*

"A tendency to rush through rough spots on the trail means the horse has some fear . . . . . the correct response is to give her practice in these areas and lots of reassurance as a reward for quiet behavior."

190

Even in unfamiliar surroundings Summer takes every opportunity to drink . . . a very good sign in a potential trail competitor.

Nancy's verdict: "As much as I like her in the arena, I like her even better out on the trail. She's sensitive but sensible. She isn't flustered by another horse coming up beside her or galloping off. She has a willing, 'go forward' attitude, a long stride for covering ground, but shows no tendency to run off or to try to take control. She listens and she's confident. Her tendency to get high-headed going down a steep hill is probably due to her conformation (higher behind than in front) which makes it difficult to collect. Maturity also plays a part. Don't rush this sensitive, young horse, and it's my opinion that you'll end up with a good partner on the trails."

TRAINING FOR TRAIL DRIVING

with Bab Verdugo

I WORKED WITH one horse that was scared of the cart. I don't know the source of the problem, but she would suddenly rear up, the owner would get excited and start yelling 'whoa.' I told him, 'Just let her rear! Don't worry, when she gets tired, she'll come down.' There's no point in hollering at a horse that's scared to death already. Quiet work brought her around."

So spoke Bab Verdugo, the Grass Valley trainer profiled in the chapter on Gold Country Horsemen. It was Bab's reputation for calmness, patience, and bringing out the best in horse and driver that made him my choice to instruct Summer and me in carriage driving on the trails. Research for this book had introduced me to the exciting revival of carriage driving as a sport. Besides all the fun, driving would give me a means of enjoying Summer while she was still too young to ride . . . and, after all, wasn't I writing a book on new adventures?

A basic ingredient of Bab's success with young horses is his tempo–"slow and easy." "Especially with a young horse, look for a trainer who's not in a great big hurry," is Bab's sound advice. The first two months of Summer's stay at Verdugo Training Stable was spent getting used to the harness, lines, and a "dummy cart." In her early lessons with the cart Bab didn't put any traces on her, just a bitting harness with the lines tied to the end of the harness. The purpose was to ease any anxiety she might have about the cart and to learn to stand quietly. Once that good habit was established, Bab put the traces on and she began to pull the cart . . . slowly, because the "dummy cart" (no wheels) is very heavy.

I was childishly eager for the first test drive. "When will she be ready to be hitched to a real cart? When can I drive?" I was beginning to sound like my teen-aged daughters as they'd approached the magic age of 16!

"The horse will be ready when I say 'whoa' and she stops instantly without any pull on the lines,"

Summer looks skeptical about our new trail adventure — she as a student harness horse and I as a student driver!

192

Summer's education was a family affair. Audrey Hubbard longes Summer in a small enclosed area, teaching obedience to voice commands which are a prerequisite to carriage driving.

Summer's quiet, sensible reaction to a real cart meant graduation from the enclosed arena to an open, graded area which Bab uses for training. While Bab doesn't believe in rushing a horse, he does believe in keeping their training interesting. Why go round and round in circles when there are interesting things you can do such as . . .

After three months of training Summer graduated from level, cleared ground to gentle grades and narrow trails lined by dense brush. First Bab had walked behind her on several training drives to introduce her to the terrain. "Get all hitched up, then hold your horses," is Bab's advice. "Ground drive them over new terrain. Don't be in a big hurry to climb in the seat. When your horse is new to trail driving look for trails with brush on either side. That will help track the horse."

After three months of training Summer graduated from level, cleared ground to gentle grades and narrow trails lined by dense brush. First Bab had walked behind her on several training drives to introduce her to the terrain. "Get all hitched up, then hold your horses," is Bab's advice. "Ground drive them over new terrain. Don't be in a big hurry to climb in the seat. When your horse is new to trail driving look for trails with brush on either side. That will help track the horse."

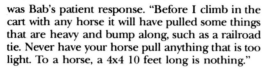

Then my big moment comes and Bab hands me the lines. We're out in the open with no fence to discourage a runaway, so Bab takes this step only after he's confident of the filly's attitude and responses. Inwardly, I'm not so confident . . . how can you ever be sure of a two-year-old? Oh, what a feeling as the horse moves forward at your command and you feel the magnificence of one horsepower at your fingertips!

was Bab's patient response. "Before I climb in the cart with any horse it will have pulled some things that are heavy and bump along, such as a railroad tie. Never have your horse pull anything that is too light. To a horse, a 4x4 10 feet long is nothing."

It had all seemed too easy. Then after several uneventful, quiet drives in the country Bab suddenly found himself in this predicament (below). Horse, cart, and Bab have come to a halt on level ground after Summer had suddenly decided to back down a steep trail instead of leaning into the harness and pulling up the hill. Some dramatic shots would have been possible if only I had been a little cooler during the blow-up! Whip in hand, Bab still had a difficult time convincing Summer to go forward.

True horseman that he is, Bab's response was to look for the reasons, instead of offering excuses for the horse's behavior. When Summer was unhitched the reason for her sudden refusal to lean against the harness was clear. Although we had picked the right time in Summer's training to introduce her to trails, we had picked the wrong day — in July heat Summer had developed welts under the harness. On a cooler day the horse would have to be reschooled over the same terrain.

The happy ending to our carriage-driving experience is that as a three-year-old Summer won the Pleasure Driving Championship at the Nevada County Fair. To be honest, only half of that statement is true. The true half is that she won. The untrue half is the phrase "happy ending." It would be more accurate to refer to a "happy beginning," because in spite of all her training as my partner in this book, Summer is still too young and inexperienced to be declared a happy ending, or final product of any kind. It will take many miles of riding before the happy ending of "Summer on the Trail" can be truly written. In the meantime, as a young trail horse prospect she is sound, beautiful, sensible beyond her years on the trail, and willing to go forward (with the one exception as noted above!). There's not much more we could ask of a four-year-old.

In looking back on my three years since the fateful auction, I would have to say that few things went as expected. This was supposed to be a story about doing things perfectly, or at least as perfectly as eager novices working with expert trainers can do them. What should happen makes good theory, but what did happen makes for a true story. For instance:

—The plan was to take it slowly with Summer in the classic sense of good horsemanship. In truth, we probably pushed her too hard. The attitude of the horse never told us, but the wind puffs did.

"Just walk," says Bab, and Summer and I are more than happy to oblige. Summer is being driven with no overcheck or sidecheck to interfere with her natural movement. In the show ring, fashion would dictate that an overcheck be used, but even with a schooled horse, in open country Bab advises nothing more than a loose side check. "If you're driving with an overcheck and the horse loses his footing on the downhill he can't recover. Then on the uphill the overcheck means the horse can't get his head down to pull. If you stymie him, he'll quit you."

Bab believes in making life interesting for novice drivers as well as green horses! This is the hardest I've concentrated on anything in years!

—On the day set aside to photograph ideal behavior for a driving horse on the trails Summer presented problems. On the day set aside to photograph 'how to handle problems with a young horse on the trail,' Summer behaved like a good old horse intent on the NATRC President's Cup!

—Most challenging of all to a confirmed trail rider is that no matter how quiet she is on the trail, what I inevitably hear from fellow horsemen is, "Looks like you've got a jumper for sure," or, "Ever thought of taking your Paint to the track?" Honestly! How could I possibly have known that the darling little yearling in the show ring would stand 15.2 hands tall in three short years?

Would I do it all again? Well, I doubt that I'll ever get the chance, now that my husband no longer fishes when there's a horse auction in the area! One thing I'm certain of—I've benefited greatly from my association with true horsemen who cared not a jot for a quick fix to a problem. Their goal was always to gain a true understanding between horse and rider. It was to their credit that although I was tempted to approach the horse from the standpoint of what would "look right in the book," they saw the horse as a living, breathing individual who needed to be taught correctly irrespective of photo sessions and deadlines. The horsemen who worked with Summer came from different backgrounds and had never met, but judging from the qualities they expressed, they might as well be blood brothers:

—Honest, intelligent responses and remarkable patience in curing confusion and eliciting the correct response from the horse.

—The presence of clear-cut goals for each training session, but the absence of hurry.

—Eagerness and enthusiasm for the job, a true love for the animal in spite of the fact that each had trained hundreds of horses.

—Willingness to work on a problem instead of just being annoyed by it.

In the company of these qualities I had as much to learn as the horse. If the filly benefited even half as much as I did from the influence of these outstanding horsemen I think I can look forward to many happy adventures with Summer on the trail!

195

Los Altos Trails Club members compete in trail events, use their horse activities as fund raisers for charities, and definitely have fun on the trails!

TRAIL RIDING FOR FUN, SPORT, AND PUBLIC SERVICE

RIDING WITH A GOAL in mind is one sure way to get increased enjoyment out of the time spent with your horse. The following description of horse activities, compiled with the assistance of Carolyn Lekberg ("I'm always looking for another excuse to get out on the trails!"), includes at least one event that is just perfect for you . . . so saddle up without delay and seek a new adventure!

American Endurance Ride Conference (AERC)
701 High Street, Suite 216
Auburn, CA 95603
(916) 823-2260

Endurance trail rides are controlled races against time over a given distance of generally 50 to 100 miles. Even though the first properly conditioned horse over the finish line is the winner, the motto of the AERC is "To Finish Is to Win." When any horse and rider cross the finish line as a team they are truly winners because: they have ridden many miles through beautiful country, enjoyed good company along the trail, and you can bet they know each other better than ever before! In addition, to finish a ride, both horse and rider must be fit and healthy, so you've both benefited from many hours of pre-ride conditioning!

AERC rides start bright and early in order to take advantage of cool morning temperatures. Generally, riders have 12 hours to complete a 50-mile ride, but with the high level of today's competition some riders may finish as early as 3½ to 4 hours after the start! The condition of horses is monitored closely by veterinarians throughout the ride. Riders also have the opportunity to talk with the vets and learn more about their horses. To top it all off a dinner, awards ceremony, and entertainment follow the ride, so no matter where you finish

in the pack you've had a full and satisfying weekend! Sound interesting? A local club to contact is Quicksilver Endurance Riders, Inc., P.O. Box 71, New Almaden, CA 95042.

North American Trail Ride Conference (NATRC)
P.O. Box 20315
El Cajon, CA 92021

An NATRC ride is a competitive trail ride that is not a race but rather a competition for best horsemanship and best condition of the horse under trail conditions. The objectives of an NATRC ride (besides having fun) are to encourage horsemanship in competitive trail-riding, to demonstrate the best methods of caring for horses during and after long trail rides, to learn the proper methods of training and conditioning horses for long rides, and to stimulate greater interest in the breeding and use of good horses for trail-riding. An NATRC ride is a great way to prepare for all your trail-riding activities. Best of all, you'll ride in the company of friendly, helpful people who care about you and your horse.

TRIATHLON
Mike Barger
19450 Almaden Rd.
San Jose, CA 95120

The Triathlon is a race in three sections. Usually it includes running, swimming, and bicycling, but recently horsemen have gotten into the act and substituted riding for the swimming portion. A triathlon can be completed entirely by one person or be divided into a three-member team, each taking one portion of the race. Triathlons are fun and require either a very well conditioned body or a measure of insanity! One local triathlon (San Jose

area) is run in Almaden Quicksilver Park and along McKean Rd. The horses and riders take their chances in the Park and the bicyclists and runners take their chances along the road. Runners travel a 6.2-mile course; the bicycle course is about 20 miles long and the rider's course is 18 miles. The human athletes are on their own, but the equine athletes are closely watched by veterinarians. The winner is the first team entirely over the finish line, but there are many categories for other awards: Iron Man (one person doing all three events), oldest team, youngest team, women's team, fastest horse, etc. If you have a great body or just want to see one, don't miss the next Triathlon!

RIDE AND TIE
Sponsored by:
Levi Strauss & Co.
Levi's Plaza, 1155 Battery St.
P.O. Box 7215
San Francisco, CA 94120
(415) 544-6000

A Ride and Tie is a race steeped in Old West tradition and necessity when two people had but one horse between them! Today's Ride and Tie combines strategy and horsemanship with long-distance running as two human team members take turns riding a third team member (the horse) over rugged, hilly terrain. As the race begins all three members take off running (one member mounted and one on foot). The horse and rider race ahead to a certain spot where the rider jumps off, ties the horse, and continues on foot . . . the horse rests until the other person comes along. The race continues in this leapfrog fashion over approximately 40 miles of rocky, dusty trail. The welfare of the horse is closely watched by the veterinarians attending the ride, but human competitors must survive on their own!

The Ride and Tie was revived as a sport in 1971 by

Bud Johns of Levi Strauss & Co. It was immediately popular with both runners and riders, and now there are over 200 rides each year in the U.S. and overseas.

POKER RIDE

A poker ride is an informal, friendly trail ride over a designated trail with an added element of spice — a poker hand is played on horseback! Riders progress through five prearranged check points at which each rider is given a playing card. The rider with the best poker hand at the end of the ride is the "winner." These rides are not races nor are they competitive, other than the poker aspect. Many times the entrance fee for the ride is the prize money for the winning hands. Local horsemen organizations hold poker rides each year just to have fun and often to benefit some worthy cause. For tips on organizing a Poker Ride contact the Quicksilver Endurance Riders at the address listed above.

RIDE FOR RESEARCH
Morris Animal Foundation
45 Inverness Dr.
Inglewood, Colorado 80112

Ride for Research is a project of the Morris Animal Foundation, a nonprofit foundation which funds research into equine health. The procedure is for riders to obtain sponsors who make tax-deductible pledges for each mile ridden. Proceeds from the ride are used to finance scientific studies in veterinary schools concerning problems such as colic, reproductive disorders, laminitis. The Ride for Research trail is chosen and marked by the sponsoring horse club. Organizational details such as ride cards and certificates are provided by the Morris Animal Foundation. The ride is not competitive except to see who can raise the most money! Prizes are awarded to the riders collecting the most pledge money, and those who raise $15 or more receive a Ride for Research shoulder patch. (Danville Junior Horsemen have a history of outstanding success with their rides — $10–12,000 raised annually per ride!) Regardless of the amount of money you collect you'll receive a certificate of participation as well as a chance to have a good time riding your horse for a good cause.

VOLUNTEER MOUNTED PATROLS

Volunteer Mounted Patrols are set up by public agencies to help patrol trails and parklands. Many patrols are also reserve units of the County Sheriff's Departments, so they are trained for crowd control and to patrol in urban environments. Other patrols include search and rescue work in their program and may be on the team with other units specializing in diving, communications, and mountain rescue. Just for fun a few patrols take part in parades, adding lots of flash and color. Mounted patrols in parks may help by clearing trails, watching for fires, assisting hikers in remote areas, and giving information to trail users. Mounted patrols have proven to be popular with park users because they are visible, giving assurance that there is someone patrolling the trails. What a great way to serve the community and enjoy your horse at the same time!

Sonoma County Search & Rescue Eldridge Posse
Sonoma State Hospital
Glen Ellen
c/o Thelma Wood
2510 Woolsey Rd.
Windsor, CA 95492

Marin County Open Space District
Marin County Civic Center, Rm. #335
San Rafael, CA 94903
(415) 499-6387

Contra Costa Cty. Sheriff's Posse
Captain Stu Safine (415) 825-3933
Joel Russell, Secretary
9437 Alcosta Blvd.
San Ramon, CA 94583
(415) 828-5073

Mounted Patrol of San Mateo County
521 Kings Mountain Rd.
Woodside, CA 94062

Santa Clara County Parks and Recreation Department
298 Garden Hill Dr.
Los Gatos, CA 95030
(408) 358-3741

Santa Clara County Sheriff's Posse Reserve Unit
70 W. Hedding
San Jose, CA 95110
(408) 299-3238

Disaster Aid Response Team
Los Gatos Police Department
110 E. Main St.
Los Gatos, CA 95030
(408) 354-5257

East Bay Regional Parks Department of Public Safety
11500 Skyline Blvd.
Oakland, CA 94619
(415) 531-9300

Folsom Lake Trail Patrol
c/o Linda Gurnee
7140 Wildwood Place
Roseville, CA 95678
(916) 791-1223

Valley of the Moon Mounted Assistance Unit
Sugarloaf Ridge State Park
2605 Adobe Canyon Rd.
Kenwood, CA 95452
(707) 833-5712

HOSPITALITY FOR HORSEMEN ON THE MOVE . . .

The horsemen on the following pages
generously contributed to the production
of this book. They share your interest
in trails and extend a warm welcome
as you explore the beauty that is California . . .

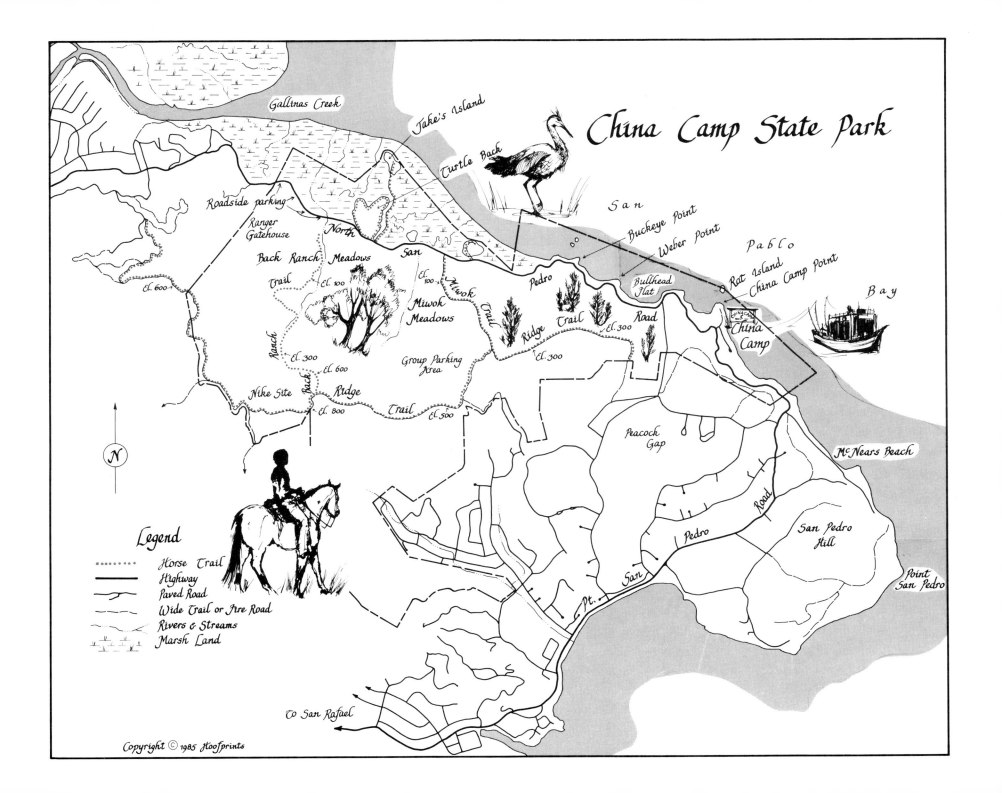

China Camp State Park

Gallinas Creek

Jake's Island

Turtle Back

San

Buckeye Point

Weber Point

Pablo

Roadside parking

Ranger Gatehouse

North

San

Pedro

Rat Island

China Camp Point

Bay

Back Ranch Meadows

El. 100

El. 100

Miwok Trail

Bullhead Flat

CHINACAMP

China Camp

Trail

El. 100

Miwok Meadows

Ridge Trail

Road

Ranch

El. 300

El. 300

El. 300

Back

El. 600

Group Parking Area

El. 300

Nike Site

Ridge

El. 800

Trail

El. 500

Peacock Gap

Mc Nears Beach

N

Road

San Pedro Hill

Pedro

Legend

San

Point San Pedro

.... Horse Trail
———— Highway
——⌐— Paved Road
– – – Wide Trail or Fire Road
⌒⌒ Rivers & Streams
ᵛᵛ Marsh Land

Pt.

To San Rafael

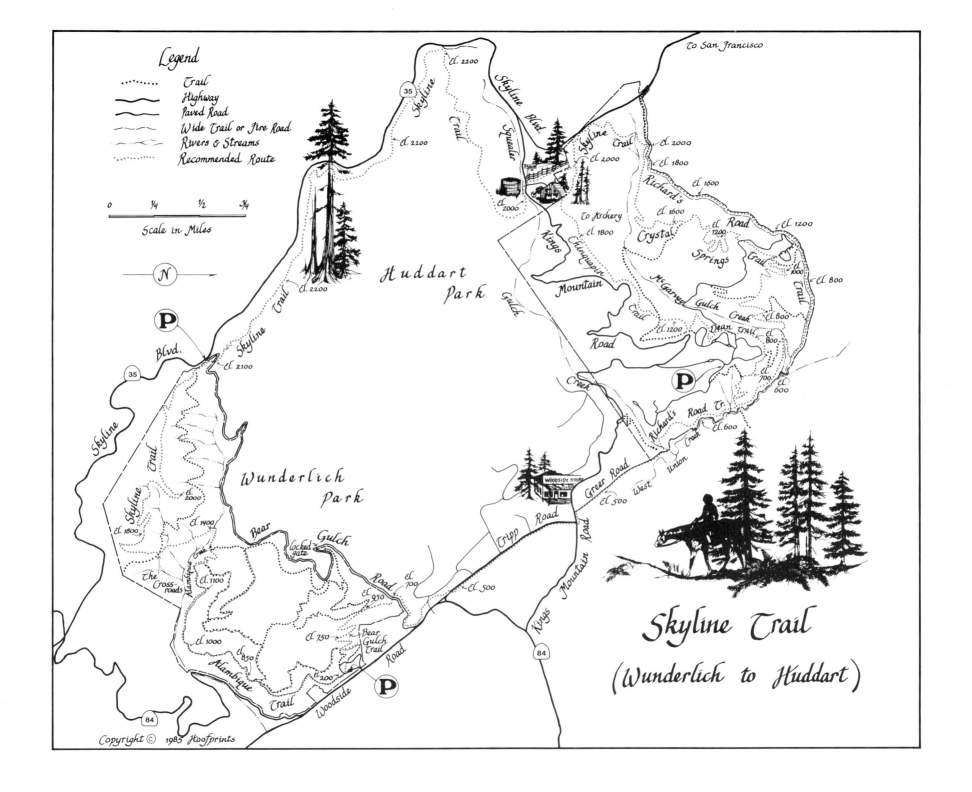

Skyline Trail
(Wunderlich to Huddart)

Legend

·········	Trail
————	Highway
﹏﹏	Paved Road
﹏﹏	Wide Trail or Fire Road
﹏﹏	Rivers & Streams
∙∙∙∙∙∙	Recommended Route

Scale in Miles

0   ¼   ½   ¾

N

To San Francisco

Huddart Park

Skyline Blvd.

Skyline Trail

El. 2200

El. 2200

El. 2000

Skyline Trail

Squealer

El. 2000

El. 2000

Richard's

El. 2000

El. 1800

El. 1600

To Archery

El. 1800

Crystal

Springs

El. 1600

El. 1200

El. 1200

El. 1200

Road

Kings

Chinquapin Mountain

Trail

El. 1000

El. 800

Gulch

McGarvey Gulch

Trail

Road

Dean Trail

Creek

El. 800

El. 800

El. 1200

El. 800

El. 700

El. 600

Creek

El. 2100

Skyline Blvd.

Richard's Road Tr.

El. 600

Union Creek

West

Skyline Trail

El. 1800

El. 2000

El. 1400

WOODSIDE STORE

Greer Road

El. 500

Bear

Gulch

Wunderlich Park

Locked gate

Road

El. 1100

The Cross-roads

Alambique Creek

El. 1100

El. 950

El. 700

El. 500

Tripp Road

Kings Mountain Road

El. 1000

El. 850

El. 750

Bear Gulch Trail

El. 200

Alambique Trail

Woodside Road

P (multiple parking symbols)

35

84

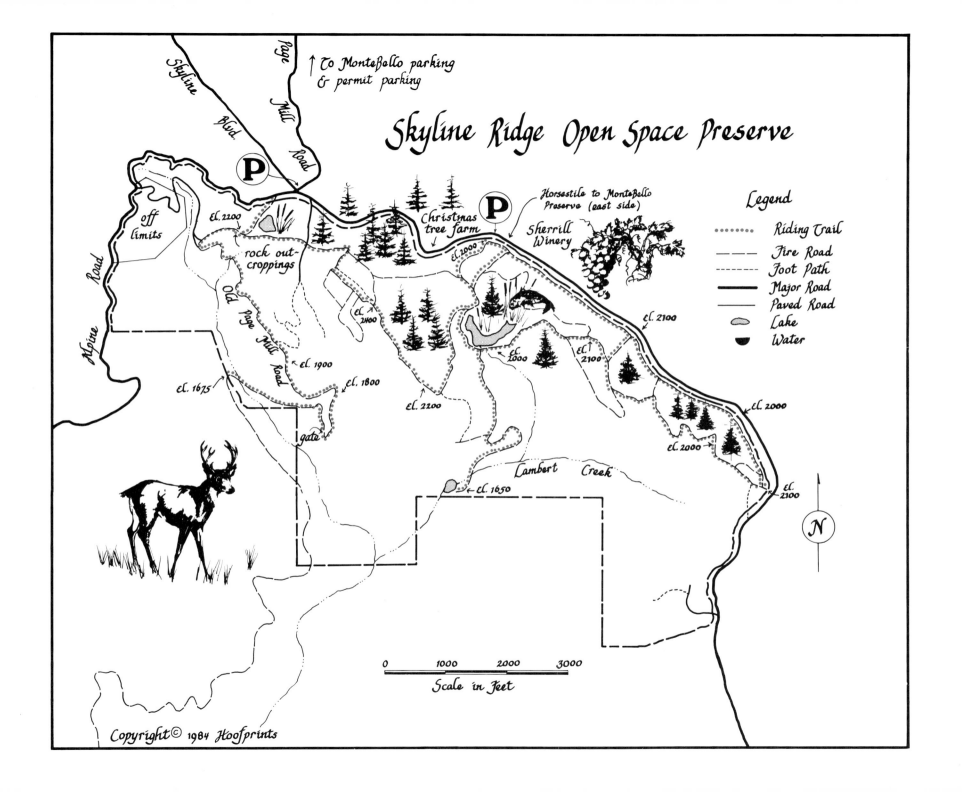

Skyline Ridge Open Space Preserve

↑ To MonteBello parking & permit parking

Skyline Blvd.

Page Mill Road

P

Alpine Road

off limits

El. 2200

rock out-croppings

Old Page Mill Road

El. 2400

El. 1900

El. 1675

El. 1800

gate

Christmas tree farm

P

Horsestile to MonteBello Preserve (east side)

Sherrill Winery

El. 1000

El. 2100

El. 2000

El. 2100

El. 2200

El. 2000

El. 2000

El. 2100

Lambert Creek

← El. 1650

Legend

········· Riding Trail

– – – Fire Road

- - - - Foot Path

▬▬▬ Major Road

──── Paved Road

🟤 Lake

🌑 Water

N

0   1000   2000   3000

Scale in Feet

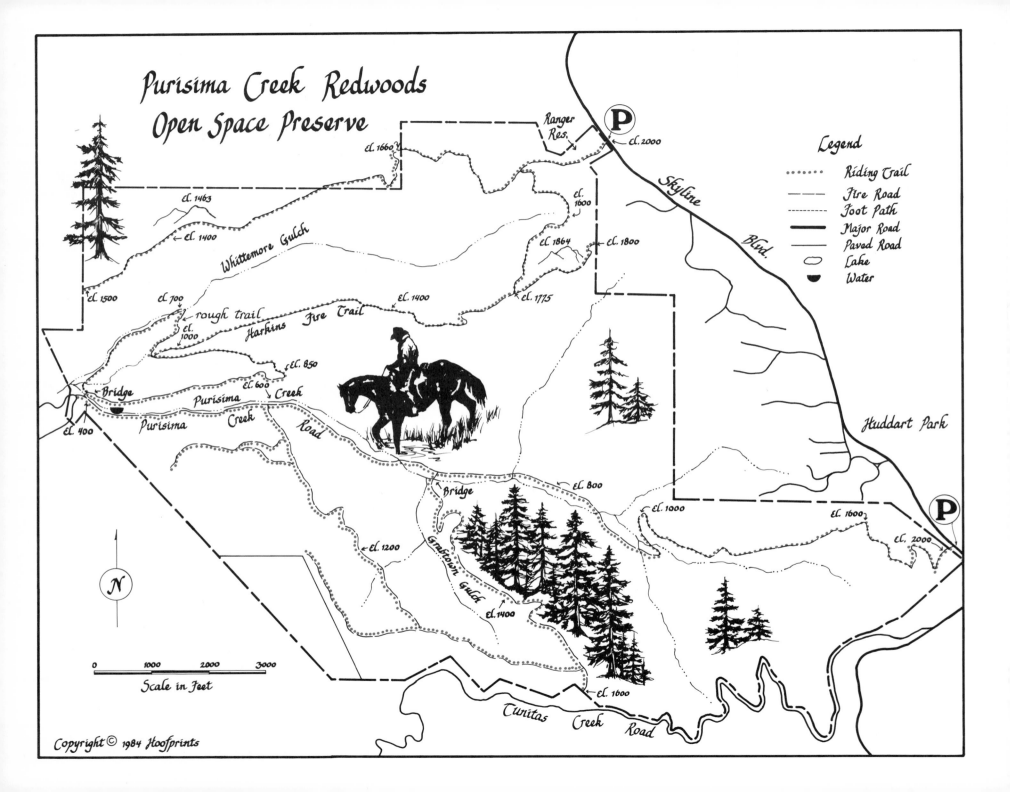

Purisima Creek Redwoods
Open Space Preserve

Ranger Res.

El. 1660

El. 2000

P

Skyline Blvd.

El. 1463

El. 1400

El. 1600

Whittemore Gulch

El. 1864

El. 1800

El. 1500

El. 1400

El. 1775

El. 700

rough trail

El. 1000

Harkins Fire Trail

El. 850

Bridge

El. 600

Purisima Creek

Purisima Creek Road

Huddart Park

El. 400

Purisima Creek

Bridge

El. 800

El. 1000

P

El. 1600

El. 1200

Grabtown Gulch

El. 2000

El. 1400

N

El. 1600

Tunitas Creek Road

| 0 | 1000 | 2000 | 3000 |

Scale in Feet

Legend

⋯⋯⋯	Riding Trail
– – –	Fire Road
- - - -	Foot Path
▬▬▬	Major Road
———	Paved Road
◯	Lake
●	Water

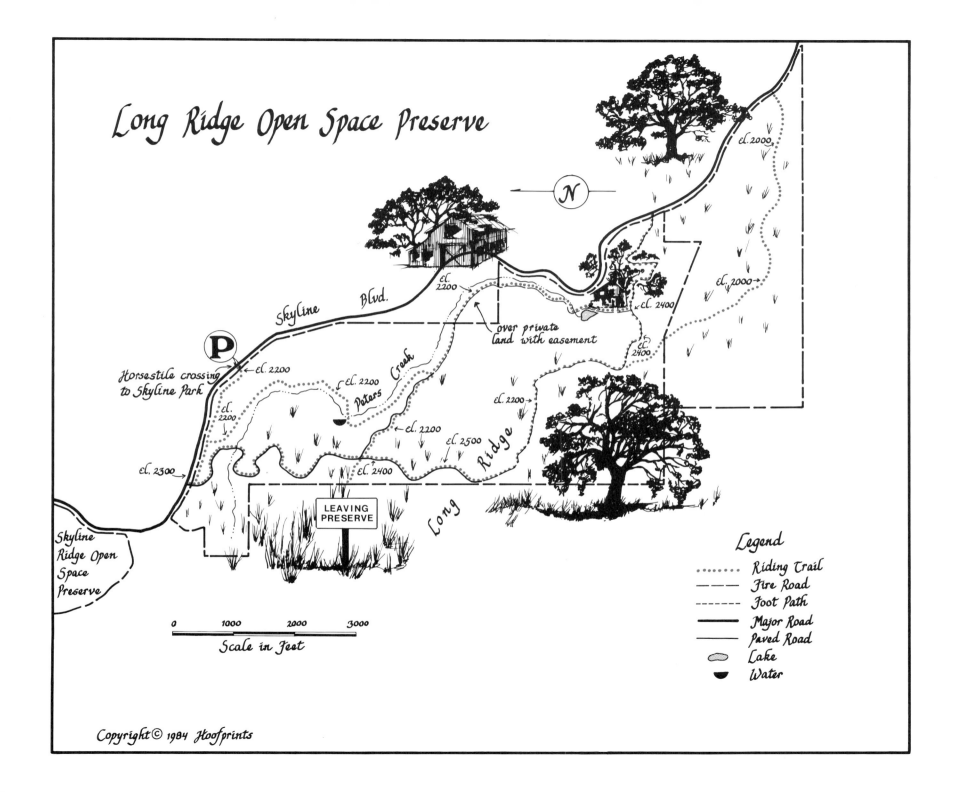

Long Ridge Open Space Preserve

N

Skyline Blvd.

el. 2000

el. 2000

el. 2000

el. 2200

over private
land with easement

el. 2400

el. 2400

P

Horsestile crossing
to Skyline Park

← el. 2200

el. 2200 →

Peters Creek

el. 2200 ↙

el. 2200

el. 2200 →

el.
2200 ↓

el. 2200 ↓

el. 2500

Long Ridge

el. 2300 →

↑
el. 2400

LEAVING
PRESERVE

Skyline
Ridge Open
Space
Preserve

Legend

.... Riding Trail
– – – Fire Road
- - - Foot Path
━━━ Major Road
——— Paved Road
⬭ Lake
⬤ Water

0   1000   2000   3000

Scale in Feet

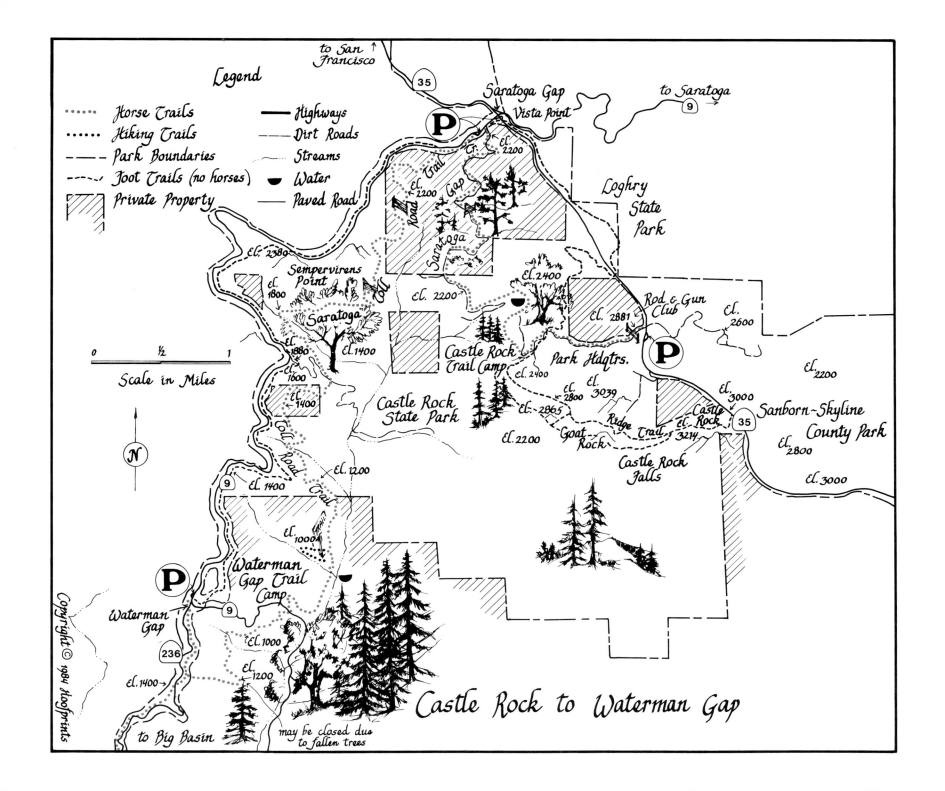

Castle Rock to Waterman Gap

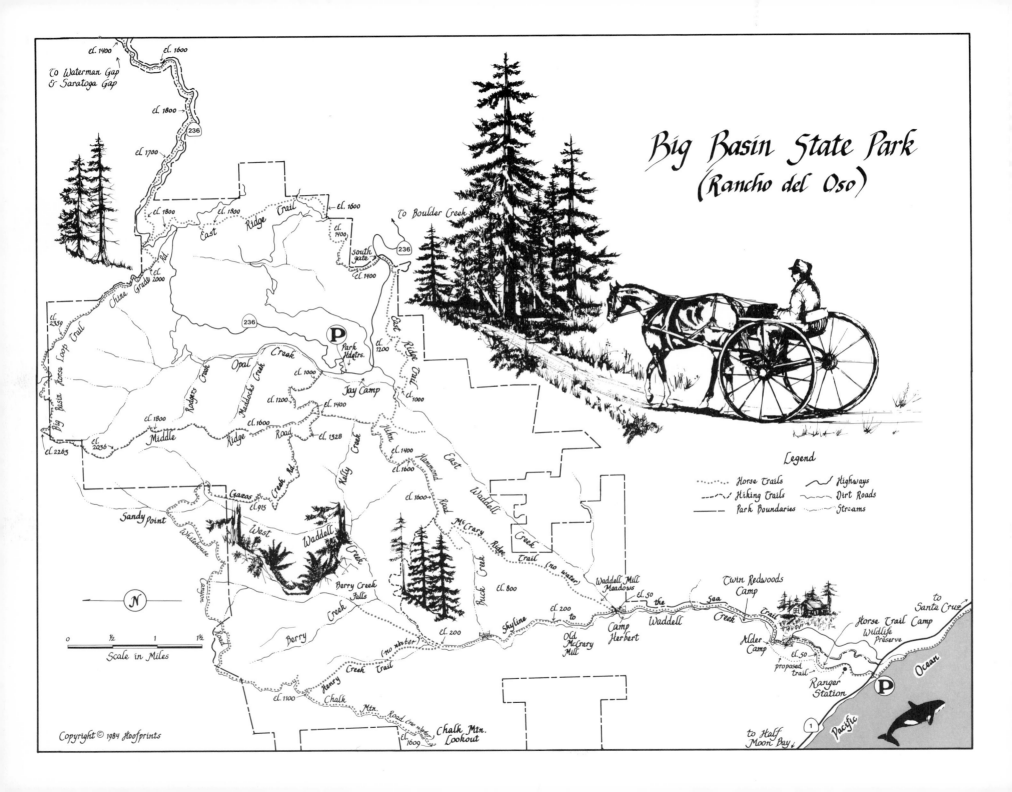

Big Basin State Park
(Rancho del Oso)

To Waterman Gap & Saratoga Gap

el. 1400
el. 1600
el. 1800
236
el. 1700
el. 1800
el. 1800
East Ridge Trail
el. 1600
el. 1400
south gate
el. 1400
236
el. 2000
China Grade Rd.
el. 2359
236
Big Basin Horse Loop Trail
P Park Hdqtrs.
Opal Creek
el. 1200
East Ridge Trail
el. 1000
Rodgers Creek
Maddocks Creek
el. 1000
Jay Camp
el. 1200
el. 1400
el. 1000
el. 1800
el. 1600
Middle Ridge Road
el. 1328
Nelly Creek
John
el. 1400
el. 1600
Hammond Road
el. 2263
el. 2036
Creek Rd.
Gazos
el. 915
East
Waddell
el. 1600
To Boulder Creek

Sandy Point
Whitehouse Canyon Road
West Waddell Creek
McCrary Ridge Trail (no water)
Waddell Creek
el. 800
Waddell Mill Meadows
el. 50
Twin Redwoods Camp
to Santa Cruz
Horse Trail Camp Wildlife Preserve
Berry Creek Falls
Buck Creek
Skyline
el. 200 to Old McCrary Mill
Camp Herbert
the Waddell Sea Creek Trail
Alder Camp
el. 50
proposed trail
Berry Creek Trail (no water)
el. 200
Henry Creek Trail
Ranger Station
P
el. 1100
Chalk Mtn. Road (no water)
el. 1609
Chalk Mtn. Lookout
1
to Half Moon Bay
Pacific Ocean

N

0   ½   1   1½
Scale in Miles

Legend

········· Horse Trails		∿ Highways
- - - - Hiking Trails		∿ Dirt Roads
——— Park Boundaries		∿ Streams

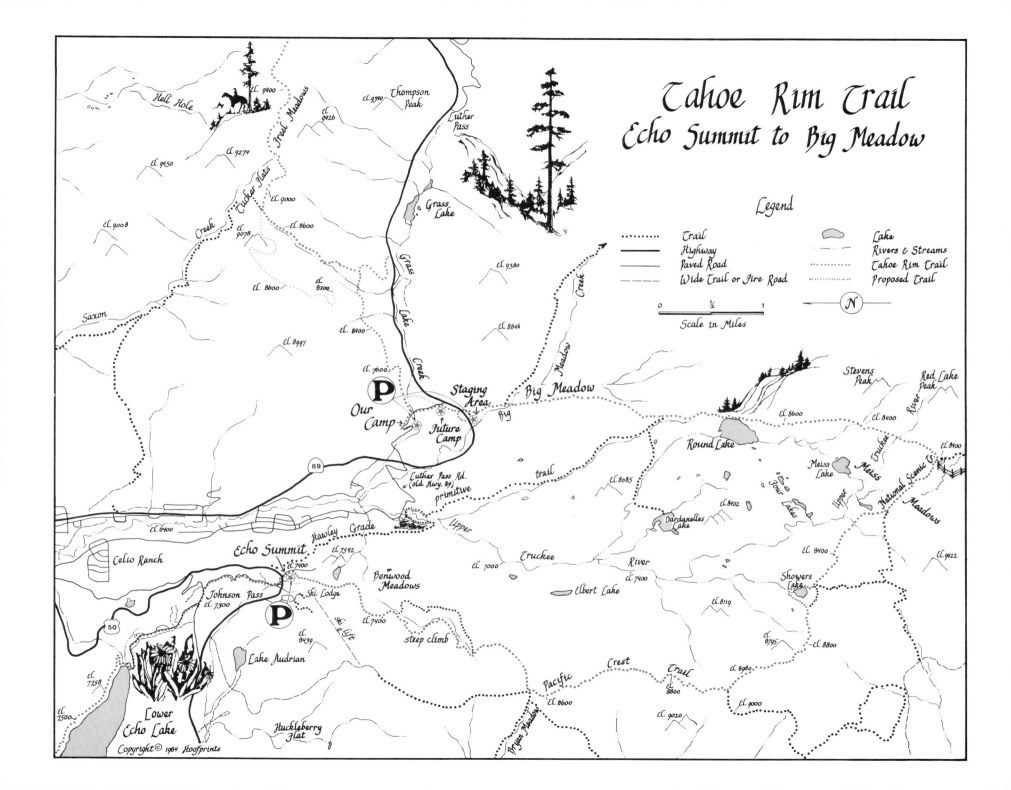

Tahoe Rim Trail
Echo Summit to Big Meadow

Legend

- ⋯⋯ Trail
- ▬▬ Highway
- ── Paved Road
- ─ ─ Wide Trail or Fire Road
- Lake
- Rivers & Streams
- Tahoe Rim Trail
- Proposed Trail

Scale in Miles
0   ½   1

N

Copyright © 1984 Hoofprints

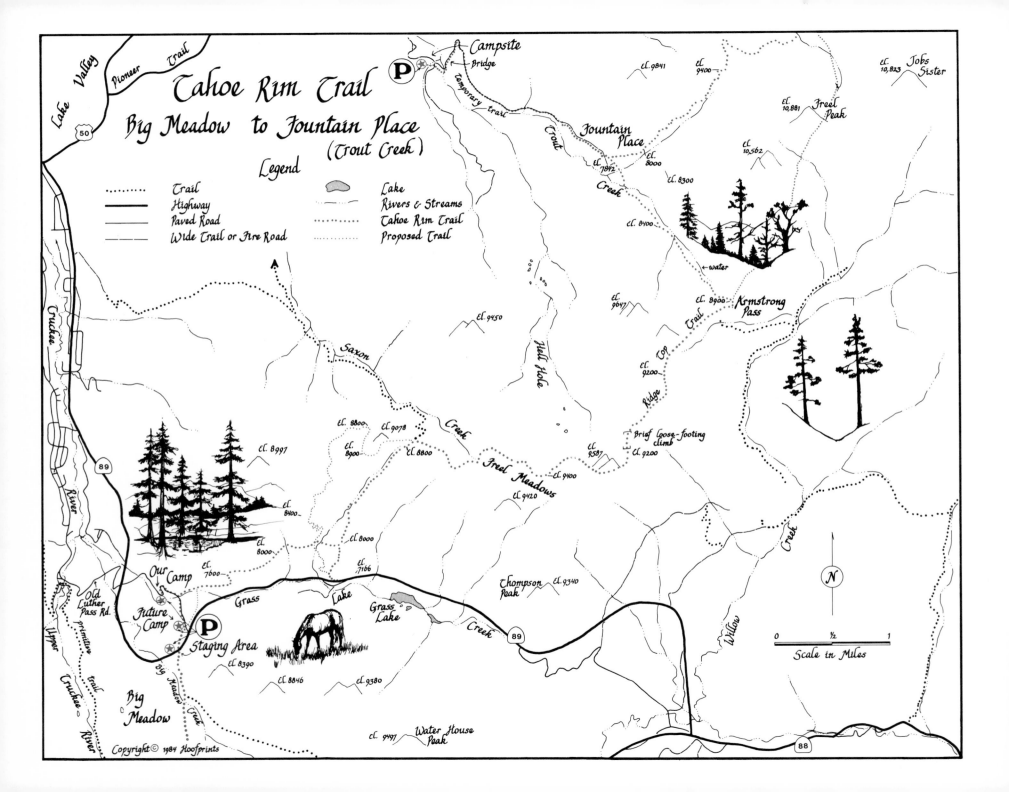

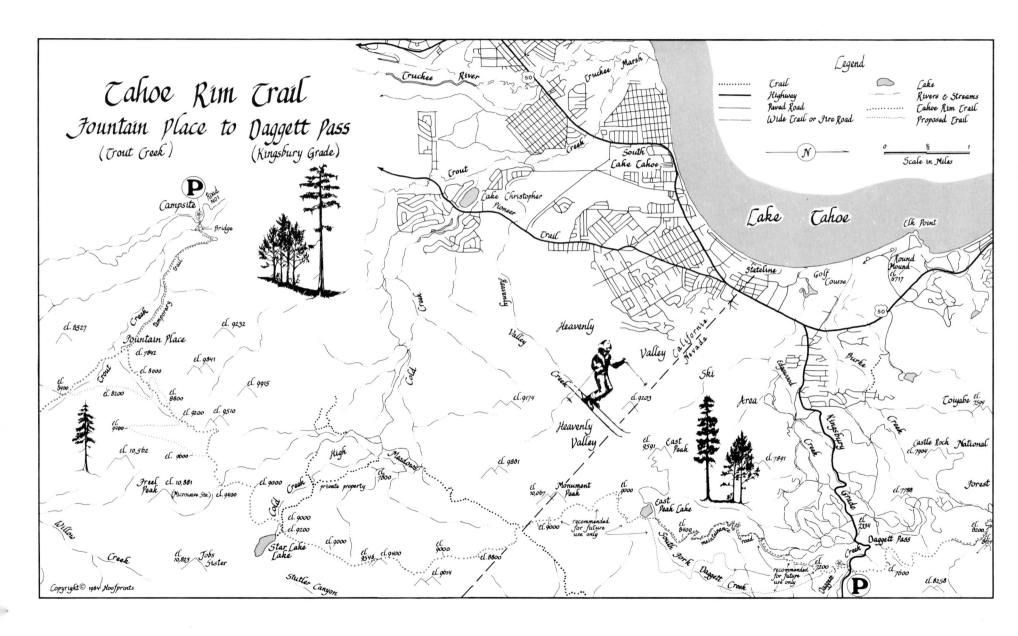

Tahoe Rim Trail

Fountain Place to Daggett Pass

(Trout Creek)   (Kingsbury Grade)

Legend

··········	Trail	Lake
▬▬▬	Highway	Rivers & Streams
───	Paved Road	········ Tahoe Rim Trail
───	Wide Trail or Fire Road	─ ─ ─ Proposed Trail

N

0   ½   1
Scale in Miles

Lake Tahoe

Truckee River

Truckee Marsh

50

South Lake Tahoe

Trout Creek

Trout

Lake Christopher
Pioneer

Trail

Stateline

Golf Course

Elk Point

Round Mound
el. 6717

50

Campsite
Road No 1
Bridge

P

Heavenly

Valley

California
Nevada

Ski

Area

Burke

Edgewood

Toiyabe el. 7594

Heavenly
Valley

East
Peak

el. 8527
Fountain Place   el. 7842
el. 9232
el. 9841
el. 8000
el. 9915
el. 8400
el. 8200
el. 8800
el. 9200   el. 9510
el. 9400
el. 10,562   el. 9600
Freel Peak   el. 10,881
(Microwave Sta.)   el. 9400
High
Meadows
private property
el. 7800
el. 9000
Monument Peak   el. 9000
el. 10,067
el. 9591
el. 7891
el. 9881
el. 9174
el. 9203

Cold Creek

Trout Creek

Cold Creek

Willow Creek

Jobs Sister   el. 10,823
Star Lake Lake
el. 9000
el. 9200
el. 9000
el. 9546   el. 9400
el. 9000
el. 8800
el. 9614
Stutler Canyon

East Peak Lake

recommended for future use only

el. 9000

South Fork Daggett Creek

maintenance   road

el. 8400

recommended for future use only

el. 7200

Daggett Pass

el. 7334
el. 7788
el. 7600
el. 8258
el. 8200

Kingsbury Grade

Castle Rock National
el. 7904

Forest

P

Castle Creek

Daggett Creek

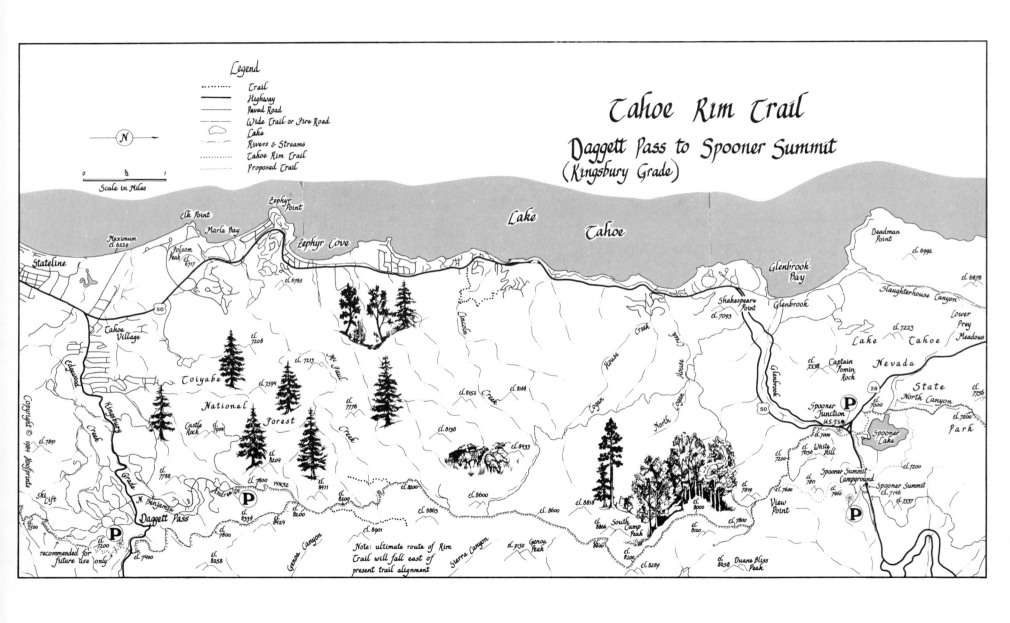

Tahoe Rim Trail

Daggett Pass to Spooner Summit
(Kingsbury Grade)

Legend

- · · · · · · Trail
- Highway
- Paved Road
- Wide Trail or Fire Road
- Lake
- Rivers & Streams
- · · · · · · Tahoe Rim Trail
- · · · · · · Proposed Trail

N

0   ½   1
Scale in Miles

Copyright © 1984 Hoofprints

Lake Tahoe

Elk Point
Zephyr Point
Marla Bay
Zephyr Cove
Maximum el. 6229
Stateline
Folsom Peak el. 8717
el. 6765
Tahoe Village
Toiyabe
el. 7208
el. 7213
el. 7594
National
el. 7776
Castle Rock
el. 7904
Forest
el. 8204
el. 7788
Ski Lift
el. 7500
N. Benjamin
el. 7200
Daggett Pass
Kingsbury Grade
Edgewood Creek
recommended for future use only
el. 7891
el. 7400
el. 7800
el. 8258
el. 8334
el. 8200
el. 8424
14N32
And Sno
McFaul
Creek
Creek
el. 8411
el. 8200
el. 8200
el. 8901
el. 8200
el. 8865
Genoa Canyon
Genoa Peak
el. 9150
Sierra Canyon
Note: ultimate route of Rim Trail will fall east of present trail alignment
el. 8152
el. 8168
el. 8138
el. 8433
el. 8600
el. 8600
Lincoln Creek
House Creek
Logan House Creek
North Logan House Creek
el. 8818
el. 8866
South Camp Peak
el. 8600
el. 8200
el. 8289
Duane Bliss Peak
el. 8858
el. 8000
el. 8120
el. 7800
View Point
el. 7819
Shakespeare Point
el. 7093
Glenbrook
Glenbrook Bay
Glenbrook Creek
Lake
Tahoe
Deadman Point
el. 6992
el. 6878
Slaughterhouse Canyon
Lower Prey Meadows
el. 7223
Nevada
State
North Canyon
Park
el. 7756
el. 7200
el. 7200
el. 7200
Captain Pomin Rock
el. 7538
Spooner Junction
U.S. 50
el. 7000
Spooner Lake
White Hill
el. 7030
el. 7811
el. 7600
Spooner Summit Campground
el. 7465
Spooner Summit
el. 7537
50
28

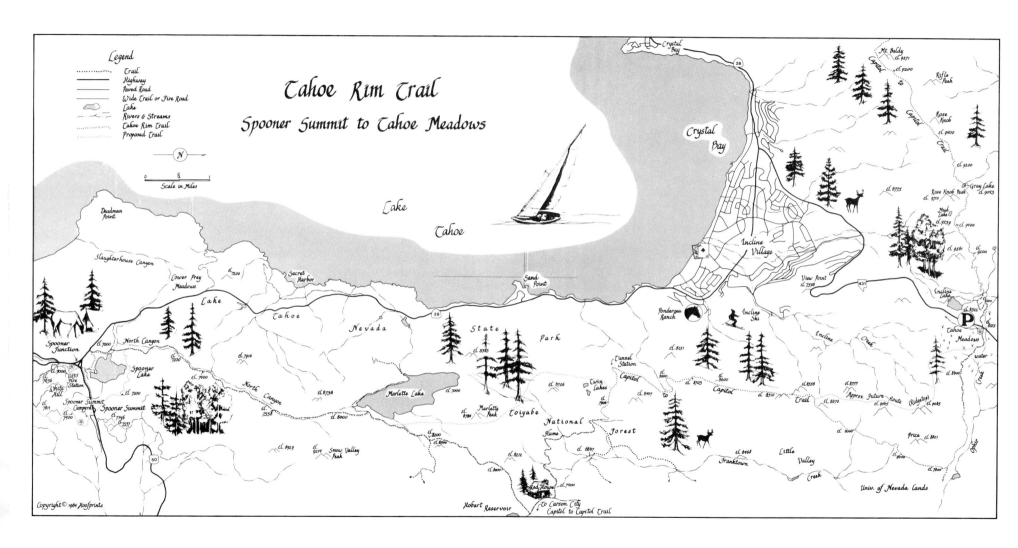

Tahoe Rim Trail

Spooner Summit to Tahoe Meadows

Legend

.... Trail
———— Highway
———— Paved Road
▭▭▭ Wide Trail or Fire Road
〰〰 Lake
〰〰 Rivers & Streams
········· Tahoe Rim Trail
········· Proposed Trail

N

Scale in Miles
0   ½   1

Lake Tahoe

Crystal Bay

Crystal Bay

28

Mt. Baldy el. 9271
el. 9200
Rifle Peak
Rose Knob
el. 9400
el. 9200
el. 8775
Rose Knob Peak
el. 9770
Gray Lake
el. 9043
Mud Lake
el. 9239
el. 9400
el. 9561
el. 9200

Incline Village

View Point el. 7598

431

Incline Lake
el. 8322
el. 8353

Ponderosa Ranch

Incline Ski

P
Tahoe Meadows

Deadman Point

Slaughterhouse Canyon

Lower Prey Meadows

Secret Harbor

el. 7200

Lake Tahoe

Sand Point

Nevada   State   Park

28

el. 8383

el. 8151

Incline Creek

water

el. 8000

Spooner Junction

North Canyon

el. 7000

Lake

el. 7916

Tunnel Station

Capitol

el. 8725

to Capitol Trail

el. 8538

el. 8777

Approx. Future Route

(Ridgetop)
el. 9065   el. 9085

el. 8000

Price el. 8801

el. 6190

el. 7800

White Hill
el. 7836
el. 7811

U.S.F.S. Fire Station

el. 7000

el. 7200

Spooner Lake

el. 7400

el. 7200

North Canyon

el. 7558

Marlette Lake

el. 8738

el. 7000

Marlette Peak
el. 8780

Toiyabe

el. 8000

el. 8706

Twin Lakes

el. 8407
el. 7900

el. 8000

el. 8510

Capitol   Trail

el. 8670

el. 8000

Spooner Summit Campground
el. 7146

Spooner Summit
el. 7537
el. 7400

el. 8829
el. 9274

Snow Valley Peak

el. 8100

el. 8800

el. 8212

el. 8000

National   Forest

Hume

el. 6867

el. 6468

Franktown

Little   Valley

Creek

Univ. of Nevada lands

50

Red House
el. 7400

Hobart Reservoir

To Carson City
Capitol to Capitol Trail

Ophir   Creek

Copyright © 1984 Hoofprints

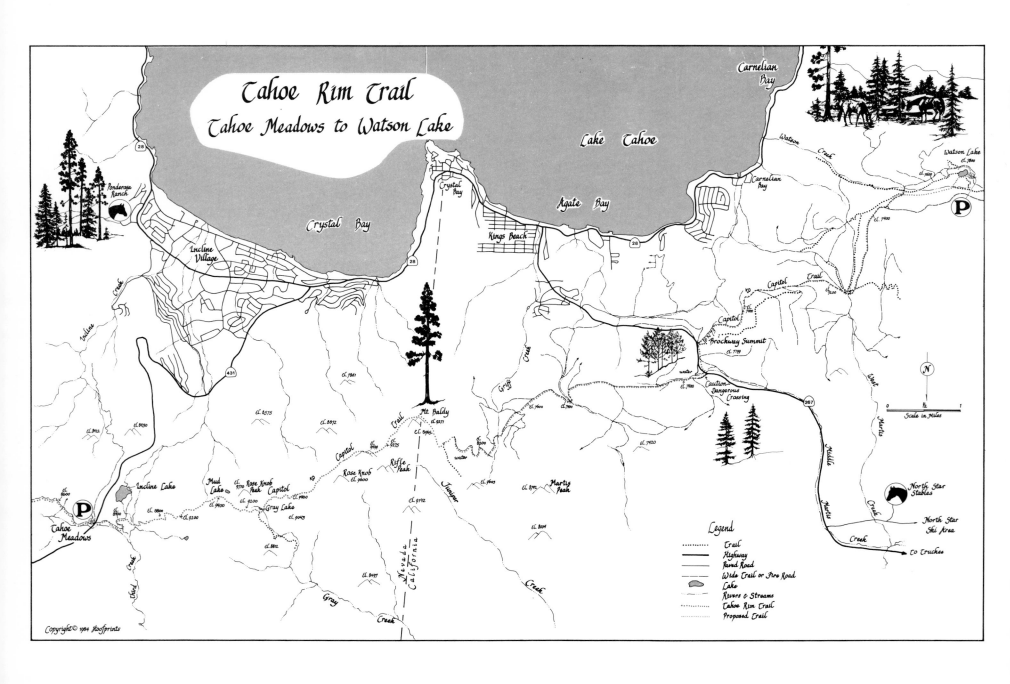

Tahoe Rim Trail
Tahoe Meadows to Watson Lake

Carnelian Bay

Lake Tahoe

Watson Lake
el. 7900

Watson Creek

Carnelian Bay

Agate Bay

Crystal Bay

Kings Beach

Ponderosa Ranch

Incline Village

Crystal Bay

Incline Creek

Capitol Trail

Brockway Summit
el. 7199

Caution Dangerous Crossing

el. 7400

Griff Creek

Mt. Baldy
el. 9371

el. 7881

el. 8575

el. 8872

el. 8945

el. 9499

el. 9275

Rose Knob
el. 9600

Rifle Peak

el. 7600

el. 7600

el. 8200

el. 7410

el. 9603

Martis Peak
el. 8711

North Star Stables

North Star Ski Area

Incline Lake

Mud Lake

Rose Knob Peak
el. 9710

Capitol

el. 9200

el. 9100

el. 9400

Gray Lake
el. 9043

el. 9112

el. 9430

el. 8922

el. 8830

el. 8200

Tahoe Meadows
el. 8900

el. 8000

Third Creek

Capitol Trail

Juniper

el. 9142

Nevada
California

el. 8497

Gray Creek

Creek

el. 8104

Middle Martis Creek

West Martis Creek

To Truckee

Co Truckee

28

431

28

267

N

Scale in Miles

Legend

Trail

Highway

Paved Road

Wide Trail or Fire Road

Lake

Rivers & Streams

Tahoe Rim Trail

Proposed Trail

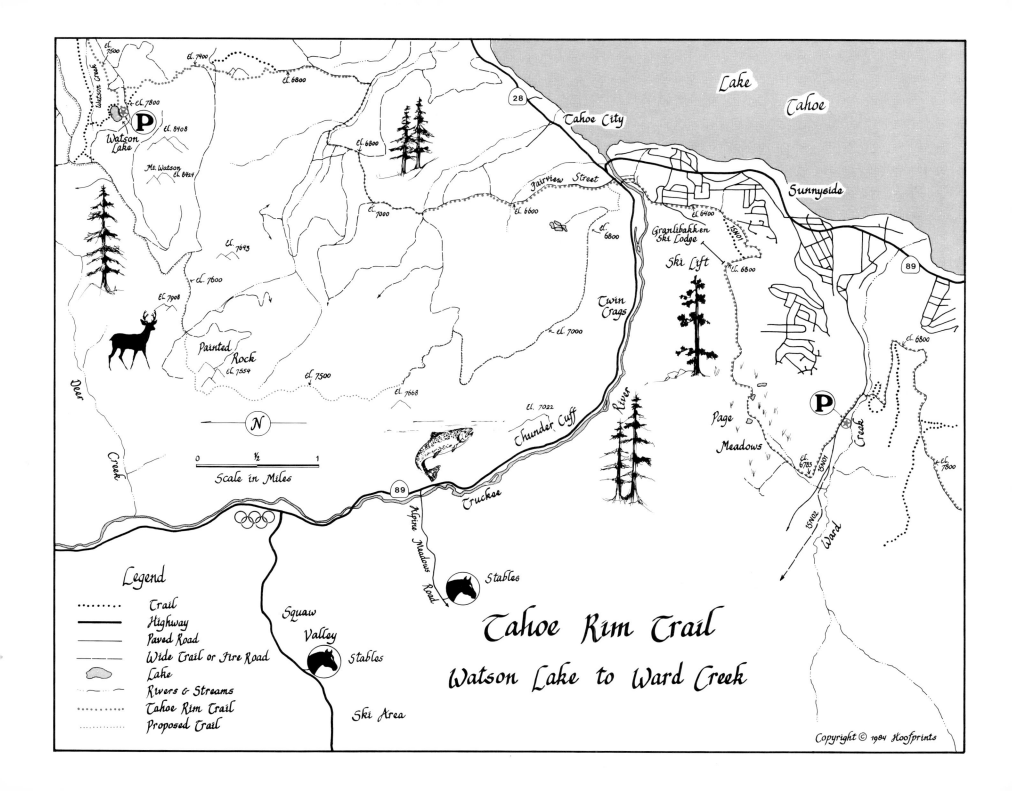

Tahoe Rim Trail
Watson Lake to Ward Creek

Legend

- ·········· Trail
- —— Highway
- —— Paved Road
- – – – Wide Trail or Fire Road
- Lake
- Rivers & Streams
- ·········· Tahoe Rim Trail
- ·········· Proposed Trail

Scale in Miles: 0 — ½ — 1

N

Lake Tahoe

Tahoe City

Sunnyside

Watson Lake — el. 7800 — P — el. 8408

Mt. Watson el. 8424

el. 7500 — el. 7400 — el. 6800

el. 6800

Fairview Street — el. 6600 — el. 6400

el. 7000 — el. 6800

Granlibakken Ski Lodge

Ski Lift

Twin Crags — el. 7000

el. 7643

el. 7600

el. 7908

Painted Rock el. 7554

el. 7500

el. 7668

el. 7022

Chunder Cliff

River

Page Meadows — P

el. 6785 — Ward Creek

el. 6800

el. 7800

Deer Creek

Truckee

Alpine Meadows Road — Stables

Squaw Valley — Stables

Ski Area

Copyright © 1984 Hoofprints

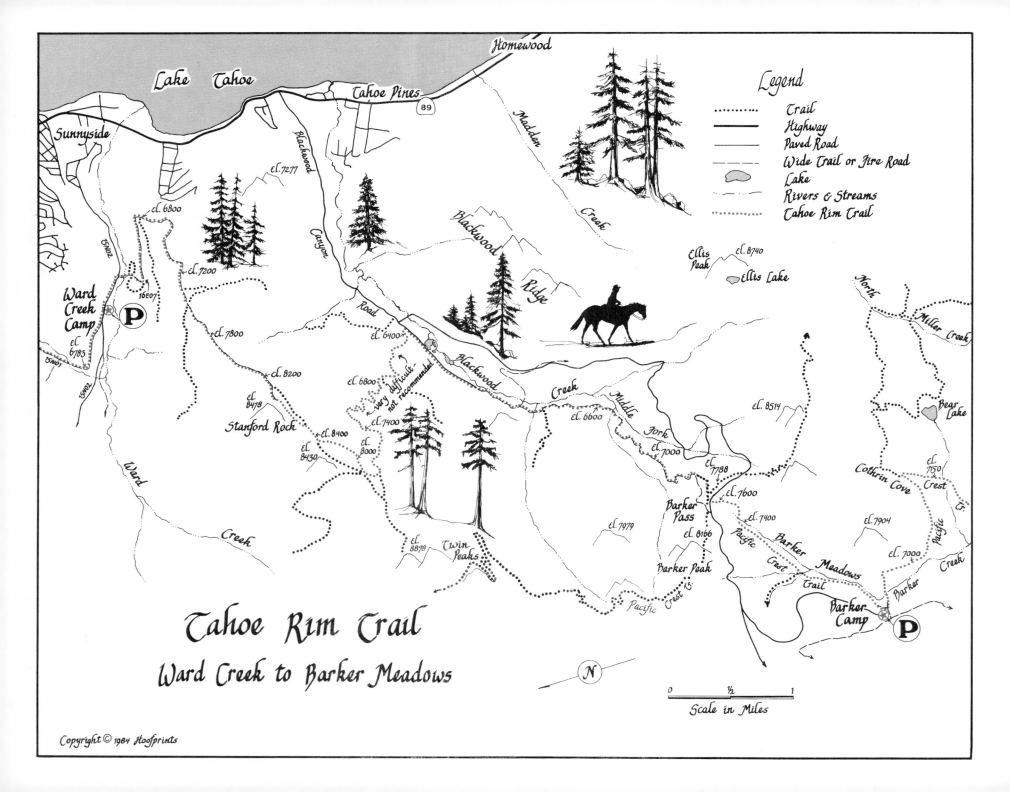

Tahoe Rim Trail
Ward Creek to Barker Meadows

Legend

··········	Trail
———	Highway
———	Paved Road
- - - -	Wide Trail or Fire Road
▨	Lake
~~	Rivers & Streams
∙∙∙∙∙∙	Tahoe Rim Trail

Lake Tahoe

Homewood

Tahoe Pines

89

Sunnyside

Blackwood Canyon

el. 7277

Madden Creek

Blackwood Ridge

Ellis Peak

el. 8740

Ellis Lake

el. 6800

el. 7200

16E07

Ward Creek Camp

el. 6783

15N02

15N01

15N02

el. 7800

el. 8200

Road

el. 6400

Blackwood Creek

North Miller Creek

el. 8478

Stanford Rock

el. 6800

very difficult, not recommended

el. 8514

Bear Lake

el. 8430

el. 8400

el. 7400

el. 6600

Middle Fork

el. 7000

el. 7788

Cothrin Cove

el. 7150

Pacific Crest Tr.

el. 8000

el. 7600

Ward Creek

Twin Peaks

el. 8878

el. 7979

Barker Pass

el. 7400

Barker Meadows Trail

el. 7904

el. 7000

Pacific Cr.

Barker Peak

el. 8166

Pacific Crest Tr.

Pacific Crest Tr.

Barker Camp

Barker Creek

N

0   ½   1

Scale in Miles

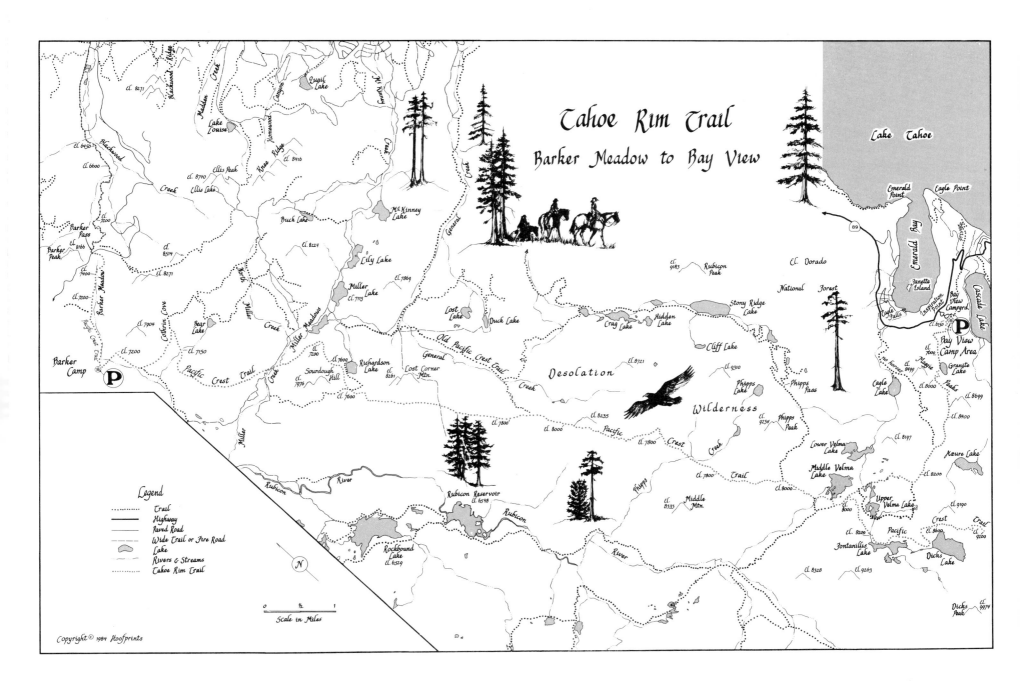

Tahoe Rim Trail
Barker Meadow to Bay View

Lake Tahoe

Legend

- .... Trail
- ———— Highway
- ———— Paved Road
- – – – – Wide Trail or Fire Road
- Lake
- ········· Rivers & Streams
- ·········· Tahoe Rim Trail

N

0   ½   1
Scale in Miles

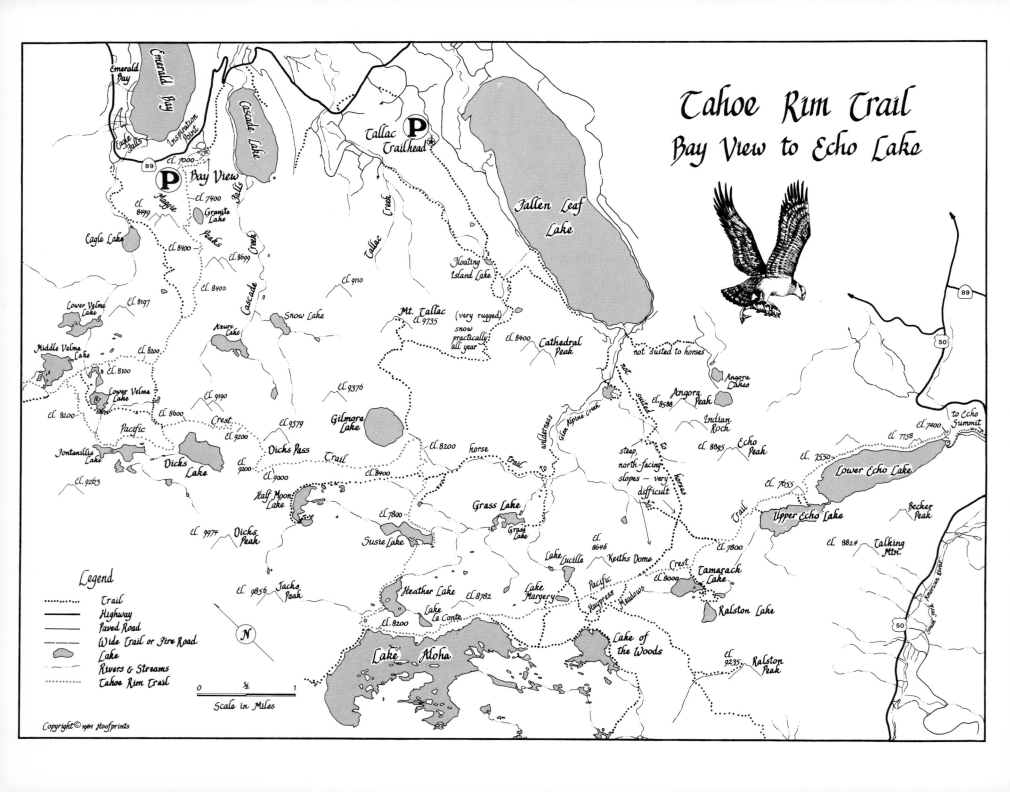

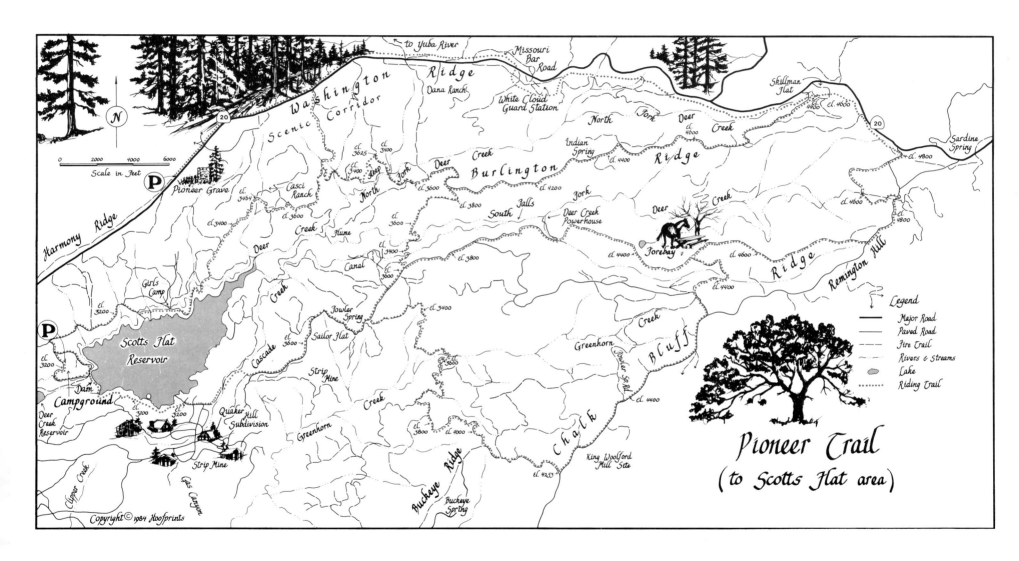

Pioneer Trail
(to Scotts Flat area)

N

Scale in feet
0   2000   4000   6000

Legend

— Major Road
— Paved Road
-- Fire Trail
~ Rivers & Streams
▦ Lake
⋯ Riding Trail

to Yuba River

Missouri Bar Road

Washington Ridge

Scenic Corridor

Dana Ranch

White Cloud Guard Station

Skillman Flat
el. 4400   el. 4600

North   Fork   Deer   Creek
el. 4600

Harmony Ridge

Pioneer Grave
el. 3464

el. 3625
el. 3400
el. 3400

Casci Ranch

North   Fork   Deer   Creek

Burlington

Indian Spring

el. 4200

el. 4400

Ridge

el. 4600

Sardine Spring

el. 4800

el. 4800

el. 3400

el. 3600

Deer   Creek

Hume

el. 3600

el. 3800

South Falls

Deer Creek Powerhouse

Fork
el. 4200

Deer   Creek

Forebay
el. 4400

el. 4600

Remington Hill

Ridge

Canal

el. 3400

el. 3600

el. 3800

el. 4400

Girls Camp
el. 3200

Deer   Creek

Fowler Spring

el. 3400

Scotts Flat Reservoir

Sailor Flat
el. 3600

Cascade

Strip Mine

Greenhorn   Creek

Chalk   Bluff

Fowler Fr. Rd.

el. 4400

el. 3200

Dam

Campground
el. 3100   el. 3200

Deer Creek Reservoir

Quaker Hill Subdivision

Greenhorn   Creek

el. 3600

el. 3800   el. 4000

King Woolford Mill Site

Clipper Creek

Strip Mine

Gas Canyon

Buckeye Ridge

Buckeye Spring

el. 4253

Copyright © 1984 Hoofprints

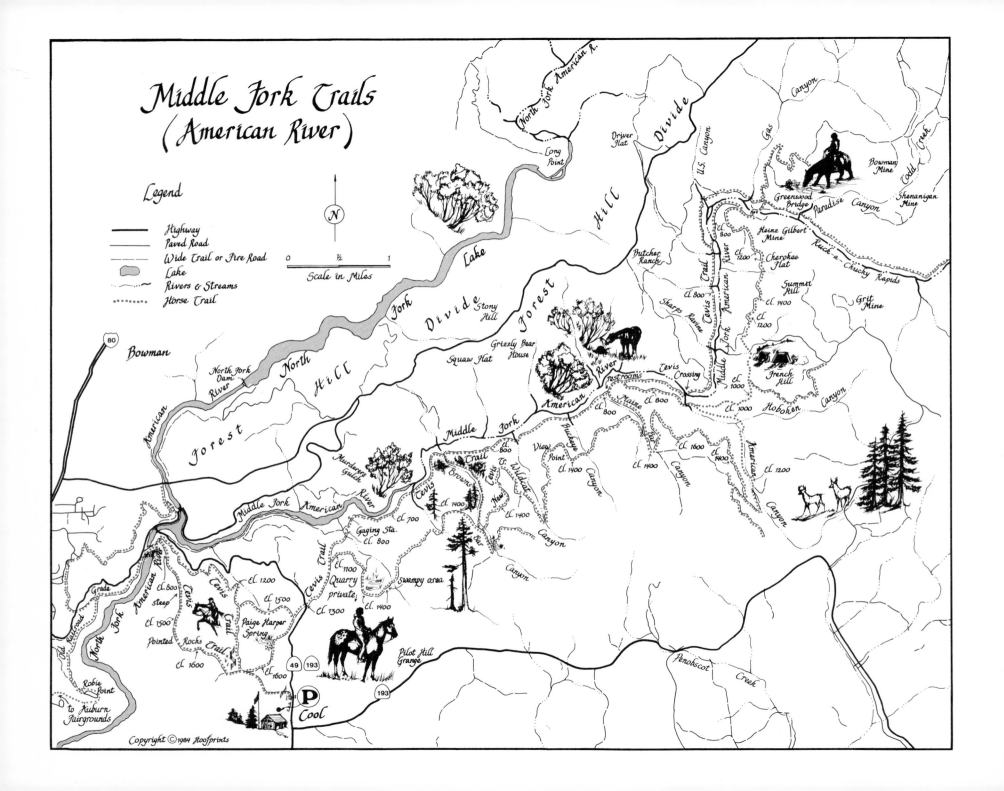

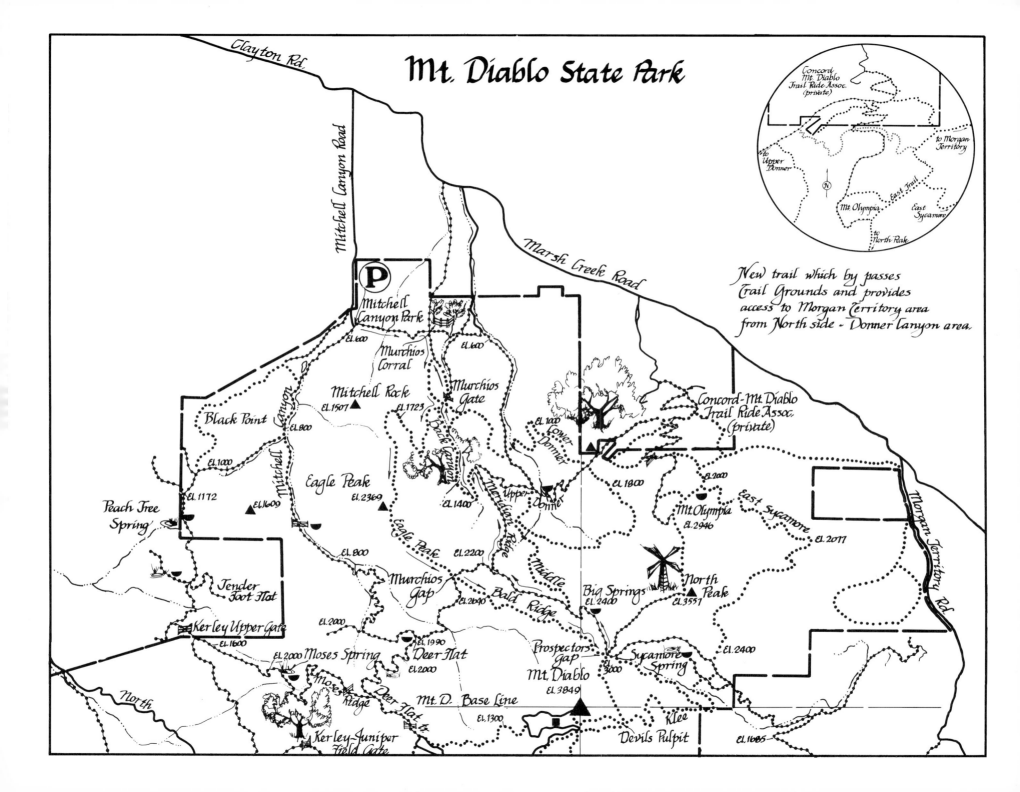

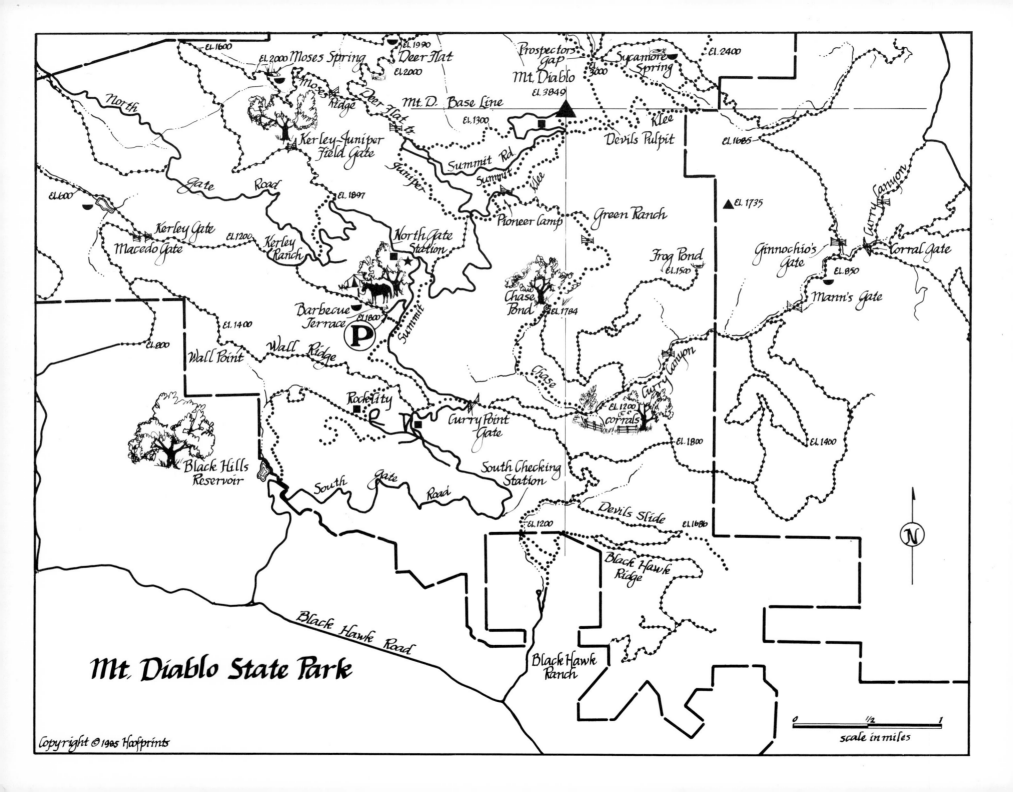

Mt. Diablo State Park

ℍoofprints

P.O. Box 5765
Redwood City, CA 94063

Name _____

Address _____

City _____ State _____ Zip _____

Please send me _____ copies of **New Trail Adventures for California Horsemen** and/or **Favorite Trails of California Horsemen** as designated below. I am enclosing $19.95 per copy plus $2.00 to cover postage and handling.

_____ copies **New Trail Adventures**

_____ copies **Favorite Trails**

_____ Total amount enclosed.

Make checks payable to HOOFPRINTS.

ℍoofprints

P.O. Box 5765
Redwood City, CA 94063

Name _____

Address _____

City _____ State _____ Zip _____

Please send me _____ copies of **New Trail Adventures for California Horsemen** and/or **Favorite Trails of California Horsemen** as designated below. I am enclosing $19.95 per copy plus $2.00 to cover postage and handling.

_____ copies **New Trail Adventures**

_____ copies **Favorite Trails**

_____ Total amount enclosed.

Make checks payable to HOOFPRINTS.

ℍoofprints

P.O. Box 5765
Redwood City, CA 94063

Dear Doni:

☐ I am familiar with a great trail you might want to consider for future editions of your trail books.

☐ I have some ideas for improving future editions of your trail book.

☐ Features of **New Trail Adventures** and/or **Favorite Trails** that I particularly like are:

☐ So far, my favorite trail ride based on information you supplied is:

Please give me your thoughts **in detail** on the reverse side or on an attached sheet of paper. I hope to hear from you soon. Thanks.

All copies will be sent to same address unless otherwise specified. If you wish to enclose your own gift card with each book, please print name and address of recipient on outside of envelope, enclose with order, and we will include it with your gift. Books will be autographed upon request.

All copies will be sent to same address unless otherwise specified. If you wish to enclose your own gift card with each book, please print name and address of recipient on outside of envelope, enclose with order, and we will include it with your gift. Books will be autographed upon request.